BEYOND
THE BOX

BEYOND THE BOX

TELEVISION AND THE INTERNET

SHARON MARIE ROSS

Blackwell
Publishing

© 2008 by Sharon Marie Ross

BLACKWELL PUBLISHING
350 Main Street, Malden, MA 02148–5020, USA
9600 Garsington Road, Oxford OX4 2DQ, UK
550 Swanston Street, Carlton, Victoria 3053, Australia

The right of Sharon Marie Ross to be identified as the author of this work has been asserted
in accordance with the UK Copyright, Designs, and Patents Act 1988.

First published 2008 by Blackwell Publishing Ltd

1   2008

Library of Congress Cataloging-in-Publication Data

Ross, Sharon Marie.
  Beyond the box : television and the Internet / Sharon Marie Ross.
      p. cm.
  Includes bibliographical references and index.
  ISBN 978-1-4051-6123-7 (hbk. : alk. paper) – ISBN 978-1-4051-6124-4 (pbk. : alk. paper)
    1. Television viewers–Effects of technological innovations on. 2. Internet. 3. Interactive
television. 4. Internet television. 5. Television–Social aspects. I. Title.

  HE8700.65.R67 2009
  384.550285'4678–dc22

                                                              2007050611

A catalogue record for this title is available from the British Library.

Set in 10.5/13pt Galliard
by SPi Publisher Services, Pondicherry, India
Printed and bound in Singapore
by Fabulous Printers Pte Ltd

For further information on
Blackwell Publishing, visit our website at
www.blackwellpublishing.com

This book is dedicated to my partner in all things TV and otherwise life and work related, Tom Skapes, and my partners in crime, Amanda Lotz, Susan McLeland, and Kelly Kessler.

Contents

Acknowledgments

My deepest thanks to the many people who offered time and energy to sit down with me for interviews. A special thanks to the over 100 survey respondents who took the time to answer questions about how they watch TV, bearing with me over the course of several years. I owe a special debt to my dear friends Kelly Kessler and Susan McLeland, whose discussions with me about *American Idol* helped me to develop the main argument of this book. A deep thanks to Dr. Janet Staiger, who inspired me to pursue work in the field of reception.

This book and its research could not have been accomplished without the assistance of the Academy of Television Arts and Sciences (Karen Herman and Price Hicks especially) and the Education Foundation of the National Association of Television Program Executives (Greg Pitts). Finally, I would like to thank my home school, Columbia College Chicago, which provided me with a generous Faculty Development Grant for my research.

Introduction

Online/Offline: What It Means to "Watch (and Make) TV" in the Age of the Internet

It's true! TWOP does control the TV!

Veronica Mars got renewed over the weekend. Its creator, Rob Thomas, is a known TWOP ass-kisser … Thomas is very selective about which sites he credits for helping spread love about the show. Over the weekend, Glark said this:

"It wasn't a big surprise to us but a friend of the site confirmed last week that internal WB research documents site TWOP as a major source for gauging reaction to their shows so all your efforts probably made a significant difference to at least some people responsible for pulling the trigger on this renewal."

Oh Mighty TWOP! The entire television programming community bows to your prowess! It is because of this site, and some "internal WB research documents," that this detective show is staying on the air!

When it's time for Q&A, I get 90% of the questions. It almost makes me uncomfortable. We're doing ComicCon, and it's the same thing … It's just, I mean, I'm a writer. It's odd to me because, in the real world – they don't do Entertainment Tonight about the writers … It's really interesting culturally, I think. (Rob Thomas, creator and executive producer, Veronica Mars, *interview, July 18, 2006)*

Granted, those of us on the boards talking and speculating about Lost *make up a small portion of the viewing audience. However, in the back of my mind I'd at least like to think that TPTB [The Powers That Be] have some poor intern slaving away reading the boards. We may represent a small portion of the viewing audience, but we are the most visible and vocal ... That, I would hope, should account for something in their world. (Posted by Leuthen)*

I did enjoy reading this [article], but one thing I noticed is that you constantly refer to the "imagined community" that Adult Swim has with its viewers, and this community is not imagined, it's called a message board. I'd suggest you visit there every once in a while ... It is very real ... Enjoy. (Posted by Kevin)

I was at a conference and we got into a minor fight on a panel as to "what is television?" So the way these things typically work is, people inside the beltway fight about it first, but then eventually it slips out into the real world. And I think it's quite possible that, for my kids [who are eight and eleven], the Internet is television is the Internet and the distinction is blurred ... But it's just now that that's starting. (Rick Mandler, vice-president and general manager of ABC's Enhanced TV, interview, June 22, 2006)

In an episode from the first full season of the cult show *Buffy the Vampire Slayer* (March 1997–May 2003), the lead heroine (Buffy) becomes incapacitated after a spell renders her weak and frightened – in fact, she has "become" the Halloween costume she wears, a Victorian era damsel, clearly in distress. As children-turned-demons under the same spell begin to over-run the town our heroine is supposed to be protecting, it is up to Buffy's best friend Willow to take charge. Willow quickly becomes frustrated with Buffy's ineffectuality and in a moment of exasperation she exclaims, "You couldn't have dressed up as Xena?!" ("Halloween," 1997).

This moment in a series that would quickly mushroom into a cult hit and become the passion of many a TV critic and academic caught my attention as a graduate student in film and television studies. Only a few months earlier, my *Buffy* fandom had emerged as I sought diversion from the work of my Masters thesis. At that time, a colleague of mine was working on *Xena: Warrior Princess* (1995–2001), and I had already become a fan of *that* show while helping her tape episodes (Parks 1997). The *Buffy* episode I describe above came next in my academic trajectory – and was in fact the one that set me on the path towards my dissertation. At first the episode registered with me primarily because of the gender issues at work. (Buffy had chosen her damsel get-up to please her new beau – who, she was worried, was finding her unfeminine in her Slayer mode.) Soon, however, I found myself entranced by the fact that this TV series evidenced awareness so quickly in its run that people who were watching *Buffy* might also be watching *Xena*. In short, that episode cemented my fandom because it recognized me as more than a *Buffy* fan.

I had been invited in, and there was no going back. As I worked away at unraveling the narrative complexities and gender dynamics of these two shows, I became involved in online fan forums for both series. Four years after I watched the *Buffy* episode that called out to me as a *Xena* fan, I found myself watching *Xena* episodes written *by* Internet fans as well as episodes *about* Internet fans.[1] One didn't need to *be* a fan to realize that both *Buffy* and *Xena* had astonishing fan bases – and I begin this book with an examination of the role the Internet played in the enjoyment of these shows for some viewers. I begin here also because, in the wake of *Buffy* and *Xena* as cult TV and Internet phenomena (along with *The X-Files*, 1993–2002, and *La Femme Nikita*, 1997–2001), I began to notice that other TV series – more "mainstream" TV series, for lack of a better qualifying term – were emerging with equally impressive online fan bases. In addition, many of these shows, through either direct textual moments or via producer and writer interviews in entertainment forums, were evidencing a heightened awareness of the existence of their fans both online and offline. What might these developments be able to tell us about what it means to watch and make TV today?

The epigraphs at the beginning of this chapter provide an indication of how the Internet has begun to alter people's experiences with television today – from viewers to producers to writers to executives. Like me, the individual fans cited here demonstrate interpellation; collectively, these quotes also demonstrate the incredible range of experiences in tele-participation that can occur when TV and the Internet meet. For fans of the series *Veronica Mars* (2004–2007) who relied on the popular TV website Television Without Pity (TWOP) for news and for a place to discuss the show, their TV experience included a sense of pride in the power they held as arbiters of taste: "Oh Mighty TWOP! The entire television programming community bows to your prowess!" Fans of *Lost* (2004–) such as Leuthen express more hesitancy about whether or not producers are paying attention to their online discussions, but clearly have confidence in their own importance as part of the viewing audience for that show: "We may represent a small portion of the viewing audience, but we are the most visible and vocal." And Kevin, an Adult Swim fan responding to an online academic discussion about the Adult Swim community (2001–), reminds those academics that for some TV viewers, part of watching TV includes keeping track of what "competing experts" have to say *about* watching TV. As Rob Thomas, creator and executive producer of *Veronica Mars*, notes, "it's really interesting culturally" – at the very least!

The above examples merely scratch the surface of online activity concerning television series, but they are indicative of the significant relationships that exist today between the Internet and TV. From dialogue in *Buffy* acknowledging a crossover fan base with *Xena*, to plotlines in *Xena* acknowledging the blurred boundaries of the imagined and real online fan communities of that series, to the executive producer of *Veronica Mars* giving a website the scoop on the show's renewal status – the Internet has become a site for tele-participation that opens up for viewers and creators myriad ways in which to experience watching and making TV. This book aims to explore the role that the Internet has come to play in both the reception of TV series *and* their production, and the reciprocal dynamics that emerge. I argue that visiting online sites linked to TV series, among other activities typically associated with "the fan," is becoming an increasingly common activity for "regular viewers." I discuss as well how TV writers, producers, executives, and marketers seem to be incorporating an awareness of such activities into the shows themselves. Viewers are responding to various kinds of calls to tele-participation – invitations to interact with TV shows beyond the moment of viewing and "outside" of the TV show itself. I break down these invitations to tele-participation into three categories – overt, organic, and obscured – working to situate these three modes within a changing industrial landscape of increased competition for viewers. Through an examination of the basic narrative structure and content of various shows, exploration of online activity concerning the same texts, and interviews with fans, writers, producers, executives, marketers, and popular critics, this book examines shifting understandings of what it means to watch and make TV in a multimedia world.[2]

Derek Johnson (2007) argues that this development of television inviting the audience in to participate can be traced to the 1980s in the

United States, as cable began to reach out to "fan groups" with channels devoted to extremely specific content. Slowly, broadcast TV responded by pursuing more niche audiences than mass. By the late 1990s, networks – both broadcast and cable – sought to retain viewers by creating a more intense relationship between the audience and a show, increasingly through multi-platforming that gave television programs life in the worlds of film, print, the Internet, etc. To a degree, one goal of this book is to trace this historical development in the world of TV by focusing on a series of programs over twelve years (1995–2007) in order to examine *how* this "more intense relationship" has developed, *why* it has developed, and to what ends.

Where my work diverges from Johnson's is in the arena of how widespread these changes have become – how common. Johnson's examples of how the television industry has been inviting viewers in to participate will resonate with my discussion of *Lost* in chapter four, but these invitations (and how audiences respond to them) exist across a wider range of programming than Johnson's work indicates. Likewise, while my approach in this book works with Jason Mittell's argument that "the consumer and creative practices of fan culture ... have become more widely distributed and participated in with the distribution means of the Internet, making active audience behavior even more of a mainstream practice" (2006: 32), Mittell's explanation that increased narrative complexity in television shows is supported by and supportive of this development does not account for "simpler" texts' invitations to participation.

My work here, then, is an elaboration on and fine-tuning of the excellent examinations of tele-participation that occur in work such as Johnson's and Mittell's. How are texts as *varied* as *Buffy*, *Xena*, *American Idol*, *Family Guy*, Adult Swim, YouTube, Current, *The O.C.*, *Degrassi: The Next Generation*, and *Lost* linked through tele-participation? How do their variations contribute to equally varying, but nevertheless related, strategies of invitation that contribute to a range of relationships rooted in tele-participation? Henry Jenkins's work in *Convergence Culture* (2006) is close in spirit to my own here, as he explores a range of texts rooted in tele-participation to different degrees, from TV to film to literature, and their audiences. Like Jenkins, I aim in this project to achieve a similarly broad look at how "consumers are encouraged to seek out new information and make connections among dispersed media content" (3), but I choose to focus on TV – however uncertain a category that is now – in order to provide a more complete examination of how convergence culture operates within this medium.

Throughout this book, I will question what kinds of relationships exist between viewers on the one hand, and writers, producers, executives, and marketers on the other. One thing that will become clear is that there is no set "assessment" of the impact I propose. Much depends on from whose perspective one is examining the relationship. At times issues of genre become paramount; at other times issues of narrative structure; and at still others the primary issue is one of who the desired target audience might be. Another point of clarification involves the scope of Internet TV fandom. In this book, I do not include a thorough examination of the phenomenon of fan fiction and other fan art, and while I do focus on specific fan bases, my primary aim is to unravel how online TV fan-like activities demonstrate an awareness of and attitude towards the originating text's creators and networks – and how originating texts and their creators and networks demonstrate an awareness of viewers' activities. Thus, while I am indeed focusing on ways in which viewers and creators use the Internet, or even "just" a sense of the Internet, to participate with the TV text, I am not coming even close to covering all of the many ways in which the Internet connects to TV. In the spirit of scholarly camaraderie, I will assume that those reading this book can seek the full scope of the Internet/TV connection through an examination of work by colleagues in my field.

Focusing primarily, then, on distinct examples of how the Internet and TV meet, I hope to demonstrate that people's experiences with watching and making TV today are increasingly inseparable from tele-participation (be that literally or conceptually). Clearly, this raises important issues of access to and literacy concerning the Internet, along with issues of who comes to represent the ideal viewer to those working within the industry – issues which I intend to address throughout the book. Along the way, this book will necessarily explore experiences of power in relation to TV: Who has it? Who *feels* that they have it? How does a sense of power translate to issues of representation – particularly for groups that may feel otherwise disenfranchised with regards to TV?

On one level, I am examining the growth of the producerly TV text – television programs that in various ways encourage viewers to feel as if they have a means to contribute to the content of that program

(Fiske 1987). How does TV today demonstrate an awareness of not only the presence of viewers, but the presence of viewers who feel as if they can – and perhaps should be allowed to – contribute to the meanings of that text? One can see the producerly text at work when, for example, an episode of *Xena* makes a plot joke out of TV viewers' desire to know whether or not Xena and her female companion Gabrielle are lesbian lovers.[3] Was Internet fandom of the show a necessary component in the decision to write such a storyline? Perhaps – perhaps not. But clearly an awareness of what many viewers were thinking about in terms of the meaning of Xena and Gabrielle's relationship was a component. How does such an example relate to a more literal example of the producerly text – such as when hopeful film and TV creators upload their own productions to the website for Current.TV so that web viewers can select those they would like to "green light"?[4]

Along with examining the development of the producerly text, I also seek to reconfigure Annette Kuhn's (1992) understanding of the social audience in light of the significant changes that have occurred within and around TV since the mid-1980s. A social audience can be thought of as a collective; people "come together" (sometimes literally) to watch a show, guided in part by the work of the television industry. "Spectators," on the other hand, are individuals who engage with a TV show but who may or may not do so with any sense of belonging to a larger collective of viewers (either symbolically or literally). This distinction between the social audience and the spectator (admittedly blurred) is useful for exploring the notion of tele-participation via the Internet. Under what circumstances and in what ways do viewers see themselves as part of a social audience? Does being part of a social audience factor into how viewers receive and interpret TV texts? How do distinctions made by producers, writers, networks, and marketers about various aspects of being a spectator within a social audience – if any – factor into the design of the TV text, and what role does an awareness of Internet fandom play in how the social audience is understood?

One of the themes that will become evident in this project is that the industry is working increasingly to create and/or sustain social audiences for their shows, looking to past examples of how and why fans developed into social audiences for guidance. One of the foremost motivations appears to be the element of sociality itself – that being part of a social audience allows individual spectators to socialize with others around a TV program. Rhiannon Bury (2005) argues that such sociality helps to create and sustain communities, especially in the age of the Internet. While I will not be exploring the concept of community per se, I will examine the importance of socializing to tele-participation, how the Internet is a dynamic in this relationship, and how the social audience can become a force to be reckoned with from the perspective of the industry.

As I mentioned above, one way in which I attempt to unravel such complexities involves the categorization of invitational strategies. As with any attempt to categorize, significant vagaries and overlaps will emerge; however, my research indicates nuances in these strategies that call for classification of some type. The first style of invitation that I focus on is "overt" – a situation in which writers' and producers' intent to activate viewer participation is easily discernible within the text of the series. For example, I spend time exploring how *American Idol*'s (June 2002–) success as a show resides in its direct appeal to viewer participation ("You vote, you decide") and how this has expanded over seasons to more actively encourage Internet participation specifically. How can this show and its corresponding Internet activity be examined to gain insight into issues of viewer power in light of past academic debates about the ability of TV viewers to carve out their own interpretations and responses to TV?

The second style of invitation I discuss I refer to as "organic," an apparently natural style designed carefully to appear as if the show (or in some cases network) is not "asking" the viewer overtly to extend the text. With organic invitations, the show/network assumes that tele-participation is an *already* occurring element of viewers' ways of watching. For example, the teen series *Degrassi: The Next Generation* (2001) – as it airs on the N network in the United States – features interstitials that mimic Internet chat and cell phone text messaging, in a manner that might seem like a foreign language to adult viewers but that is clearly understood easily by the show's desired demographic. How might such strategies indicate a generationally influenced shift in the ways that TV producers and marketers understand their audiences? How might the actual messaging that occurs on websites associated with the series feed back into this loop?

The third category of invitation that I utilize is perhaps the messiest due to its complexity and ambiguousness, and that is the style I refer to as "obscured." By obscured, I mean to describe a style of invitation that is apparently careless, operating at a primarily aesthetic level; in other words, any invitation to participate resides primarily in the *narrative structure and content* of the show itself through a certain "messiness" that demands viewer unraveling. From an outsider's perspective, it can appear as if fans are seizing upon textual elements that occur by chance, allowing for specific pleasures of "insider status," puzzle-solving, and prediction and speculation. For example, the ABC series *Lost* features intricately designed back-stories woven into episodes in atypical ways; the show features as well myriad and obscure clues as to the potential meaning of characters and their stories via references that range from the philosophical to the popular. This narrative design in no small way demands the Internet as a site in which viewers can seek information, engage in their own theory-making, and (as seen in the epigraph quote by Leuthen) voice concerns and ideas to producers and writers – or, at the very "least," to interns. The ratings success of this series, and the importance it has played in reviving ABC as a player in the industry, make the exploration of this series' invitational strategies all the more intriguing: What can we learn, and what might the industry be learning, from a show that has landed in the Top Ten while engaging in a style of invitation that is most akin to that found in the traditionally denigrated domain of cult TV?

While I engage in the categorizations I have laid out above as a means of organizing and addressing variations, I seek as well to thread these modes of invitation together. To use an outdated analogy, these varying strategies all to some degree appear to be rooted in an understanding of the Internet as the water-cooler of the new millennium. While Phillip Swann (2000) argues that the proliferation of program choices via the expansion of cable and satellite has made it harder for people to discuss any given show around the water-cooler at work (with so many shows on, what are the chances that one's co-workers will have watched the same thing you have?), the Internet seems to operate for many viewers as their water-cooler (who needs co-workers when you can reach out across geographical boundaries to chat about that episode online?).

I also use the water-cooler analogy because I argue in this book that the Internet has reinvigorated elements of oral culture – specifically, storytelling as understood by Walter Benjamin (1968). On one (and perhaps the most obvious) level, most TV-oriented websites clearly invite the viewer to *participate* in the interpretation and understanding of a story – that has been told to them *by* TV. According to Benjamin, the element of participation is a key dynamic of storytelling.

On another level, I argue that the Internet – through stoking participation – in turn influences the storytelling that emerges from TV, such that TV as a storyteller in turn stokes participation on the part of those listening. In short, the Internet's placement "between" sites of production and sites of reception creates a sense of proximity among those at work in these sites that in turn encourages a sense of reciprocity and closeness between industry professionals and viewers (see Johnson 2007).

While I will discuss Benjamin's understanding of storytelling further on, here I simply note that for Benjamin, one of the most elemental dynamics of "good" storytelling is some measure of reciprocity between the storyteller and the listener – such that the distinction between these two positions is somewhat muddled in the larger scheme of things. In order to explore this dynamic of reciprocity, I weave throughout this book stories offered to me by writers, producers, marketers, Internet professionals, and network executives – along with stories and opinions I gathered from viewers of the shows I examine. In the many interviews I conducted and surveys I designed, I sought greater understandings of how those who consume media imagine and relate to those who produce and promote media, and of course vice versa.

Beginning in 1999, I began a series of email conversations with adult viewers of *Xena: Warrior Princess* and *Buffy the Vampire Slayer* for my dissertation, which focused on the representation of female friendships on these two series. I found the majority of these respondents through postings I placed on fan sites for the shows; as I began developing this work for publication, the changes occurring with the Internet and television kept bubbling up and encouraging me to examine viewers of different programming that had significant online presences. I began to wonder: What might be different from the era of *Xena* and *Buffy* – when most series with online presences could easily be labeled "cult" – and the era of what media management and consulting firm Pricewaterhouse Coopers called "the rise of lifestyle media" (2006) – when the idea of a social audience for a television show existing through the Internet was seen as an about-to-be "given"? What new understandings of television were emerging for viewers and industry professionals? How might understandings of fandom and fan activities have changed? Or broader senses of what constituted a good storytelling experience?

To begin exploring these questions, in 2005 I designed a survey about television viewing and Internet activities and, through online postings at fan and industry sites for the series I had decided to explore, as well as at the numerous more generalized media entertainment sites that had grown online since 1997, I invited viewers to take part in the survey. In an attempt to broaden my sample beyond those already online, I also solicited involvement from college students at my home institution of Columbia College, Chicago. Those who completed the survey were then invited to participate in follow-up email conversations that were show-specific, most of which occurred via a temporary LiveJournal site that allowed participants to speak online with each other, as well as with me, if they wished.[5]

Across these multiple years and surveys, I received survey responses from a total of 143 individuals, 65 from the 1999 survey and 78 from the 2005 survey. Among the first group of earlier viewers, I relied primarily on 40 respondents; among the second batch, I relied on all 78 and engaged in follow-up exchanges with 56.[6] The majority of respondents in both samples identified as White, female, and US citizens. The end result of this drawn out process was a rich series of exchanges among myself and participants that offers a sense of what has changed in terms of the relationship between television and the Internet and how these changes have created and/or sustained broader changes within the television industry. Combining the surveys with my interviews of industry professionals, I discovered an excitement about television and its power to promote a participatory experience that is creating new (and often confusing) notions of storytelling and ownership. I also found creators and consumers eager to share their stories with a readership beyond myself. I hope those reading this book take heed of the voices found throughout its pages, considering my own voice as but a guide through this invigorating terrain of tele-participation.

Cult Television and Extension of the TV Text

Fictional worlds, of necessity, always exceed *the texts that describe them. (Gwenllian-Jones 2004: 92; my emphasis)*

One of the more intriguing relationships I found across the earlier and later years of my audience research revolved around viewers' sense of whether or not they were watching "acceptable" or mainstream television, and whether or not they perceived their TV-related activities to be "typical." Thus, in order to situate this project further, here I examine briefly the role that cult TV has played in academic understandings of the social audience. Cult television shows historically have been the primary sites around which viewers have participated with the TV text, and most academic research concerning fan activities has centered on such programs.

Scholars writing about cult TV fandom often disagree as to the minutiae of what constitutes a cult television text and as to what constitutes cult TV fandom, but many describe a form of tele-participation that necessarily includes a show that "prompts" (somehow) a need for viewers to ponder the world of their program in all its complexity. This "pondering" might take any number of forms: creating a fanzine, joining a club, contributing to fan-based encyclopedias, writing slash fiction ... but whatever the form of tele-participation might be, a general scholarly consensus has emerged that cult TV is uniquely poised to prompt such activities and that true cult TV fandom demands this tele-participation.

While Sara Gwenllian-Jones, in the above quote, seems to imply that *any* fictional television show can prompt such activity, most scholars writing about cult TV fandom (Gwenllian-Jones included) reserve a special place for cult TV in the pantheon of television fandom. There seems to be something "different" about such texts and the fandom they inspire. For example, Gwenllian-Jones argues elsewhere that cult television can be defined by a series of narrative traits that induce tele-participation that – in today's TV viewing world – leads a fan naturally to the Internet:

> From 1990 onwards, a number of television series have been produced and marketed precisely in order to attract particular microcultures and to foster within them *not just regular viewers* but also a high proportion of fans ... Intertextuality, metatextuality, self-referentiality, story-arc and stand-alone episodes within the same series, an exaggerated play of fracture and textual excess and generic interconnections with wider subcultures (science-fiction, fantasy, horror, conspiracist, ufological) are knowingly employed to seduce viewers into intense engagements with the fictional worlds and fantastic logics of the cult television series' diegesis. The wide open, *producerly* texts of these series appeal not so much to their audiences' desire to be entertained as to its need to be imaginatively involved. (Gwenllian-Jones 2003: 166; my emphasis)

This somewhat overwhelming list of narrative traits is representative of many other scholars' assessments of "what it is" about cult TV texts that promotes cult fandom.[7] I agree with the general argument that shows that become cult programs tend to share specific narrative traits (such as those listed above) and that these traits are conducive to tele-participation. However, I am more interested in exploring here briefly if there are elements found in cult TV and in cult TV fandom that are not necessarily exclusive to the domain of cult. How have more recent TV shows perhaps borrowed from the strategies of cult television and its fandom to create more mainstream programming that *does* attract "just regular viewers"? Indeed, how might such narrative strategies currently be reconfiguring the very idea of "the regular viewer" to more closely approximate "the (cult) fan"?

One valuable line of inquiry can be extrapolated from Matt Hills's discussion of cult TV fandom. Hills (2002) argues that one important element in defining a cult text is that the audience claims the text as in fact cult. This inclusion of the viewer serves two useful purposes. First, allowing for viewer distinctions helps to delimit definitions of cult TV that rely solely on textual characteristics. Second, highlighting the audience clarifies that part of defining cult TV must of necessity include the audience and their experience with the text. For the purposes of what this book will examine, Hills provides a useful guideline: in attending to the activities of the audience (rather than focusing *primarily* on the structure and content of the text), we might find that social audiences today engage in activities and relationships with non-cult TV programs in very "cult-like" ways.

Hills himself hints at this possibility when he struggles to make a distinction between soap operas and cult TV by arguing that a characteristic narrative element of cult TV is an "endlessly deferred narrative" (134). Yet, many scholars describe soap narratives in exactly this manner.[8] More to the point, listening to the social audiences of soap operas *and* of cult texts might reveal competing perspectives. For example, in my own audience research on *Buffy* and *Xena*, many fans of these shows assessed their texts' narratives as soap-like (Ross 2002). By consistently keeping in play the social audience, their interactions with the TV text, and the text proper, it becomes apparent that a good deal of what scholars describe when discussing cult TV (and cult TV fandom especially) resembles the descriptions forthcoming in this book – in terms of both what social audiences are doing *and* in terms of what writers, producers, networks, and marketers are doing. For example, both Hills and Gwenllian-Jones (with her co-editor Roberta E. Pearson, 2004) describe cult TV fans as members of communities that tend to produce tertiary texts such as fan fiction, music videos, or websites and that tend to engage in tertiary activities such as traveling to visit sites from a show, or impersonating a character. As Hills (2002) puts it, "an important part of being a cult fan … involves *extending the reader-text* … relationship into other areas of fan experience" (22, my emphasis).

Yet, most of the shows I examine cannot easily be labeled cult. My point is not so much to argue that academic definitions of cult TV are flawed; rather, it is to suggest that specific facets of cult TV narratives *and the tele-participation that intermingles with these facets* may be as important in other kinds of programs as they are in cult programs. By emphasizing the dynamic of "extending the reader-text," we can begin to imagine possibilities beyond (without leaving behind) the cult. As S. Elizabeth Bird's (2003) research on an online fan community for *Doctor Quinn Medicine Woman* demonstrates, even the most "unlikely" of television shows can inspire intense tele-participation. In addition, Hills points out that a wide range of fandom and fan activities exists, making fandom in general difficult to define; by emphasizing the concept of the social audience, we can also begin to imagine possibilities of tele-participation beyond (without leaving behind) fandom.

Based on my observations of Internet activity related to television, activities and textual strategies that used to be primarily the domain of cult TV and its fans are increasingly a part of TV making and viewing more generally, suggesting the importance of audience and industry research today to understanding both "TV" and "TV fandom." To take one example, Will Brooker's examination of the official *Dawson's Creek* (January 1998–2003) website and how some viewers used it revealed that for most participants, the website extended the TV text of *Dawson's Creek*, but to a limited degree. Website users primarily turned to the site for basic information on the show, rather than for chatting about the show with others.

Brooker describes the website as a prime example of a program

> deliberately overflow[ing] the bounds of television … rais[ing] important questions about the experience of watching television, and the concept of the television audience. To what extent has the nature of watching

television changed due to dedicated websites that offer an immersive, participatory experience? (Brooker 2004: 569–70)

In short, Brooker discovered that the importance of the website to regular viewers was limited – that, for this group of participants, "the nature of watching television" may not have changed much, regardless of whether or not a "website that offered an immersive, participatory experience" existed.

Brooker's study is important in three key respects. First, the website for *Dawson's Creek* is designed in a manner similar to websites that preceded it for programs designated "cult." Second, this similarity suggests that the managers of this site have a vision of the social audience as likely to respond to such a "cult" appeal online – even though most critics have firmly and consistently labeled the series a teen soap opera. And third, regardless of what the managers of this site may have assumed or desired, in the case of Brooker's subjects at least, viewers were not responding to the site in its fullest capacities.

Hills (2004), in fact, refers to *Dawson's Creek* as an example of "mainstream cult." The distinction he is making between cult and mainstream cult is "between fan cultures that construct their own intertextual links between programmes ... and fandoms that largely follow intertextual links put in place by the media industry to court such fans" (63). In other words, many of the activities fans of this show engaged in resembled those of cult fans – but these activities were not likely to have occurred if not for the strategies evident within the text and/or on the website.

Still, Brooker's actual audience research (as opposed to, in this case, Hills's textual and industrial analysis) suggests that "cult-like" strategies are no guarantee of cult-like consumer behavior. If "overflow" exists but tele-participation is limited to the degree that Brooker describes, why study it? To begin with, perhaps it is not as limited as Brooker suggests (thus the scope of this book in terms of approaching a variety of shows). In addition, the fact that industry professionals seem to be seeking tele-participation and extension of the TV text suggests that the tele-participating viewer is becoming a prototype – and real or imagined, the *perception* of the social audience is often as important as the *actuality* of the social audience when it comes to what the industry will offer.

TV, like other arts, is a *shared* practice, bounded by the limits (in the US) of a commercial industry that today includes the Internet. As Raymond Williams argues:

> The relationship between the making of a work of art and its reception is always active, and subject to conventions, which in themselves are forms of (changing) social organization and relationship, and this is radically different from the production and consumption of an object. It is indeed an activity and a practice ... only accessible through active perception and interpretation ... We have to break from the common practice of isolating the object ... We have to discover the nature of a practice and then its conditions. (Williams 1980: 47)

As with any shared *practice*, then, there will be a range of constantly shifting activities. What I propose to examine in this book is such a range. In the spirit of Williams, I seek to "discover the nature" of practices involved with TV and the Internet and the conditions (including the limits) of those practices, refusing to isolate the object of TV from the audience *or* from the industry. And in the spirit of Hills and Brooker, I seek to discover the *changing* nature of the practices associated with television in the age of the Internet.

Managing Tele-Participation: Industry and Viewers

> *"Individual" viewing encounters a variety of institutional practices, from the director watching back-episodes of a soap opera before plotting his first block, through the producers watching the first assembly of an episode, to school children in the playground competing to retell the previous night's story. (Tulloch 1990: 19)*

> *To gauge the response of his viewers, [Dan] Schneider [creator of Nickelodeon's* Zoey 101*] said, he reads Internet message boards. (Arthur 2005: 6)*

Although these two quotes commenting on the relationship between TV creators and viewers are separated by 15 years, they collectively zero in on a common dynamic between professionals and "regular consumers" that reaches far back in time: few consumers leave a text at its reading, and few producers leave a text at its point of official completion. This is especially true for something like series television, which relies on a continuity from episode to episode that makes the text "never-ending" from both a creative and reception context. One can see this relationship at work as well in newspapers' publications of serial stories and comics, and also in the marketing of stars from the era of classical Hollywood cinema. We are facing a relationship with long and vibrant roots in media that historically precedes television.[9]

Magazines in particular became a favored site for the filmgoer of the 1940s and 1950s who wanted to follow something specific about a film in more detail, and therefore it is hardly surprising that a primary forum for tele-participation has been the same. Cult TV shows especially have capitalized on the magazine format, offering fans details on everything from dialogue to upcoming casting decisions to interviews with producers, writers, and stars. Some fans turned also to fanzines – homemade fan creations offering fan fiction and fan commentary.[10] Today, more mainstream magazines cater to fans of specific shows as well; *Entertainment Weekly* has become noted for its periodic "fan issues" on series ranging from the cult show *Buffy the Vampire Slayer* to the top hit *Seinfeld*.

Another forum for fans of cult programs that has reliably produced interaction with producers, writers, and stars has been the convention. In 1971:

> Creation Entertainment [began] a 34 year tradition of producing the world's leading conventions for fans of genre television and films. Creation has organized over 2,300 events in major cities throughout the globe. Creation is also the acknowledged leader in the manufacture of fine collectibles, apparel and autographed items for fellow fans! As fans ourselves, we take pride in delivering the best! (www.creationent.com/)

Some of the earliest TV series Creation Entertainment produced conventions for were *Star Trek* (1966–9) and *Doctor Who* (1963–December 1989, first run) – both cult programs.[11] Such conventions have traditionally focused on cult TV programming, whereas more mainstream fare has sought other venues. Series featuring teens, for example, have taken advantage of the American mall to bring stars (with producers hidden in the background) to teen viewers assumed to be primarily interested in the characters and their actors rather than their creators.

With the proliferation of access to the Internet and the World Wide Web, viewers of any number of styles of programming could create and find sites offering many of the advantages of entertainment magazines, fanzines, and conventions. While at first the history of such sites appears to have belonged to the cult TV show, the reader will see in the remainder of this book that "regular"/"non-cult" sites have proliferated to much the same degree as those for cult programs. An important differentiation exists between those online sites created by the industry and those created by viewers – a differentiation similar to that which exists between most fan magazines and fanzines: official publications, be they online or in print, have agendas and advantages different in kind from those created and maintained by viewers (such as official sites providing easier access to creators and copyright permissions). Nevertheless, a largely, though not always consistently, symbiotic relationship has emerged between the industry-industry sites and the viewer-viewer sites that allows each "group" to use the other for their own ends – with the balance of power almost always residing in the hands of the industry. While I will examine this "delicate ecosystem" in future chapters, my point here is to more generally explore how the Internet especially has become a site at which the industry and its needs intermingles with the viewers and their needs more thoroughly than before.

This intermingling of producer/pursuer and product/consumer/ pursuer is an important area of change to consider. As Philip Napoli points out, "the pursuit of [media audiences as an economic product has affected] … the structure of media industries and the behavior of media organizations" (2003: 6). Tele-participation has become an increasingly crucial element in industrial strategies to capture the ever-splintering audience, as well as a crucial element in viewers' expectations for television. The Internet, meeting television *and* meeting the viewer, is an important part of this historical reconfiguration of television in its broadest sense. As computer technology developed to make the creation and maintenance of websites easier beginning in the 1990s, broader cultural and societal changes occurred as well – from an increased emphasis on computer literacy in the classroom and demands for digital divides to be bridged (through initiatives such as bringing the Internet to public libraries), to shifts in the dynamics of family life.[12] It didn't take long in the bigger scheme of things cultural and social for the Internet to become naturalized for many – or at least for those who "count."

Concurrently, changes in technology directly related to the television industry also began to occur. The development of digital cable and satellite in particular has created what John Ellis (2000) refers to as a shift from a television era of scarcity to one of proliferation and fragmentation. The resulting increased competition for viewers in the midst of a splintering general audience led to new conceptions of the social audience – *and* new conceptions of the industry itself. Today, there exists an increased importance of the niche market, discrete collections of viewers demarcated most often along lines of age (especially 18–49 and teen), gender, race, and income. One need only look at the full cable spectrum of channel choices to see how many stations break down along specific lines of viewer demographics (Lifetime for women, Spike TV for men, The N for young adults, BET for African Americans) and/or lines of content assumed to correspond to desired demographics (Food Network, Travel Channel, BBCAmerica). Competition has only increased as new technologies allowing the development of DVD, digital video recording, and video streaming have offered alternative modes of viewing to consumers with the means.

To more directly link such broad changes to the project at hand, one can "imagine the possibilities" – many of which have come to fruition – in terms of channels devoted to specific social audiences. The Sci-Fi Network emerged on cable in 1992 and continues today as a site for the distribution of primarily cult science-fiction and fantasy shows, with the attendant assumption that viewers seeking out this channel are willing to pay for it. The N bills itself exclusively to young adults as members of a social audience seeking a network they can *literally* relate to: one promotional bump airing during commercial breaks features a teen girl annoyed by her kid brother receiving a pager text message *from The N* which reassures her that someday things will get better.

I raise this context here to demonstrate the complexities of what can occur when technological, cultural, social, and industrial changes converge: the viewers to whom The N and Sci-Fi pitch themselves have little trouble navigating such systems of relationships, even though it is unlikely that the average viewer of a program on either network knows the web of corporate bonding that exists beyond it. This seamlessness demonstrates the degree of finesse with which the television industry has learned to *manage* such changes as the ones I describe in this book – a level of expertise that extends to, and may even rely on, the Internet (Johnson 2007). Further, some viewers I spoke with for this book *do* indeed understand the complexities of ownership/production and distribution *because the Internet has made such information available*. Typically, viewers seek out such information as they work to solidify their sense of being members of a social audience – for example, when trying to obtain permission for stills, or when trying to save a show from cancellation. The overall picture is one of a fine balancing act between the power of the industry on the one hand and the power of viewers on the other, and throughout this book I work to lay out the industrial frameworks within which the various invitational relationships I explore take place.

An Aesthetics of Multiplicity

Robert C. Allen and Annette Hill (2004), in a discussion concerning the future of television, make two astute observations about the nature of this medium. First, "change … is not something about to happen, but something that has been a part of the experience of television since its introduction" (537). The impact of the Internet on TV creating and viewing, while unique in its specific manifestations, is part of a historical continuum that includes fears of TV "dying" accompanied by heightened expectations for TV's ability to radically alter the society and culture within which creators and viewers live. Second, "transformation[s] of television … [take] place in relation both to those with the money and inclination to invest in the latest technology and those for whom television still means a few broadcast channels" (537). In other words, while the specific slice of change I am studying here is just that – specific and a slice of much broader trends and patterns – this does not necessarily mean that such developments have not/do not/will not come to have significant impact on those who may not be involved directly with such change. In fact, this may be one of the more pertinent elements of this book: when the inclinations, abilities, and actions of the few impact the many, we are dealing with crucial issues of power and privilege.

The complexities of television demand an adequately complex methodological approach. As a primary starting point, I take the concept of invitation beyond its colloquial use of asking someone to attend some event; here, invitation is best understood as a key factor in designating the *relationship* between viewer, text, and creator as a reciprocal one. The industry has come to learn that viewers want to be "invited to the party," so to speak. Creative professionals have responded to this growing knowledge with invitations to tele-participate – and as with any "formal party," certain expectations arise on the part of both the hosts and the invitees.

As Janet Staiger (1992) points out, spectators have relationships with texts; the text is not purely determinative of meaning. This is even more the case when the Internet operates as a forum in which a viewer's relationship with the text can include a relationship of some type with creators and promoters of that text. A web of interactions emerges that encompasses myriad relationships: between viewers and creators, between viewers and originating texts, between creators and originating texts, between originating texts and the Internet, and between/among viewers, creators, promoters, the originating text, and the Internet. As well, both industry professionals and spectators exist in sociohistorical contexts that contribute to meaning and understanding – contexts that include personal narratives, shared cultural narratives, and even individual understandings of industrial narratives.

This understanding of invitation demands that various constitutive elements be examined simultaneously; thus, I interview and examine not just viewers, but also writers, producers, marketers, and critics (who ostensibly serve as a public nexus between viewers and the industry). More specifically, I work to bring these narratives together, seeking to examine how TV in conjunction with the Internet serves the needs of all these various narrative contributors – and what happens when needs are *not* met. How does TV in conjunction with the Internet feed what John Ellis describes as a "deep human need for association and personal fulfillment, as like-minded individuals try to find each other" (2000: 64)? If human beings rely on TV in conjunction with the Internet for this sense of community, how does this serve the needs of an increasingly fragmented TV industry that relies on niche marketing? How does the industry respond when a social audience feels that the industry is disrupting their community, or when a social audience

RSVPs to an invitation in an unexpected manner? How does the social audience respond when they feel that the industry's invitation has been misleading or revoked?

In this book, I work to highlight and make manifest the range and complexity of the relationships that exist today among a wide variety of people and entities via the Internet. John Caldwell refers to the strategic industrial components of such relationships as "second-shift aesthetics" (2002: 132) that seek to establish a relationship with the viewing audience. Working from this descriptive label, and factoring in those resulting relationships, we are dealing overall with what I refer to as an aesthetics of multiplicity. At the broadest level, the range and complexity of these relationships itself represents an aesthetics of multiplicity, whereby the lines of communication among different people and entities begin to intersect in constantly shifting ways – a web of relationships operating most often like the connections that occur on an Internet site. At a more specific level, within episodes and within Internet sites about television programs, an emphasis on multiplicity emerges as the norm in the creating and viewing of television; the "text proper" of the TV series becomes inextricable from the text of the Internet site – which itself multiplies as sites link to other sites, message board topics spur additional topics, etc. The text and the creators and the viewers become inseparable from each other.

To return to the genre of soap opera in relation to the extension of the TV text, I refer briefly to the work of Jennifer Hayward (1997). Soap operas, with their paradigmatic structure, feature stories focused on the relationships that exist between characters of a large ensemble and the associations that exist between stories. Soap operas' aesthetics of multiplicity works to sustain the social audiences which emerge, allowing for and indeed promoting an experience of TV viewing and creating as an experience of "retelling." Between creators, viewers, originating texts, and the Internet, there emerge stories *about* stories as the constantly multiplying elements of this genre prompt what Hayward refers to as "radical oscillation" among viewers (150–1). Viewers "bounce," so to speak: among characters and their multiplying storylines, among emotional and cognitive responses to those characters and storylines – which themselves bounce due to the ever-changing nature of soap operas via their seriality. I would argue that the Internet offers an additional realm of radical oscillation: surfers bounce literally from site to site and from link to link within any given site as they expand upon the paradigmatic structure which the originating text offered to them initially on their TV screens. In this book I will take time to examine how the paradigmatic structure of many shows today is refracted in the paradigmatic structure of the Internet and individual websites – and how this structuring prompts radical oscillation among viewers (that is in turn refracted back to them by the originating texts as the texts' creators respond to this oscillation with oscillations of their own).

I also explore what radical oscillation might garner the viewer from a psychological perspective. Hayward (1997) argues that radical oscillation prompts pleasures of participation as viewers can actively "take up" *various* positions of identification in order to explore the relationships and associations that may exist between characters and stories. The resulting awareness that "all perspectives are partial, colored by place and context" encourages viewers to embrace a philosophy in regards to their text's stories that they "must seek knowledge of all points of view before making judgments" (4). While only audience research can determine (and then only ever incompletely) if paradigmatically structured TV stories do indeed prompt viewers to such an awareness, as Hayward points out, soap operas have traditionally prompted among viewers "ritual[s] of (often collaborative) reading or viewing" – rituals made much easier by the presence of the Internet (137).[13] It takes no small stretch of the imagination to argue that the Internet "naturally" offers multiple arguments and an awareness that multiple perspectives exist. Of course, what viewers do with this awareness of multiplicity is an entirely different matter, as intertwined as all this multiplicity is with industrial invitational strategies.

Feminist epistemologist Lorraine Code's (1991, 1995) concepts of second-person knowing and epistemic negotiation fit into Hayward's arguments nicely. Discussing women's gossip as a form of storytelling, Code describes a mode of building knowledge among women that positions knowledge as a joint endeavor: one can never truly understand something or someone without exploring others' (second-persons') positions or stories. Through informal conversation, be it oral gossiping or online debating, participants create and explore knowledge through constant readjustments that emerge through negotiations and retellings of stories. For Code and for Hayward, this matrix of multiplicity creates something useful in a political sense – from a "simple" awareness that knowledge is not finite, to the endorsement of a way of understanding that circumvents traditional conceptualizations of knowledge as "set" and unidirectional in terms of how it is "passed on."

While I agree that such an understanding of knowledge and its processes has indeed historically been the domain of those outside of traditional power structures, I would argue that to some degree the Internet as an extension of the TV text – with its role in an aesthetics of multiplicity – is contributing to a broader embrace of such a philosophy. In line with Henry Jenkins's (2006) use of Pierre Levy's notion of collective intelligence, I agree that many of the activities that surround tele-participation promote the notion that "none of us can know everything; each of us knows something; and we can put the pieces together if we pool our resources and combine our skills" (4). Those engaging in tele-participation become focused on the nature of knowledge and truth itself, faced with the multiple perspectives at work in collective knowledge-building.

Walter Benjamin (1968) might argue that such a matrix of multiplicity can be traced back to perhaps the earliest days of human civilization, when oral storytelling dominated as a mode of communication. In his essay "The Storyteller," Benjamin argues that storytelling and the story should contain something useful for the listener: a means in which to participate in the storytelling so that the story may suit their needs. "Good" storytelling prompts retellings of the story – retellings that may involve changes as befit the context in which the stories are circulating. Stories and storytelling should offer "less an answer to a question than a proposal concerning the continuation of a story which is just unfolding" (86). This "lack of ending" invites the listeners to become a part of the story by continuing its trajectory themselves. This basic description resonates strongly with Hayward's points about soap operas (perhaps the ultimate "continuing stories") and their correlative radical oscillation prompting an awareness that "all perspectives are partial." The description resonates as well with Code's description of knowledge-building through second-person knowing and epistemic negotiation, and of course with Jenkins's discussion of collective knowledge.

In addition, I would argue that TV series in general suit Benjamin's discussion of storytelling – in spite of the fact that he insists that storytelling (in the way he describes it) is "dead." The TV series must continue, from episode to episode and from season to season. Certainly, some types of TV stories rely on continuation more than others. However, when factoring in the Internet as an extension of the TV text, Benjamin's contention that storytelling has become a lost form of communication begins to crumble a bit. If, as Benjamin argues, story-telling relies on "the ability to exchange perspectives," the Internet as an extension of the TV text may be contributing mightily to a revitali-zation of storytelling (83). Indeed, given the predominance of televi-sion viewing in American culture, how can we understand the dynamics of storytelling and what it means to people *without* studying TV? The importance of TV – or perhaps more precisely, the ubiqui-tousness of TV – in American culture today suggests that it is in and of itself "something useful" for viewers.

As viewers, one of our primary pleasures involves feeling a sense of connection with the position of a character – with the place that a char-acter holds in the narrative: What is their "story of desire?"[14] It is *story-telling itself* that resonates with us; hearing or reading or seeing a story "reminds us" that we, too, desire to have a story worth telling. Further, the more narrative positions a story offers – the more options for iden-tification offered – the higher resonance the originating text has for the viewer. Perhaps more pertinent to the research at hand, the more a narrative invites viewers to feel as if they are a part of the storytelling experience, the higher the resonance with the viewer. And when this narrative has expanded beyond the "TV text proper" through various invitational strategies, a sense of contribution and ownership multi-plies. Thus, storytelling such as this, interwoven with notions of con-tribution and ownership, becomes about more than immediate gratification – it is about pleasurable work.

Still, some TV texts prompt more work than others – and not every-one wants the workload. In this book I focus on the fact that many *popular and successful* shows of a wide variety of genres are prompting pleasurable work, relying on the Internet to encourage and endorse the strategies they use as they seek to connect with those viewers will-ing to work. The strategies at hand operate to manage the significant shift that has occurred in industry understandings of the social audi-ence as comprised of ever-smaller and more isolated groups. John Ellis (2000) argues that television has been developing an increasingly indi-vidualized mode of storytelling due to the increased competition resulting from an explosion of channels and viewing options. "The mode of address of programmes [has become] less universalistic and more specific," appealing to viewers in what appears to be a direct, personally designed manner (71). Perhaps more importantly, these direct appeals are, in fact, multiple and shifting *from the perspective of the viewer*, according to Ellis:

> At the level of individuals, the new consumerism is one of *multiple and shifting identifications*. Within this market of ever more differentiated and targeted commodities, it sometimes seems that individuals can establish their styles and identities from a *vast range of possibilities*. (65, my emphasis)

Thus, somewhat paradoxically, we are living in an era that emphasizes the perception of *narrow* "tailor-made" invitations (niche marketing), even as we glory in an aesthetics of *multiplicity* that appears to offer us endless choice.

Without transgressing further into a discussion about a psychological need to have choices, suffice to say that in today's marketplace television viewers seem to be responding to two storytelling strategies rooted in an aesthetics of multiplicity: (1) offers of choice in a myriad of ways and forms such that an individualized connection is discerned, and (2) offers of a sense of participation and perhaps even community such that the potential alienation prompted by intensified individualization is lessened. And of course, successful storytelling strategies serve the marketplace of the TV industry as much as (if not more than) they serve the marketplace of TV viewers. Any embrace of second-person knowing, radical oscillation, or collective knowledge on the part of the industry is accompanied by a sense that "something useful" will emerge economically. And if what is ultimately most useful to the social audience is in tension with what is most useful to the industry, the relationships in this aesthetics of multiplicity will become strained, forcing new strategies of storytelling to emerge for all those involved.

The Big Picture

Online fandom has attracted substantially more attention from journalists, scholars ands crucially, the culture industry itself. (Gwenllian-Jones 2003: 168)

This is some serious watching (and writing and producing and marketing) we are talking about here. I will be exploring a complex set of relationships – both real and imagined – that may raise more questions than provide answers. While I will in fact be arguing that the Internet has significantly altered the manner in which TV is created and understood, and at times explore directly the question of how the social audience has an impact on storytelling, the primary focus of this book is concerned less with cause and effect and more with attempting to unravel the ways in which modes of communication and storytelling are influencing understandings of "TV." Along the way, multiple areas of inquiry will emerge. Are we dealing with a primarily generational shift in how TV and storytelling are understood? Are these new understandings the domain of a privileged few? Has the Internet as a venue for storytelling as Benjamin describes it contributed to a shift within television that offers more to viewers – or that merely reconfigures what we have seen for decades already on TV in terms of representation and storytelling?

I have organized this book around case studies – programs that I believe exemplify a convergence of TV and the Internet through tele-participation. Clearly, not every TV series inspires extensive online fandom, and not every TV series (postmodern though our TV world may be) evidences awareness of this fandom. I am not claiming that this extension of the TV text is indicative of where TV is going in general (a topic I will discuss in the conclusion); I am, however, claiming that tele-participation occurs more regularly and on a more widespread basis than we might suspect, largely because the industry has been working to promote and manage this trend.

Chapter one examines *Buffy* and *Xena* in light of the academic history surrounding understandings of tele-participation via cult TV texts and to some degree soap operas. Across chapter one, I claim that the development of the Internet as a tool for TV viewers demands a reconceptualization of Annette Kuhn's (1992) idea of the social audience to accommodate a more persistent and complex sense of interactivity that emphasizes the socializing element of the audience – exemplified by the adult fandom of *Buffy* and *Xena*. Shifting from the niche market cult content and fandom of *Buffy* and *Xena*, I examine in chapter two the overt style of invitation at work in *American Idol* and to a lesser degree in *The Family Guy* and the Cartoon Network's Adult Swim block of programming. With *American Idol*, I examine how the show taps into a rhetoric of "freedom of choice" that permeates extensions of the show as well, resulting in a sense of shared ownership among viewers. This theme of shared ownership operates with *Family Guy* also, and I examine the unusual trajectory of this series and how fan power propelled this, taking the show from cancellation to syndication on the Cartoon Network's Adult Swim to a return with original episodes on its original network (FOX). Finally, I explore the relationship between the notions of freedom, choice, and ownership with the rise in viewer-created video content online, via sites such as YouTube.com.

I continue discussion of these themes into chapter three, examining the Canadian TV series *Degrassi: The Next Generation* and the US TV series *The O.C.* Because these two shows are teen-driven and loosely soap operatic, in chapter three I explore elements of generation, genre, and narrative structure in conjunction with processes and pleasures of identification (both in relation to the shows and to the Internet). In particular I examine the emergence of online social networking in conjunction with these two series, considering how this development is operating with the way that these programs and "teen networks" are reaching out to millennial viewers with organically oriented invitations to tele-participation.

The shows I have mentioned previously are all significant to the establishment and maintenance of the respective networks on which they have aired (with the exception of *Xena*, which was a syndicated program); in chapter four I develop earlier discussions of network branding and network power, concurrent with a close examination of the ABC series *Lost*. This show provides an interesting opportunity to explore several dimensions of TV watching today. As a series that falls best in the mode of the fantastic (which I will discuss in this chapter), *Lost* has much in common narratively with cult fan shows of the past. Yet, it was a Top Ten hit in its debut season and one of the shows responsible for raising ABC in key demographic ratings after a long-term slump. The show also has inspired a rapidly developing and complex Internet presence similar to that for *Buffy* and *Xena*. I use this show (and its attendant complex situating within the fantastic, within a "Big Three" network, and within the Internet) to demonstrate the mode of invitation that I refer to as obscured, focusing on how the TV industry has been watching this series and its successful invitations as a potential model for future developments of tele-participation.

I begin to build up to a concluding chapter by considering more specifically the broader landscape within which these particular shows have existed, looking closely at issues of the TV industry, tele-participation, and power. I offer tentative conclusions about TV watching and making in the US today, exploring shows that were "Internet darlings" yet that failed (e.g., *Joan of Arcadia*, *Wonderfalls*), and successful fan campaigns to save shows via the Internet (e.g., *Roswell*, *Farscape*). I also use the concluding chapter to explore the possibilities of future modes of making and watching TV, focusing on industrial professionals' and popular TV critics' thoughts about TV/TV watching today. Will the Internet (and the cell phone and the video game and the digital video recorder and the iPod ...) continue to become integral to our understandings of and experiences with TV? If so, what issues does this raise in regards to access and literacy and power and socialization? What issues does this raise for writers and producers and networks facing increasing demands from viewers? What issues does this raise for social audiences and more "isolated" viewers with their increased expectations as they face the fine-tuned strategies of an industry unlikely to relinquish much control over tele-participation?

My intention with this book is not to use these shows and their online fandom as exemplary modes of tele-participation, nor to hold up these models of tele-participation and invitational strategies as in any way typical for all of TV making and watching. Nor do I wish to naively celebrate the power of the social audience, or to cynically bemoan the eternal might of the television industry. Rather, I hope to use this project to examine what I perceive as a shift in the way some people think about and experience TV, from viewers (including those who may not use the Internet), to writers and producers, to networks, to marketers, and to critics – and the dynamics of the relationships that have begun to develop among these constituents via this shift. It is only through sharing the stories of those involved intimately *with* cultural storytelling that we can begin to appreciate the complexities of television in this new era. Exploring change and what that even means within television/television studies is part of our cultural and academic heritage. Given the many joys and disappointments that TV brings us in our everyday lives, a richer understanding of this medium and how it tells us stories about our world and ourselves seems, in the spirit of Benjamin, to be "something useful" for us all.

Notes

1 Producers approached Melissa Good, a *Xena* fan well known online for her fan fiction, to write the Season 6 episode "Legacy" (November 4, 2000); that same season featured an episode in which fans of the series brought the "real" Xena and Gabrielle to life via cloning ("Send in the Clones," April 28, 2001) and one in which an academic conference on mythological figures is interrupted by two fans asking the executive producer of the series to extend the show for one more season ("Soul Possession," June 9, 2001).

2 My deepest gratitude goes out to Janet Staiger, Amanda Lotz, and Matt Hills for their excellent suggestions about making a distinction between Louis Althusser's concept of "interpellation" (1971) and the relationships I am describing in this book, which fall better into the dynamics associated with an "invitation."

3 In the Season 6 episode "You Are There" (February 10, 2001) a TV tabloid reporter attempts to get the answer to this question – in spite of the fact that TV did not exist in Ancient Greece, where most of the series is set. (And in fact, no answer is forthcoming when "technical difficulties" cut the feed and the reporter's transmission is interrupted.)

4 In the summer of 2005, Al Gore launched the cable network Current.TV, which offers "viewer-created content, or VC2 ... [that] anybody can join in to produce ... or watch and vote" (www.current.tv/).

5 Both sets of surveys were submitted to the Institutional Review Boards at the universities from which I was conducting my research and were approved. The 1999 survey consisted primarily of open-ended questions soliciting opinions about a range of topics (from why a viewer might think Xena and Gabrielle were lovers, to how a viewer might define quality TV). The 2005 survey offered a mix of objective questions that allowed me to look for trends among respondents in terms of the types of activities they were engaging in, with a small amount of open-ended questions focused on opinions about why TV-oriented websites existed, why specific shows or types of shows had strong online presences, and the appeal of the Internet for TV viewers. The follow-up queries were entirely open-ended, and focused on a mix of show-specific elements and more general themes such as definitions of quality TV and good story-telling, and opinions about whether or not viewers had the right to be heard by producers, etc.

6 The discrepancy in the first sample resulted from a decision to exclude earlier responses from participants who later stopped participating due to a variety of factors, ranging from discomfort with topic matter as I shared

work (particularly chapters on sexual orientation) to simply "disappearing" from the Internet.

7 See, for example, Hills (2002); Jenkins (1992); Lancaster (2001).

8 See, for example, Allen (1985); Ang (1982); Brown (1990); Modleski (1982).

9 For an excellent discussion of the relationships between producers, distributors, critics, and readers of Charles Dickens novels and Milton Caniff's comics in newspapers, see Hayward (1997). Extensive work exists on the phenomenon of classical Hollywood stars as a text in their own right; I refer the reader to Schatz (1997); Stacey (1994); Gledhill (1991).

10 In addition, many fans have since become editors of full fan magazines, replete with publishing deals and regular publication dates – as opposed to fanzines' more haphazard, low volume publications. For a solid overview of the history of fanzines, see Romenesko (1993).

11 Comic-Con International began in 1969, and, while primarily featuring comics, has been hosting cult TV fans and creators with links to comics (however weak) since its earliest years.

12 For example, Bird and Jorgensen (2002) discuss how teen use of the Internet for homework, entertainment, and communication with peers has impacted relationships among family members.

13 See also Baym (1998).

14 Elizabeth Cowie (1997) argues that film viewers (and I would argue this applies to TV viewers as well) "go to" their visual stories because of a psychoanalytic drive to find pleasure in identification. Importantly, Cowie describes the process of identification as one of identifying with the *position* of characters – rather than the common perception that viewers identify with someone like them in terms of sex, sexuality, race, etc.

References

Allen, R. (1985) *Speaking of Soaps.* University of North Carolina Press, Chapel Hill.

Allen, R. C. and Hill, A. (2004) Introduction to Part Seven: Transforming Television. In Allen, R. and Hill, A. (eds.) *The Television Studies Reader.* Routledge, New York, pp. 535–42.

Althusser, L. (1971) Ideology and Ideological State Apparatuses. In *Lenin and Philosophy and Other Essays.* Trans. B. Brewster. Monthly Review Press, New York, pp. 127–86.

Ang, I. (1982) *Watching Dallas: Soap Opera and the Melodramatic Imagination*. Trans. Della Couling. Routledge, London.

Arthur, K. (2005) Tweener TV Dials in to Teen Wishes. *Chicago Tribune*, Tempo. August 8.

Baym, N. (1998) Talking About Soaps: Communicative Practices in a Computer-Mediated Fan Culture. In Harris, C. and Alexander, A. (eds.) *Theorizing Fandom: Fans, Subculture and Identity*. Hampton Press, Cresskill, NJ, pp. 111–29.

Benjamin, W. (1968) *Illuminations*. Ed. H. Arendt, trans. H. Zohn. Schocken Books, New York (orig. pub. 1955).

Bird, S. E. (2003) *The Audience in Everyday Life: Living in a Media World*. Routledge, New York.

Bird, S. E. and Jorgensen, J. (2002) Extending the School Day: Gender, Class and the Incorporation of Technology in Everyday Life. In Consalvo, M. and Paasonen, S. (eds.) *Women and Everyday Uses of the Internet: Agency and Identity*. Peter Lang, New York, pp. 255–74.

Brooker, W. (2004) Living on *Dawson's Creek*: Teen Viewers, Cultural Convergence, and Television Overflow. In Allen, R. and Hill, A. (eds.) *The Television Studies Reader*. Routledge, New York, pp. 569–80 (orig. pub. 2001).

Brown, M. (1990) Motley Moments: Soap Operas, Carnival, Gossip and the Power of the Utterance. In Brown, M. (ed.) *Television and Women's Culture: The Politics of the Popular*. Sage, London, pp. 183–98.

Bury, R. (2005) *Cyberspaces of Their Own: Female Fandoms Online*. Peter Lang, New York.

Caldwell, J. (2002) Interactive Audience? In Harries, D. (ed.) *The New Media Book*. BFI, London, pp. 127–44.

Code, L. (1995) *Rhetorical Spaces: Essays on Gendered Locations*. Routledge, New York.

Code, L. (1991) *What Can She Know? Feminist Theory and the Construction of Knowledge*. Cornell University Press, New York.

Cowie, E. (1997) *Representing Woman: Cinema and Psychoanalysis*. University of Minnesota Press, Minneapolis.

Ellis, J. (2000) *Seeing Things: Television in the Age of Uncertainty*. I. B. Tauris, New York.

Fiske, J. (1987) *Television Culture*. Methuen, New York.

Gledhill, C. (ed.) (1991) *Stardom: Industry of Desire*. Routledge, New York.

Gwenllian-Jones, S. (2004) Virtual Reality and Cult Television. In Gwenllian-Jones, S. and Pearson, R. (eds.) *Cult Television*. University of Minnesota Press, Minneapolis, pp. 83–97.

Gwenllian-Jones, S. (2003) Web Wars: Online Fandom and Studio Censorship. In Jancovich, M. and Lyons, J. (eds.) *Quality Popular Television: Cult TV, the Industry and Fans.* BFI, London, pp. 163–77.

Gwenllian-Jones, S. and Pearson, R. (2004) Introduction. In Gwenllian-Jones, S. and Pearson, R. (eds.) *Cult Television.* University of Minnesota Press, Minneapolis pp. ix–xx.

Hayward, J. (1997) *Consuming Pleasures: Active Audiences and Serial Fictions from Dickens to Soap Opera.* University Press of Kentucky, Lexington.

Hills, M. (2004) *Dawson's Creek*: "Quality Teen TV" and "Mainstream Cult." In Davis, G. and Dickinson, K. (eds.) *Teen TV: Genre, Consumption and Identity.* BFI, London, pp. 54–67.

Hills, M. (2002) *Fan Cultures.* Routledge, New York.

Jenkins, H. (2006) *Convergence Culture: Where Old and New Media Collide.* NYU Press, New York.

Jenkins, H. (1992) *Textual Poachers: Television Fans and Participatory Cultures.* Routledge, New York.

Johnson, D. (2007) Inviting Audiences In: The Spatial Reorganization of Production and Consumption in "TV III." *New Review of Film and Television Studies vol.* 5 (no. 1 April), 61–80.

Kuhn, A. (1992) Women's Genres. In Caughie, J. and Kuhn, A. (eds.) *The Sexual Subject: A Screen Reader in Sexuality.* Comp. Mandy Merck. Routledge, New York, pp. 301–11 (orig. pub. in *Screen* vol. 25, no.1, Winter 1984: 18–28).

Lancaster, K. (2001) *Interacting with Babylon 5: Fan Performances in a Media Universe.* University of Texas Press, Austin.

Mittell, J. (2006) Narrative Complexity in Contemporary American Television. *The Velvet Light Trap* (no. 58 Fall), 29–40.

Modleski, T. (1982) *Loving With A Vengeance: Mass-Produced Fantasies for Women.* Methuen, New York.

Napoli, P. (2003) *Audience Economics: Media Institutions and the Audience Marketplace.* Columbia University Press, New York.

Parks, S. (1997) Pleasurable Contradictions: Perceptions and Negotiations of *Xena.* Unpublished Masters thesis, Ohio State University.

PricewaterhouseCoopers. (2006) *The Rise of Lifestyle Media: Achieving Success in the Digital Convergence Era.*

Romenesko, J. (1993) The Zine Explosion. *American Journalism Review* 15 (no. 3 April), 39.

Ross, S. (2002) Super (Natural) Women: Female Heroes, Their Friends, and Their Fans. Dissertation, University of Texas at Austin.

Schatz, T. (1997) *Boom and Bust: American Cinema in the 1940s*, vol.6. University of California Press, Los Angeles.

Stacey, J. (1994) *Star Gazing: Hollywood Cinema and Female Spectatorship.*
    Routledge, New York.

Staiger, J. (1992) *Interpreting Films: Studies in the Historical Reception of
    America Cinema.* Princeton University Press, Princeton, NJ.

Swann, P. (2000) *TV dot Com: The Future of Interactive Television.* TV Books,
    New York.

Tulloch, J. (1990) *Television Drama: Agency, Audience and Myth.* Routledge,
    New York.

Williams, R. (1980) *Problems in Materialism and Culture: Selected Essays.*
    Verso and NLB, New York.

1

Fascinated with Fandom: Cautiously Aware Viewers of *Xena* and *Buffy*

I think Xena *has a cult following similar to those that develop for movies such as* Rocky Horror *or* Labyrinth. *The Internet provides a space for these subcultures of fans to meet. (Jenny)*

[Buffy] *is a show that appeals to a strange cross-section of people ... I think it picks up people who watch shows that have failed: you're picking up the kind of people who watch "convention" shows.* Star Trek, Babylon 5 *fans. The kind of people represented in* Galaxy Quest. *These are not "prime-time" people. They don't watch* ER. *And the people who watch* ER *don't watch these shows. Tere (my emphasis)*[1]

"Prime-time" people. "Convention show" people. "Subcultures" of fans. The above descriptive quotes from Jenny and Tere tap collectively into themes dominant in this chapter, in which I explore the TV series *Xena: Warrior Princess* and *Buffy the Vampire Slayer*. As I discussed in the introduction, these two programs were part of a historical moment, if you will – part of a transitional shift from the Internet being associated primarily with small cult audiences of small cult shows to viewers and professionals in the TV industry embracing the Internet more widely as an integral part of what we call television. In order to make the leap across this moment, then, from cult text and cult fandom to something "different" later, it is necessary to examine what "cult" means and what it looks like in relation to these two programs and their fans.

As both Jenny and Tere note (Jenny referencing "cult" directly), part of "cult" involves tele-participation – meeting online and going to conventions, for example. "Cult" also seems to involve a recognizable social audience – an audience filled with "certain kinds of people." One fascinating pattern in the responses of many of those who answered survey questions for me about these shows is that they often saw themselves as part of a social audience of *Xena* and/or *Buffy* viewers – while also working to distance themselves from other social audiences for the same series. In particular, these fans struggled with these shows' cult status – or, more precisely, they struggled with the idea that they themselves were likely to be perceived as cult fans. There were, in short, many exceptions to the rule among this group, with respondents explaining that they were different in how they approached their relationship to these shows (compared to "others"). Many respondents expressed awareness of how fandom for these shows operated but were cautious about taking on the mantle of fandom themselves, finding the idea somewhat distasteful. Thus, a primary theme I explore in this chapter is the relationship between notions of taste and quality in terms of fandom/cult fandom, as well as in terms of the TV text proper.

In this chapter, I focus on the role that the Internet played in the enjoyment of *Xena* and *Buffy* for this group of respondents (whom I found primarily via the Internet), striving to unravel how the dynamics which emerged can be connected to understandings of cult TV, cult TV fandom, and tele-participation. How do these viewers, in their discussions of the shows and their relationships with them, reveal academically accepted understandings of cult – and how do they suggest something other than cult fandom as academics discuss this? How important are the concepts of taste and quality to discussions and understandings of cult TV and cult fandom and tele-participation – both academically and for viewers? Another corresponding theme evident in my respondents' relationships with these programs is that of power: How does the Internet and the ways in which it opens up tele-participation factor into a viewer sense of ownership of the text – and a sense on the part of viewers that they have a right to be heard by creative and industry business professionals? Finally, how do the patterns I note with regards to these two series indicate what was on the horizon for ways in which different clusters of people involved with TV conceptualize television making and viewing? What changed and what remained?

I explore *Xena* and *Buffy* as both models of cult television and fandom and as foreshadowings of emergent forms of invitational strategies to tele-participation that are influenced heavily by the Internet. I argue that these two programs reveal the need for scholarship about television creation and reception to incorporate considerations of interactivity – that *Xena* and *Buffy* and the ways in which viewers related to them through the filter of the Internet were part of a cadre of shows which began to set new standards for viewers and industry professionals alike as to what TV could be and what it could mean to "watch TV."

"There's something different going on here": Tele-Participation and the Internet

For the uninitiated, I offer a brief examination of the significance of these two series to television studies and reception studies specifically. *Xena* and *Buffy* were contemporaries, with *Xena* emerging as a spin-off of the syndicated series *Hercules* in 1995, and *Buffy* emerging as an early WB mid-season replacement in 1997, after a movie in 1992. Industry analysts and television scholars have often credited both shows for starting a "Girl Power" trend on TV that included series such as *La Femme Nikita* (1997–2001), *Charmed* (1998–2005), and *Alias* (2001–5). *Xena* focused on the titular character seeking redemption for previous evil deeds she had committed as a warrior in areas surrounding Ancient Greece; the series was known for its high level of campy physicality, its reworkings of Greek, Roman, and Christian mythologies, and perhaps most famously for the sexually ambiguous relationship that existed between Xena and her traveling companion Gabrielle (a female bard). *Buffy* focused on the titular character coming to terms with her calling as a Slayer while still in high school (and later college) and the unique relationships formed in her life with friends, family, and enemies because of her responsibilities.[2] Both shows generically offered physical action, fantasy/supernatural features, humor blended with melodrama, and intense romantic and sexual storylines.

In the late 1990s, such themes and images were unusual in terms of the larger TV landscape. This rarity, combined with the fantastic nature of the programs and their placement as syndicated/small network shows, had much to do with their adoption as cult texts. Both of these programs can be placed within a lineage that includes the *Star Trek* franchise and *The X-Files* (1993–2002); like these series, official fan magazines published by presses known for covering cult shows (Topps, Titan) coexisted with conventions promoted by established entertainment venues such as Creation Entertainment. However, *Xena*'s and *Buffy*'s lead female character base and consistent storyline focus on issues of gender distinguished these shows for many of their fans – and for scholars as well. *Buffy* in particular spawned an astonishing academic sub-industry of sorts, with literally thousands of books and articles emerging, as well as an annual academic and fan conference, international in scope.[3] (*Xena*'s academic response base was more contained – and existed more online than "in public.")

An important element in the academic attention given to these series is that fans of the programs were aware of and contributed to the academic rhetoric that emerged so quickly. This "one-two punch" makes it unsurprising that mainstream entertainment news began covering the series as well – also relatively quickly. From *Entertainment Weekly* to *Entertainment Tonight*, to major national newspapers and smaller local ones, if people weren't watching it was difficult for the average TV viewer to have not at least heard something about these series, their heroines, and their fans. Still, in my analysis, the dynamic that solidified both series as unique in the grander scheme of things TV was the concurrence of these programs – and all their cult-like elements – with the rise of the Internet in homes across developed nations. In 1997, 18 percent of homes in the US had Internet connectivity; by 2001 this number had risen to 50 percent – with numbers higher among households with college students and/or with incomes of $100,000 or more (Murphy 2006).

Xena was one of the first television shows to promote website use, advertising its website via Universal Pictures at the end of every episode; by the second season of the show, the first endorsed fan site emerged with Whoosh!/The International Association of *Xena* Studies (www.whoosh.org), featuring academic and fan-based articles, interviews, episode summaries and analyses, and artwork. When the show began airing in repeats on WE in 2001, viewers were encouraged to chat online while episodes aired – and a live chat ticker scrolled across the TV screen to reveal what viewers were saying while they were watching. Such synergy is resonant with the manner in which I described overt modes of invitation in the introduction to this book, wherein appeals to the viewer to engage in tele-participation are clear and direct ("visit our website").

Buffy, alternatively, while having a substantial Internet presence, thrived online more through word of mouth and through self-initiation on the part of viewers as opposed to via direct appeals from the networks on which it aired. It was not until *Buffy* switched to UPN that consistent appeals to the viewer operated at a more overt level for tele-participation online – and this was primarily (and importantly) a move on the part of UPN to make viewers aware that the *network* understood that a highly developed online fan base for the show had developed during its five years on the WB.[4] UPN developed a sophisticated web presence for the show, noting to fans who visited their new site that professionals at the network had designed it to "help familiarize *Buffy* neophytes with the show's rich mythology, while also providing the show's massive internet-based following with tantalizing never-before-seen photos and exclusive cast and producer interviews" (www. upn.com, 2001). This awareness that Internet fans existed demonstrates to a degree organic modes of invitation as I described this earlier, in which online tele-participation is assumed to be an already occurring part of how the viewer interacts with the text.

Organic strategies of invitation at times made appearances in the *content* of both programs also, as I alluded to briefly in the introduction to this book. *Xena* led the way in this regard as well, with several episodes offering storylines that focused on the existence of *Xena* fans. "A Day in the Life" in Season 2 obliquely paints a picture of both female and male fans of the star, for example, when Xena and Gabrielle come across a peasant man and woman who are both enchanted by Xena. The husband (Hower) is so entranced with Xena's leather ensemble that he falls in "love" with her – prompting his wife Minya to replicate Xena's outfit and demeanor in an attempt to woo him back. Online fans thrilled to the attention producers appeared to be paying to academic and popular critiques that had been circulating about Xena's clothing – and thrilled even more to the attention producers appeared to be paying to fans' online discussions of the lesbian tension building between Xena and Gabrielle. (The episode featured a shared nude bubble bath, as well as not-so-subtle dialogue about Gabrielle being a better mate for Xena than Hower.)

In the final season of the series, two episodes in particular used the fantastic and comedic framework of the show to acknowledge its modern-day fan base, and the attention that the media had begun paying to *Xena* fans. In "You Are There," while Xena and Gabrielle are attempting to deal with the disastrous results of the Greek Gods losing their powers, a television tabloid reporter inexplicably is present, following their every move. The reporter has an agenda: he wants to determine "for the millions of viewers who have been wondering" if Xena and Gabrielle are lovers. In the final moments of the episode, Xena and Gabrielle agree to an interview in a local tavern; unfortunately, as Xena begins describing the relationship, the battery pack for the camera dies and the feed is lost. Fans will never know if Xena and Gabrielle are, in fact, lovers.

Several episodes later, in "Send in the Clones," a story emerges set in the new millennium. A former enemy of Xena's, Alti, has survived as an immortal to become a cloning expert. Alti works with fans of the show *Xena* to clone Xena and Gabrielle. (Gabrielle's writings have survived through academic research in archeology and history and become the basis for the TV series.) One woman is a fan of Gabrielle (played by the actress who portrayed Minya the jealous peasant wife in "A Day in the Life," which, by the airing of this episode, had become a lesbian fan favorite); another woman is a fan of Xena (played by an actress who had previously "been" Xena in past season episodes – once as an actress auditioning to play Xena in a play written by Gabrielle).[5] Both women are dressed like Gabrielle and Xena to some degree, with the Gabby fan clearly representing those who read Xena and Gabrielle as a couple. (She at one point wonders aloud if the clones should be shown old *Ellen* episodes.) The Xena fan reads Xena and Gabrielle as friends. A third male fan is unsurprisingly a fan of both Xena and Gabrielle – especially as lesbians to whom he can offer male "Twenty-First-Century lovin'." The episode works to poke fun at the stereotypical categories of *Xena* fans while also acknowledging, through its very premise, that it is the fans who keep Xena and Gabrielle "alive" by watching the show actively: the fans provide the clones of Xena and Gabrielle with memories by downloading *Xena* episodes into their brains, arguing as they do so over which episodes best represent the women and the show.[6]

Buffy episodes with organic homages to fans were much more subtle than those offered by *Xena* – to the point where it is not easy to determine if, indeed, an homage was definitively present. However, fans online discussed several episodes after they aired within a framework of assuming that they were examples of how producers and writers were attending to fan fiction and chatroom trends. For example, one multi-season story arc involves Buffy's best friend Willow becoming a lesbian while in college (Season 4). Two episodes in Season 3 ("The Wish" and "Dopplegangland") appear to hint at what is to come when Willow becomes a "kind of gay" vampire in an alternate universe (as Willow herself describes her Doppelganger). Fans online who had been engaging in slash fan-fiction writing (when characters not typically aligned romantically within the show proper are written as involved sexually) saw these developments across episodes as evidence that Joss Whedon (the executive producer of *Buffy*) was responding directly to their stories – many of which involved Willow-on-Willow and Willow-on-another-woman romances.[7]

To those not familiar with the show's online fan base this may seem like viewer wishful thinking; however, from very early on in the series, Joss Whedon, other writers, and even stars of the show had made a habit of visiting the show's official fan chatroom – The Bronze – within the WB's forum for the show. While I will be discussing the unique dynamics and history of The Bronze (named after a club that the characters in the show frequented while in high school) later in this chapter, here I note that researchers focusing on the unique dynamics of this chatroom have noted the frequency with which the series' creative professionals visited the boards – at times interacting with fans online directly.[8] Thus, the idea that the industry was writing the show "with" fans to some degree is not as far-fetched as this might seem. And as seasons progressed, references to media fandom began to emerge with a regularity rivaling the final season references of *Xena*.[9]

Perhaps the most famous nod to fandom was the Season 4 episode "Superstar," in which a minor character named Jonathan becomes the star of the show for one episode. Jonathan (played by actor Danny Strong) had by this point in the show's run become an Internet darling for *Buffy* viewers, operating as a cult icon of sorts within the originating text (including Danny Strong as an actor). For die-hard fans, Jonathan first appeared in the un-aired pilot of the series, speaking briefly with Buffy outside the teen club, The Bronze. Jonathan then appears sporadically throughout the first two seasons as a classmate of Buffy and her friends, emerging in Season 3 to help headline "Earshot," an episode about a potential school shooting in which he is contemplating suicide. This episode may have inadvertently cemented Jonathan's/Danny Strong's importance to the online community for the show; because the original airing was scheduled close on the heels of the Columbine High School shooting in Colorado, the WB delayed the airing – setting off a massive Internet sharing campaign of the episode via Canadian fans (and not a few Los Angeles insiders).

Thus, by the time "Superstar" aired, Jonathan/Danny had become a cult figure. In this episode, it is Jonathan who is the hero of Buffy's world; the opening credits of the episode even feature images of Jonathan engaged in actions that typically belong to the realm of Buffy. Now a lonely college student, Jonathan has figured out how to engage in some witchcraft and he casts a spell that makes everyone around him see the world through his eyes – and in his eyes, he is the hero. Buffy must come to Jonathan for assistance and decision-making, and everyone is enamored of Jonathan's sexy Bond-like demeanor. He can sing (and has CDs to sell), he can write (and has books to sell), he starred in *The Matrix*, and (surprise, surprise) he is credited with having invented the Internet. In the end, however, Buffy regains her perspective and Jonathan is relegated back to the sidelines of the show (until he reemerges as part of a cult fan anti-hero team that works to take Buffy down in the sixth season).

As Justine Larbalestier (2002) discusses in *"Buffy's* Mary Sue is Jonathan,"* many Internet fans of the series read "Superstar" as what fan-fic writers call a "Mary Sue" story. Mary Sue stories – generally evaluated negatively by seasoned fan-fic writers who see these stories as evidence of novice writing – are ones in which the author writes himself or herself into the world of the show in such a way that the original star is dethroned. The fan-fic story, in short, "stars" a character – highly idealized and ridiculously heroic – assumed to be a manifestation of the author and of the author's own fantasies:

> You will never find an ugly Mary Sue, or a stupid one ... When she dies, the universe mourns. This is the wish fulfillment fantasy of the author, often to the extent that the character is named after them. It has been said in *Star Trek* terms that Mary Sue is smarter than Spock, braver than Kirk, more empathetic than Bones, and sleeps with all three. (Rust 2003)

As Linda Rust notes, this vision of fans is not complimentary – in a manner akin to the literal fans who help clone Xena and Gabrielle in "Send in the Clones." Yet, for many fans who themselves critique Mary Sue stories, this episode is a nod to their own knowledge-base about fan-fic, as well as a nod to the very presence of Internet fan fiction (and therefore the existence of an Internet fan base).

Both programs, then, demonstrated a growing awareness across their runs of the role that the Internet was playing in how their core audience was watching. However, for most of both series' runs, the more dominant mode of invitation at work in the shows was of a kind with techniques of obscured invitation. In short, while *Xena*'s promotion of its website was indeed an example of overt invitational strategies, and while *Buffy*'s UPN website and both series' "fan homage" episodes make assumptions that fans are active online already (indicating a sense that organic modes of invitation could be effective with viewers), it was the messy and rich mythology of both shows that prompted many viewers to become so interactively involved with their shows. In fact, even within the episodes I discussed above, the "joke" works because viewers are watching their show's mythologies being turned upside down with new, "modern" interpretations.

This component of mythological complexity within the world of the series' story is what most scholars working on cult TV point to as the definitive narrative element prompting cult fandom.[10] In particular, Matt Hills (2002) emphasizes the "endlessly deferred narrative" of cult texts leading to fans building communities and engaging in tertiary activities – or activities beyond the realm of the plots of the series proper.[11] The *episodes* I discussed above clearly offer visions of fans engaged in such activities (*Xena* fans gathering clips of the show, a fan of Buffy-the-character writing a new "story" with the help of a spell), lending more specificity to my argument that these series recognized the existence of fans – and specifically that the shows recognized the existence of *cult* fans. And my descriptions of actual online fan activities suggest that these visions are not misplaced.

Indeed, the complex storytelling at work in both series seems to demand unraveling and a "playing with" – and the Internet provides a convenient and pleasurable forum in which viewers can puzzle out the world of these programs. How are characters related to each other? What kinds of obscure references are at work? What clues may be appearing as to future plot points? As Philippe LeGuern (2004) argues, cult texts produce communities that maintain enthusiasm for endangered shows through rituals of performance rooted in demonstrating a mastery of a show's encyclopedic knowledge-base. The cult TV show's complex worlds sustain an " 'encyclopedia' of the fictional world that forms ... the basis for interaction with the deterritorialized fiction itself" (Gwenllian-Jones 2004: 91). The massive amount of information required to "get" the show becomes a source of further interaction – a source for reworking the original text, be that reworking through new creations (e.g., fan fiction) or reworking through discussion and elaboration.

Marianne Cantwell's (2004) work with online *Buffy* fans in Australia in the show's final season demonstrates how the pleasures of online fandom for this series revolved around fan knowledge. She also argues that the circulation of fan knowledge allows for a more intense experience with the series from the perspective of the fan, because fan knowledge is rewarded within the show and within fan communities. Cantwell's emphasis on intensity is intriguing, given my respondents' tendency to remove themselves from anything approaching intensity in terms of self-reporting. Such differences suggest the continued value of addressing variations potentially rooted in geography/nation as well as method (Cantwell's lurking, my survey questioning). But perhaps more pertinent is the fact that Cantwell's subjects all belonged to an established online community board, and one that she studied in 2003. It may be that Cantwell was seeing an indication of the shift that I argue began to occur with the dynamics of tele-participation as both *Xena* and *Buffy* ended (2001 and 2003, respectively): a stronger sense among viewers and industry professionals that extending the experience with a show was becoming more common and more accepted.

The fans I worked with for both series focused primarily on talk as the most pleasurable "tertiary activity" they engaged in, distancing themselves from the more dominant emphasis in cult scholarship on literal productivity via creative artwork or literal excess activity via convention-going or visiting locations associated with the show. This is not to paint a picture of these *Buffy* and *Xena* fans as unaware or dismissive of such activity; in fact, some of them engaged in such activities. Rather, it is to paint a picture of nuance: for these fans, it was going online to discuss the characters and the stories that sustained their interest and passion – a form of interacting with the text past its origin that truly requires the presence of a *group* (i.e., social audience). The complicated nature of these shows – especially the cult element of the endlessly deferred narrative and the more soap operatic element of complexly interweaving interpersonal relationships – prompted viewers to go online first to keep themselves aware and then to discuss such elements with those who would understand:

Buffy seems to provoke a fairly strong viewer response online … If you watch it, you tend to be really, really into it, and this enthusiasm and investment can be shared easily with other fans on the Net. Because *Buffy*'s plots are fairly complex and drawn-out, *the program invites itself to be dissected at length*, and the Internet's a great tool for this. (Karen, my emphasis)

As the episodes have unfolded on *Buffy*, we've learned how the "Buffyverse" works. I think the mythology helps to make the show more complex and challenging for viewers (and I use "challenging" in a good way!) … I like how in a given episode, we usually learn something about the main storyline of the season, a bit about some smaller storylines, and a few things just specific to that episode. It gives the show a continuity that makes me invested enough as a viewer to keep turning on my TV, week after week. (Hannah K.)

I think that most people have not taken the time to watch and appreciate the complexity of *Xena*. As each season went on, I think it became more difficult to follow for a casual viewer; it seemed that each episode built on previous ones. This would make it hard to enjoy if you didn't have the background *or take the time to go online and find it*. (Tina, my emphasis)

Thus, in line with scholarship on cult fandom, these viewers emphasize the complexity of these programs' structures and webs of information, highlighting as well that this results in viewers needing to work at unraveling their texts. Viewers must be devoted in order to understand their shows' universes, and this cultural competency grants them an insider status. Yet, these descriptions of the series and the work they require resonate also with scholarship on soap opera fandom – a genre traditionally not afforded the moniker of cult (or the moniker of "complex," for that matter).[12] As Mary Ellen Brown (1990, 1991) stresses in her work on soap opera fans, the paradigmatic structure of soap operas prompts viewers to seek out others with the same cultural competencies, often leading to the development of Annette Kuhn's social audience (1992) – a collective of viewers aware that they are, indeed, a collective centered on a TV text. Nancy Baym (2000) has noted the same tendency among soap fans online specifically. Thus, something "beyond cult" appears to be occurring. In the following section I will explore how these two programs and their fans figure in the world of cult even as they inspire activities and attitudes indicating that something beyond cult fandom is beginning to develop.

"There's something (more) familiar going on here": Cult TV, the Culture of TV, and Taste

Having chatrooms and posting boards where you can talk about Buffy makes watching the show more interesting. *You have someone to talk to or you can get information. (Lillie, my emphasis)*

The Internet makes everything easier, quicker, more readily available. If I had to write in by mail or wait for some sort of mailing regarding Xena, *God knows I wouldn't keep up on it! But the Internet makes everything so available* – it's easy to be a fan. *(Angela, my emphasis)*

Both Lillie and Angela demonstrate one of my key arguments about the importance of the Internet in relation to shifts that began to occur in the late 1990s with regards to how television could be watched and understood: the tele-participation that the Internet allows for *changes* the experience of watching the show and the experience of interacting with the show. The show becomes more pleasurable for Lillie and fandom becomes an option for Angela. The Internet provides an immediacy and sense of ease for viewers who go online, creating "something more" of something that is familiar – fandom.[13]

Kirsten Pullen (2000) emphasizes this point in her examination of *Xena* fans in the late 1990s, noting that the web in general allows for the spread of more material and information concerning cultural texts, as well as providing a larger community for fans to work with. This "more-ness" is the glimmering of an aesthetics of multiplicity. The TV text begins to extend more quickly and in a more complicated fashion than with earlier cult texts, potentially expanding the cult fan base for a show – and thus beginning to fracture the notion that cult fandom revolves around a small and loyal group of viewers.[14]

Many of my respondents from this stage of my research emphasized the convenience factor of the Internet, with the discovery of other fans being almost a surprise of sorts:

> On the Internet, you can easily connect with other like-minded individuals whereas otherwise you might have limited access because of geography. *I would never have known about the popularity of* Xena *without the Internet.* (Tina, my emphasis)

As Janet Staiger (2000) notes, a significant element in extending a media text past its moment of reception is the sense of connection that can emerge through discussion of the text with others. Most of my respondents eventually discussed the enjoyment of finding a community of viewers; their responses to questions about their Internet involvement indicate that they "stumbled across" others with whom they could interact – sharing familiar opinions and perspectives in increasingly systematic and intense ways the longer they "played" online.

However, the very fact that most respondents assumed going into their online activities that there would *not* be many others out there "like them" indicates the sense that they themselves felt they were dealing with a cult text (as academics define this). The vast majority of my respondents in fact sought out the Internet because of the anonymity it could provide for them as viewers of programs with "low cultural status" (read: viewers of programs with cult status). In addition, adult fans of *Buffy* felt they were a special sub-audience by virtue of the show being marked as a teen show, while *Xena* viewers who read the Xena-Gabrielle bond as a lesbian one felt similarly. There was a relief evident among respondents that can be attributed to the Internet providing them with a safe forum for discussion:

> I think that the net is such a popular place for "groupies" because there is a fairly small [*Buffy*] following, and people like to laugh about that. So, the ones who love the show but don't know each other can get together and chat about what they like about the show without having people snickering about [them]. (Hannah M., runs a *Buffy* site)

> We go to the Internet because we are afraid of what others think. (Tarmo, on *Xena*)

> The lesbian overtones of the show [*Xena*] make it good to discuss on the Internet. The Internet gives lesbians a space to expand the X & G [Xena and Gabrielle] relationship in the directions they would like to see it go. (Pat)

> I suspect part of the success of the Internet is because of the anonymity the net provides. There are a lot of closet *Buffy* watchers out there. (Belinda, fan and television critic)

This sense of being part of a select group of viewers resonates with academic discussions of cult fandom.[15] As Philippe LeGuern (2004) argues, part of being a cult fan is being underappreciated – and the show being underappreciated as well. Along these lines, however, two motivations for underappreciation emerge: (1) the text is rare and hard to find and/or (2) the text (and its fans) are seen as belonging to a low cultural taste group (9–10). For *Xena* and *Buffy* and their fans, in spite of the shows' "residences" on smaller networks/syndication, it is LeGuern's second motivation for underappreciation that appears to dominate. In fact, both *Xena* and *Buffy* viewers show evidence of being part of a social audience *because* they are teased about their status as fans. A distinct "us vs. them" rhetoric begins to emerge collectively when examining statements of viewers who first discuss being made fun of – and then discuss how this disparagement led them online. For some of my respondents, a sense of pride emerges in their fandom; the viewers who take time to appreciate the shows are special because they are able to overcome disparagement and continue watching. Yet for most it is the Internet and the safe space it provides that allows them to escape the disparagement and that then additionally provides them with proof of the wider worthiness of the series.

Thus, a central tension emerges among the *Xena* and *Buffy* fans I worked with. On the one hand, they demonstrate familiar understandings of cult TV and fandom via their sense of belonging to a small, loyal group of followers. On the other hand, they evidence opinions that their shows are worthy of mainstream acclaim. Both *Buffy* fans and *Xena* fans spent extensive energy explaining to me why more people were not watching; it was an issue of television viewers' and at times critics' misperceptions – as opposed to the shows being "built" for cult status and therefore for a small but loyal audience:

> I have four housemates who think that [*Xena*] is awful and as a result force me to convince them of the merits of the show in order for me to get to use the TV ... I just basically tell them that while it may not be your mainstream drama, or your run-of-the-mill comedy, it is entertaining. Even if you're not into myth, even if you're not into the whole Xena/Gab relationship, and hell – even if you've never watched an episode before, most people can sit down and find at least one thing that they enjoy about an episode ... In the case of my housemate who's joined me on the "dark side," well, she simply "fell" for my line about how *the show tackles universal themes* – love, hate, redemption, etc. (Jenn, my emphasis)

> People who have not watched *Buffy* assume unfairly that it's stupid ... I tell people who won't watch it that the subject matter is fascinating; *real life problems are explored* through a supernatural frame. I also tell them it's

a really funny show with great drama, too. I would then go into the juicy details about Buffy and Spike and Buffy and Angel. (Lillie, my emphasis)

The people who watch *Xena* and *Buffy* love them. The people who don't watch generally don't know anything about [these shows]. It's like *The Last Temptation of Christ. A lot of people make an unfair judgment* ... without bothering to find out about the content. (Tere, my emphasis)

Obviously there is a small lesbian fan base for this show [*Xena*]. But also action-adventure fans, sci-fi fans, women and children ... Anyone who has a good sense of humor and wants to escape reality for one hour per week. (Tina)

The dynamic at work in these arguments is evidence of one of the more contradictory components of cult television and cult fandom: many viewers take pleasure in the fact that they are part of a specialized social audience while also working to defend their text as worthy of a broader social audience. This is amusingly evident with Tina, who begins with an argument that *Xena* is for a "small lesbian fan base" – but also a series of other social audiences that collectively merge into something "beyond cult" – and much larger. This is not to imply that these viewers are hypocritical or confused; rather, I mean to point out the difficulty of applying academic notions of cult TV and cult fandom wholesale. Indeed, most viewers I worked with seemed hyper-aware of the fact that they both enjoyed and were dissatisfied with being cult fans of cult texts: there was enjoyment in being part of a like-minded social audience and displeasure in having to secretly seek out this social audience online; there was enjoyment in being part of a social audience that "got it" – and frustration in being unable to get others to see things their way. As Mark Jancovich and Nathan Hunt (2004) stress, cult fans desire popularity and/or cultural recognition of the value of their text and their fandom – but ironically, true popularity poses a threat to "true" cult fandom.

Correlated to this tension of pleasure in being a member of a select group while desiring wider acceptance of the text the group admires, fans of *Xena* and *Buffy* simultaneously mark themselves as separate from the mainstream television industry's understanding of quality (they can see what the industry – including critics – cannot); and on the other hand they defend their shows in relation to accepted under-standings of quality. As Jancovich and Hunt argue, "Cult texts are defined through a process in which shows are positioned in opposition to the mainstream" (27). Yet, cult TV fans often position themselves paradoxically as having elevated or different tastes while also subscribing to standards of taste that are – if not mainstream – then at least "establishment":

> I think it [*Buffy*] is the most well-written show on television ... It's such a different, original show. The show also seems to respect the viewer. What I mean by that is, when I watch a show like *Dawson's Creek*, I am disgusted by how boring, plain, and predictable it is. With *Buffy*, they seem to know that we want something better than that. (Lillie)

> The writing [on *Buffy*] is terrific, and the show presents a successful combination of interpersonal drama and supernatural action ... Whenever I catch glimpses of other "narrative" programs (*Everybody Loves Raymond*, *Alias*, *Law and Order*, *Ally McBeal*, etc.) I'm struck by how poor the writing and character development is ... I know that Buffy doesn't fit the traditional formula for quality television, but even in the current not-great season, its standards are way above other shows I watch. (Karen)

> In terms of quality, I do think *Xena* stood out from others. There were very few episodes which seemed like little thought was put into them. (Tina)

Writing "smartly" and in an "original" fashion has long been considered a marker of quality for critics in the television industry. In fact, when TV is disparaged more generally it is often because scholars see it as a "literate light" medium. Thus, when fans explain that their shows are quality because of the writing and originality, they are seeking at some level to align themselves with critics who traditionally value these traits. Still, one can see moments of distancing from critics – such as when Karen compares *Buffy* to other critically acclaimed programs, and finds the other programs lacking. And indeed, critics largely ignored both *Xena* and *Buffy* with rare exceptions when it came to publicly recognizing them with awards,[16] leading to extreme defensiveness among viewers:

> I think the show [*Buffy*] is overlooked by the traditional television industry because (1) There's a general snobbery towards it and (2) I don't think the industry knows how to categorize it. (Belinda, freelance TV critic)

> I think critics ignored *Xena* because the show has had controversial subjects that it has handled in a "normal" fashion. I never saw any TV

promos highlighting "the lesbian kiss" (*Friends, Ally McBeal*) or interracial relationships. *Xena* did those and handled them with a maturity not often found in TV. It didn't "sell out" for sensationalism, and critics do not know what to do with that. (Tina)

As for lack of awards, I see it as due to who makes up the organizations that give out the awards – namely older white men. They are not the sorts of people who tend to watch *Buffy*. They tend to watch all those damn cop and hospital shows that get nominated year after year … I think those judges probably don't understand at all what's going on. (Hannah K.)

The show [*Xena*] has not been nominated because (like *Buffy* and *Hercules* and even *Sliders* and *Roswell*) it has not been taken up by a very well known station. Such as NBC, ABC, whatever. Critics do what the big networks want them to do. (Gabby)

Thus, the fans I worked with often spoke of their shows defensively, seeking to prove that these shows were "quality" and therefore worthy of critical and popular respect – even as they sought to discount critics' and mainstream viewers' perspectives. This double-edged defensiveness resonates with academic descriptions of cult fans' attitudes towards critics. The prevailing argument that critics were missing the boat for unsubstantiated reasons indicates an agreement with Charlotte Brunsdon's (1997) discussion of quality television, in which she argues that determining "quality" – even among professionals – is a subjective practice immersed in power relations (133). While Brunsdon focuses primarily on cultural power (industry professionals are accorded the "right" to determine what is quality), fans make very concrete claims as to bias and power – economic, racial, gendered, aged … and beyond. Yet, even as the critiques of the critiquers fly, an agreement emerges in these responses as to what constitutes quality. In part, my respondents' statements resonate with the criteria for quality that John Mepham lays out (as discussed by Brunsdon 1997: 134–7). A quality television show aims to provide diversity, to tell stories that are usable within the larger culture (a point of agreement with Walter Benjamin (1968) that I shall return to), and to tell the truth about some element of society or culture.

The question then becomes, of course, what is "useful" and what is "the truth?" This muddled area can, Brunsdon notes, lead to a great deal of variation among critics, with many dismissing specific genres wholesale – particularly those genres that do not feature realist paradigms or traditional aesthetics. This is likely why many of my respondents felt it necessary to defend these series' use of the fantastic – while urging critics to look past this element. This tension is indicative of cult TV fandom as well: cult fandom is, as Matt Hills puts it, a performative cultural struggle in which viewers claim an identity run through with "cultural defensiveness" (2002: 12). To a significant degree, the cult social audience emerges out of defensiveness, creating a situation in which the viewer *cannot* escape the critical (and industrial and cultural) confines against which they struggle without this social audience dissolving.

As Brunsdon (1997) argues, however, this "Catch-22" occurs at a more generalized level with TV that can take us beyond a discussion of cult. Spectators always interact with "others'" perceptions of them and their text and this relationship informs the way spectators watch. In short, there is no escaping what Brunsdon refers to as the "landscapes of taste" within which television is understood (148). S. Elizabeth Bird (2003), for example, describes online fans of *Doctor Quinn, Medicine Woman* as defensive about their series' quality because of mainstream perception of the show as light romantic silliness – with that defensiveness often taking on the mode of proving how the series met standard definitions of quality that critics were overlooking.

While cult scholars often emphasize landscapes of taste when they describe cult fans as reacting against the industry and mainstream critics and viewers, this can elide the fact that fans also react against their own potential cult status. For example, respondent Jenn states that "all 'good shows' have a solid and broad fan base. *Even The X-Files was just a cult show* for the first few seasons" (my emphasis). The most common generic reaction against cult classification involved the notion of "excess." My respondents stressed the importance of "reining things in," so to speak; for example, they discussed the generic blending within both series as useful for its ability to keep any one genre from excessively dominating the aesthetics of the text. One respondent who was an avid fan of both programs even offered the following caution:

> These shows appeal to all ages. Anyone who likes to laugh at campy stuff. Sci-fi and fantasy readers, D & D [Dungeons and Dragons] players, convention goers … I think if someone were looking for a lesbian relationship on *Xena* though, they might be disappointed. I suppose that's okay *as long as the fans are not the violent kind*. I think that's a real

danger. Is the fan in question the kind who takes this so seriously that he or she will start stalking? There are a lot of those out there on the Internet. (Tere, my emphasis)

While extreme in its assumptions – and rare for my respondents' general concerns – this quote reveals the slippery slope that exists even among fan bases when it comes to assessing other fans. As easily as friends and family and critics disparage them for "just" watching, viewers themselves can turn cultural and social hierarchies back against their own social audience, seeking to draw boundaries between themselves and those with excessive tendencies.

Pierre Bourdieu (1984) (who ironically replicates this tendency in his dismissal of television) seeks to explain Western European cultures' paradoxically excessive obsession *with* excess. Excess is associated with the uneducated and uncontrollable masses of the Industrial Age, during which classification and demography became paramount as means of controlling both population and rebellion. Bourdieu explains that classification became a part of European culture, contributing to a ladder of capital with economic capital at the top as capitalism spread, and relational capital (bonds between citizens) at the bottom. More importantly, however, the forms of capital within the ladder developed their own internal hierarchies; and regardless of the form of capital, the tendency towards hierarchies reveals a fear of those without power amassing power on their own – power enough to overthrow the hierarchy and thus the establishment.

Within culture and the arts, of course, television falls at the bottom of the cultural capital ladder. Within television, specific genres fall at the bottom – particularly those with cult status and/or those that inspire fandom. Within fandom, hierarchies emerge such that one can paint a face red and holler drunk at a football game, but noses will be turned up at those who follow a soap opera for generations. And even within focused social audiences for a particular program, activities considered "excessive" (i.e., "cultish") are often pushed to the bottom of the fan ladder of capital – even when the program itself is considered to be cult. Among my respondents, then, "cult's" muddled and tension-inducing status is somewhat familiar. Fans debated the propriety, for example, of purchasing items associated with their shows; DVDs and books are appropriate, but dolls and mugs might be *too* excessive. For some, purchasing any product is fine – but displaying products publicly (in an office, for example) is excessive.[17]

Importantly, what was once considered "cultish" or "excessive" (using the Internet to further interact with a TV text) is quickly becoming normative. In 1999, when I first began this research, respondents were hesitant about involvement with their shows online, often seeking to explain that what they did do online was not truly "active" or "participatory":

> I think that the Internet, and *Xena* sites, can contribute to an obsession – if that is a trait that the fan already struggles with. If I didn't limit myself, I would spend hours surfing *Xena* sites. (Tina)

> I am not active – but I'm a lurker online. (Belinda, *Buffy* fan)

> I follow some of the discussions about *Buffy* that occur on the web, but I don't really participate. I enjoy reading what other people have to say, though. I surf several *Buffy* sites. I follow a couple of message boards, read *Buffy* fan-fic, and swing by a few general sites for *Buffy* news ... I'm probably way too addicted to fan-fic ... I've also collected a lot of music used on the show from one website. *But again, I don't really participate in Internet fandom.* (Hannah K., my emphasis)

> I'm not really active. I check out the [*Xena*] websites to see about upcoming episodes but that's about it. I do read some of the stories on various websites – it's fun reading. *But no, not active.* (Angela, my emphasis)

Here the prevalent definition for being active online incorporates a subtle conceptualization of "lurking" (reading rather than posting) as an activity that is, somewhat intriguingly, not active. Regardless of the level of enjoyment, regardless of the thought processes involved in seeking out specific sites or even in the "act" of reading itself, there emerges a desire among my earlier respondents to root their fandom firmly in the originating text rather than in the extended text. In short, reception was not assessed as an active process; rather, active processes involved the creation of another product for reception – fan stories, sites themselves, etc.

Yet, these are the same fans who describe their reception of the TV text proper as "enjoyable *work*" – something that implies reception to be active in nature. This paradox suggests to me as a researcher a desire among some respondents to distance themselves from the "excess" of the Internet; tele-participation meant extending the TV text beyond the boundaries of acceptable reception. Importantly, my younger respondents were less likely to formulate their online activities as passive, and instead spoke avidly about the enjoyment of chatting online and even the empowerment of a show prompting them to learn the skills necessary to create sites or learn about Instant Messaging. In following chapters I will further examine the importance of generation to an embrace of the Internet; however, even among older TV viewers, the respondents I interacted with just six years after this initial group were much more likely to discuss their online activities as, well, active.

One significant element in this dismissal of lurking in terms of active participation revolves again around the notion of hierarchies. A stellar example of how internal fan hierarchies can stifle fans' sense that they are contributing to the formation of a viable social audience emerged with the first official *Buffy* website, The Bronze. The Bronze was created via the WB website in 1998, and quickly became *the* site for fandom. As Andrea Zweerink and Sara Gatson (2004) describe in their ethnographic assessment of this site, The Bronze quickly developed its own rules of etiquette, set up by those members able to host literal Posting Board Parties when members would physically meet, often in the Los Angeles area. In particular, it appeared to many "outsiders" joining The Bronze that unless you lived in California or could afford to travel there for conventions (and therefore were able to attend private parties with people working *on Buffy*), you were not truly a fan. Battles emerged online over who "mattered" on this site, the criteria often favoring the ability to prove heightened intellect in discussions, as well as the ability to post often and immediately – thus appearing to favor those with jobs that allowed them to post during work hours.

Given that The Bronze was developing right alongside the spread of the World Wide Web in general, it is not surprising that those new to the Internet might be intimidated by the intricate rules of this site (which included how to read and respond to threaded posts, and understanding verbiage such as "shout-outs" and "emoticons"). Further, those establishing the rules insisted that contributors "worthy" of attending Posting Board Parties be willing to discuss more than the show, extending their fandom to include disclosure of personal activities and experiences not necessarily connected to the program. Such practices were seen as a means of "proving" a devotion not just to the series, but to the community of The Bronze. Thus, again, hesitancies about "excessive" online involvement could have easily come into play for many exploring this site.

Complaints about the rules and exclusions of The Bronze mirror anxieties about excessive behavior in fandom more generally. To a significant degree, respondents expressing hesitancies about fan activities often spoke in terms that would sound familiar to Walter Benjamin (1968), stressing that creating sites and updating them immediately, or writing fan-fic, or attending parties (etc.) were not "useful" activities – and therefore were excessive. While those involved in such activities would certainly argue the point, the more relevant observation is that disagreement existed *among fans* as to what was reasonable activity and as to what activities constituted "true" fandom. Further, these disagreements align with academic differentiations of cult fandom and "regular" fandom (with "excess" aligning with "cult") – even though the originating text is the same. Thus, on the one side there is "active" and "cult" and "insider" and on the other there is "lurking" and "regular" and "outsider" – this last descriptive most ironic, given cult fans' own complaints about marginalization.

These variations also point to the complexity necessary when attempting to understand the social audience. One can see academically the need to accept the paradox of social audiences existing to a degree in the formation of concentric circles: there may be a social audience of *Buffy* or *Xena* fans, but within these initial social audiences, smaller, constantly shifting social audiences emerge – sometimes clashing and sometimes coalescing with each other – all the while remaining part of the broader social audience associated with the originating text. Among my own respondents, individual spectators could have widely varying interpretations of everything from a storyline's meaning to an understanding of what activities amounted to active fandom; but when "push came to shove" the sense of being part of a social audience of *Buffy* or *Xena* viewers rose to the top. Thus, for example, individual *Xena* fans might have disagreed as to the nature of the relationship between Xena and Gabrielle – and argued vehemently about this – but if the issue of the show being cancelled arose, the allegiance in question became that of the broader social audience of *Xena* viewers. In short, to return to Benjamin, when the primary storytelling was threatened quite literally, members of the social audience could put aside their differences in order to pursue "something useful." Namely, the continuation of the story.

"There's something useful going on here": The Pleasures and Politics of Ownership

As I've mentioned to many of you, a town meeting is being planned to gather all interested parties to meet and discuss a plan

*of action to see our fav UPN shows in the fall ... I think it's
becoming clear that in order to make sure something meaningful
happens ... this group is going to have to take matters into its own
hands. (Belinda, author of the* Austin Chronicle's *"TVEye"
column, personal email)*

I would argue that one of the primary things the online popularity of
Xena and *Buffy* reveals is that a dimension of cult TV and cult fandom
exists that most of academia has not considered – but that the industry
has begun to. This is that the tele-participation so often linked to cult
TV texts is the primary point of pleasure for viewers; and in a media
world that includes the Internet, this pleasure can continue (indeed, it
can thrive) "in spite of" popularity. It is this tele-participation – con-
versing and debating and sharing perspectives with other members of
the social audience – that can bring disparate viewers together when
the originating text is threatened in some way. *Buffy*'s Internet history
with its parent company of Twentieth Century Fox provided an initial
clue as to the impact of the Internet on understandings of television in
relation to interactivity when Twentieth Century Fox began shutting
down fan-created websites for the show. In 1999, FOX began targeting fan sites for many of their programs (the company had also targeted *X-Files* sites in 1996), but the quickly growing and fervent
Internet fan base for *Buffy* was what captured headlines and galvanized
viewers the most.

Those creating and visiting sites were dismayed at the attack, while
fully comprehending the legal issues involving copyright. Internet fans
argued that most fan sites do not make money off of their content and
that they in fact provide a public relations service by promoting viewer
involvement with the text. As Sara Gwenllian-Jones describes it: "For
fans, the ubiquity and public character of popular culture makes it in
some respects unownable. By this rationale, once a popular cultural
text enters the public domain, it becomes, to an extent, public property" (2003: 170). In short, fans feel that once the storyteller has put
the story "out there," they, as listeners/readers, are free to continue
the storytelling as they see fit. In the case of the Internet, this includes
the right to create and maintain websites discussing the show and to
produce tertiary texts (such as fan-fic). However, whereas Gwenllian-
Jones describes viewers as perceiving the text as ultimately "unownable," I would argue that there is instead a sense among viewers that the
text is *shared* property. I would argue further that the Internet has

contributed significantly to this sense of shared ownership, and that it is this sense of shared ownership that can prompt fans to lay claim to their status *as* fans – including those who otherwise might dismiss such public claims as excessive.

This was particularly evident to me in the spring of 2001, when I was in the midst of wrapping up my initial research on *Xena* and *Buffy* fans. At this time I was living in Austin, Texas, where *Buffy* aired on the local WB affiliate station. An unexpected bidding war arose over the series between WB and UPN when WB announced that they felt the asking price for the series' renewal was too steep; UPN met the asking price and overnight viewers found out that this program would be on a new network the following fall season. Fears first arose due to comments from star Sarah Michelle Gellar that she would leave the show if WB did not renew, as well as angry comments from executive producer Josh Whedon about the WB's abandonment of the series. A larger issue, however, quickly became apparent in Austin (among other cities): in this town, there was no UPN affiliate station. No UPN meant no *Buffy* (or *Roswell*, another show that had moved networks, and also *Star Trek: Enterprise*).

Over half of my respondents did not have access to UPN where they lived, or, if they had it, it was with poor visual reception. I had been working in my research as well with Belinda Acosta, a local TV critic and *Buffy* fan; when word of the deal spread, fans of the threatened series began contacting Belinda via her column, asking for information and ideas about what could be done. A series of initiatives began as fans, including myself, took matters into their own hands to ensure that something meaningful (something useful?) would happen. Different social audiences – people who watched different programs, people who kept their fandom offline, and those who were active online – came together via Belinda's column and subsequent email list. We worked to gather information about the closest UPN affiliate, the local cable company's policies involving serving the public interest, state and federal must-carry laws – and more. Viewers coupled research with tele-activism, as little information was forthcoming from official channels; Belinda approached a local independent cinema house (The Alamo) that agreed to look into broadcasting satellite feeds of UPN at their theater, and members of the email group began strategizing with some of my respondents in better situations elsewhere to exchange tapes and online downloads. One diligent participant even unearthed topographical maps of the city to unravel issues of picking up signals from nearby cities.

In less than two months, people who had for years never told close friends and family members that they were fans of *Buffy* (or *Roswell* or *Enterprise*) or who had only ever "lurked" online had begun to meet in public settings, started letter-writing campaigns, and found the Internet to be their new best friend as they researched legal and industrial policies and set up a website for the exchange of information. Then, Time Warner Cable in Austin announced in the city's larger newspaper (*Austin American Statesman*):

> Ultimately, the return of UPN came about because of pressure from the public, a long-awaited retransmission agreement between KBEJ's owners and Time Warner, and a contract between Time Warner and Belo to give the cable company a share of the ad revenue. (Holloway: 2001)

Or, as members of what had become tagged the "UPN to Austin" group interpreted it:

> ALL of us who wrote letters, made phone calls, designed websites … and basically showed we were out here and cared – we should pat ourselves on the back. WE did it. (Belinda, personal email)

> Well, I feel like we should have a party. Or at least a drink. I've really appreciated all the work that we did and the constant updates online … It's comforting to know that we won't be missing any *Buffy* episodes (or *Roswell*, or *Enterprise*, or heck, even *Smackdown* if that's your thing!). Bottom line: we're going to see the programs we want *because we went out and did something useful* – and that's good news. (PC, my emphasis, personal email)

The "UPN to Austin" group exemplifies the role of the Internet in maintaining a social audience and allowing communication within that social audience. Because different shows were involved, one can also see how social audiences shift and reorganize, merge and diverge, when reasons to do so occur. As Belinda described the situation in a later article, "there was something to get worked up about, and it involve[d] the fundamental question of who owns the airwaves" – something prompting disparate social audiences to coalesce (Acosta 2002: 42). Further, as PC notes, this social audience "did something useful"; and while this may not be what Benjamin (1968) envisioned when he

discussed storytelling offering something useful to its listeners, I believe
that for these listeners that is beside the point.

Indeed, Belinda made the connection between tele-activism and
Benjamin's storytelling explicit in the conclusion of her article on
television fandom (which discussed the actions of this group):

> I listened to each fan's explanation as to why he or she follows *Buffy*,
> *Star Trek*, or *Roswell*. Some admitted to having a crush on this character
> or that actor. But more than that, I heard the excitement in their voices
> when a favorite episode turned out to be the favorite episode of another,
> formerly faceless fan. I observed the delight in finding a like-minded
> soul, and *the pleasure of retelling morsels of the tale*, and the warm gener-
> osity of bringing newcomers up to speed. Could it be that with all our
> computers, beepers, wireless messaging, email, voice mail, faxes, and cell
> phones, all created to bring information to us as fast and furiously as
> possible, that the need to admire the embroidery of a well-crafted story
> is stronger than ever? (Acosta 2002: 42; my emphasis)

As is evident in Belinda's argument above, it is, after all, the originating
text that prompted viewers to come together; and any and all talk that
led to the actions of saving the show(s) was inextricable from the story
of the texts themselves. Part of the pleasure of these programs for these
viewers was the ability to "retell morsels of the tale," and the Internet
then and today provides a forum for this. And while Belinda hypothesizes that the very tools of technology that *allow* for tele-participation
may be what drives the *need* for the same, the fact remains that these
tools (the Internet, text messaging, etc.) were central to this group's
ability to, well, keep their stories continuing – for the "pleasures of
retelling" to continue.

Benjamin argues that storytelling has been dead for some time in
most cultures because of these very technologies. Our new technologies (beginning with film and extending to TV and the Internet) have
disrupted the benefits of oral culture, in which storytelling was a "live"
art; the bard would reveal a story to listeners who could respond immediately, incorporating the local culture and its needs into the story.
As Benjamin (1968) puts it, "storytelling is always the art of repeating
stories" (91) – and through this "retelling of morsels" (as Belinda put
it), the "ability to exchange perspectives" is engendered (83). This,
then, is the "something useful" Benjamin stresses: through the
exchange of perspectives, listeners can reinterpret the stories that come

their way, *participating* in the process of storytelling as they listen and then retell.

Certainly this description resonates with the concept of shared owner-ship; a true story belongs to both the author and the readers, including the right for the readers to retell the story as suits their community's needs. And as John Fiske (1987) would point out, stories that are pro-ducerly – stories that engender among viewers a sense that they can contribute to their meanings and trajectories – inspire a loyalty that many cultures tend to dismiss as excessive. In the examination of cult television programs offered to this point, scholars have described cult texts as "nat-urally" inviting producerly viewer involvement because of cult TV shows' complexities. Yet Fiske chooses the soap opera as his model for pro-ducerly shows – significantly pointing out that what this genre offers is a metatext of sorts through what he labels the "vertical intertextuality" of publicity and commentary on items as varied as star contracts, writers' plans, and the like (117). The non-cult soap opera has long offered tele-participation through soap magazines and conventions. Yet, Benjamin would not endorse this form of storytelling as true storytelling. In line with my earlier discussion of Western culture's fears of excess, Benjamin's model for modern storytelling is Brechtian theater, which prompts retelling through rational discussion that leaves little room for the concurrence of intense emotional investment that accompanies fandom.[18]

Cult television programs and the non-cult soap opera clearly do not fit within this non-emotive rubric of reception. Yet, the majority of my *Xena* and *Buffy* respondents expressed pleasure in both Brechtian analy-ses and more affectively oriented analyses – and it was this *combination* of aesthetic pleasures that cemented their commitment to the program:

> We tend to discuss the good and bad points of particular plot lines and character trajectories, and we talk about our hopes for what the writers will do. Also, we talk about the extra-show stuff, like the writing style and the professional activities of the actors, insofar as they impact the story. Conversations tend to run like this: "God, I wish 'blank' would happen! Can you believe last night's episode when so-and-so did that? I'm not sure what the writers are thinking – I wonder if so-and-so is leaving the show? Do you think they used that song to make a point? Why was there no music in that scene? ..." (Karen)

Here, Karen exemplifies one element of what I mean when I argue that television today is operating via an aesthetics of multiplicity. From production factors to aesthetic choices to character and narrative developments, all infused equally with emotion, the complexity of these programs offers much to discuss. Importantly, much of the discussion relies on information increasingly found online. And much of the discussion *itself* occurs online, further extending the aesthetic components to include (*á la* Benjamin) the world of the listener and the world of retelling, such that new perspectives can be incorporated in order to provide something useful:

> At first when I watched *Xena*, I thought I would never be able to get past the warping of history and myth. But the more I read online and talked with other fans, the more I came to enjoy this … What is history, anyhow? Just a story we tell. Are the stories in *Xena* so ridiculous? Columbus discovered America. Black men want to rape White women. Richard the Lionheart was gay while his mother was a nymphomaniac. Our understanding of "history" is as reductive and inflected with anachronism as anything Sam Raimi or Rob Tapert comes up with … But in this show, it's a way of remaking the world and negating the power of those dominant historical narratives taught in school. (Jenny)

Evidenced here is Benjamin's insistence that a true story offers "less an answer to a question than a proposal concerning the continuation of a story which is just unfolding" (1968: 86). For Jenny, the story of *Xena* continued in a different direction after she expanded her experience of the narrative online – and found her interpretation mingling with other viewers'. Cult texts in and of themselves tend to offer this experience of multiplicity through their continuing serial structures and ever-expanding mythologies. Yet, as John Ellis (2000) argues, television itself offers a "constant process of making and remaking meanings, and of exploring possibilities" via the narrative's daily/nightly/weekly return (79). And when factoring in the narrative returns and continuations that can occur through Internet retellings, we appear to be facing something amenable in spirit to Benjamin's useful storytelling.

Conclusion

> *Fandom is … a spectrum of practices engaged in to develop a sense of personal control or influence over the object of fandom* in response to subordinated social status. *(Harris 1998: 42; my emphasis)*

Or, as [a] newsgroup poster put it: "We are the people – We have the Internet – We have the power – Any questions?" (Wen 1999)

Matt Hills (2002) argues that cult fandom is marked by a "common affective tie" among fans, and that online forums have been allowing for an intensification and validation of emotional bonding centered on a television program (180). While Hills does not specify as to whether or not such bonding over a story is useful, other scholars working in areas of popular culture fandom not considered cult have proffered that such bonding is useful for disenfranchised groups in particular. Janice Radway's (1984) work on female romance readers and count- less works by feminists studying soap opera fandom, for example, have stressed the importance of women using their fandom of belittled texts to forge a space for themselves in which to discuss their concerns as women, or even "just" the value of having an activity that centered on themselves rather than others (i.e., husbands and children). I myself offered this assessment in my work on *Xena* and *Buffy* fans, positing that a primary appeal of the shows and the fandom surrounding them involved viewers finding a space for the discussion of stories about feminist and queer desires (Ross 2002).

I do not wish to discount this line of arguing, yet I am mindful of the slippery slope that exists between empowerment and a *sense* of empowerment that can distract one from the need for actual empow- erment. In other words, if women reading romance novels or watching soaps receive *momentary respite* from any gendered disenfranchise- ment, but never seek to alter the conditions of their status in society, one can hardly argue that that "break" from sexism is of any real value. However, recognizing this important distinction between a momen- tary *sense* of empowerment and empowerment that leads to actual action does not mean that debate and discussion of issues important to culture and society do not occur, or that debate and discussion never lead to anything concretely useful.

Further, I think it is important to consider the value of any kind of debate and discussion – even about things that may seem mundane:

> I've also made some cool friends through the Internet via the forums for the show *Farscape*. It was nice to talk about the show to folks who enjoyed the show and as an added bonus, I got to make some new friends. It was also interesting to listen to how different folks interpreted

what they saw and also to have things pointed out that I might have
missed or not considered. (Kirbosi)

Kirbosi's pleasure in finding other perspectives – other continuations
of the story – is the type of tele-participation that many choose to over-
look because it does not indicate anything overtly political. Yet, the
"UPN to Austin" group emerged from just such beginnings. While
such activity will not occur all the time (or even when needed), it may
be that such "mundane" socializing is a precondition for more clearly
political action.

Or it may be that fandom is simply useful because of the socializing
it prompts. One thing that has remained central among respondents
across my research is pleasure in discussion (as well as, of course, the
displeasures of debates shut down). This suggests that a primary appeal
of the Internet especially is its ability to provide space for what Radway
(1984) refers to as an "interpretive community" – a site at which members of a social audience can ponder meaning, be it aesthetic, philosophical, or metaphorical (8).

The messiness of understanding what, precisely, constitutes cult
television and cult fandom is inextricable from the messiness of comprehending fandom and even TV viewing in general. As much as there are
shifting social audiences, there are clusters of fear surrounding those
social audiences; as much as Western cultures prize the collective, we also
fear the power collectives can amass when we are not a part of that "in-
group." And as much as scholars and fans may argue that fandom (of any
kind) is a legitimate cultural activity, we feel compelled to qualify that
with a focus on "usefulness" and "value" that can only ever be about
revolution or disrupting the status quo. Perhaps, when it comes to "cult"
and "fandom," we should heed the advice of scholar Philippe LeGuern:
"The question is less one of knowing what 'cult' [or 'fandom'] is ... than
one of bringing to light the uses that are made of it" (2004: 19–20).

For my initial group of respondents, "cult" raised worries about
excessive fan behavior; for my later group of respondents, the distinction between "fan" and "cult fan" and "hit" and "cult hit" was much
more wide-ranging and less infused with worries about excess.[19] While
there still seems to be a general agreement that there are degrees of
fandom, the idea of cult shows being inextricable from a "small but
loyal social audience" rooted in defensiveness seems to be significantly
shifting among fans themselves:

You can be a "cult" fan of a popular show – it is all about the attention you give it. I think a "cult" fan tends to be the "uber-fan;" you know, the obsessive completist who has to know everything and own everything. (PanPan)

What makes a show a "cult show" is a good question. For me, it's one that continues to have fans well past its cancellation. Or it's a show that has an avid fan base – a passionate fan base – no matter how big that fan base may be. (Fehrscaper)

I don't know if anything currently on TV would be called "cult." I would guess *Lost* is achieving cult status. Perhaps *Desperate Housewives* or the *CSI* shows. But "cult" usually attaches itself to "genre" TV – sci-fi and fantasy like my favorite show *Roswell*, or *Xena Warrior Princess* or *X-Files*, or the grand daddy of them all, *Star Trek*. (Loretta)

The respondents I worked with for my more recent research were fans of a broader range of shows, and while many of their programs would likely be labeled cult by scholars, this group of fans on the whole were less likely to categorize fans according to criteria of what was excessive in terms of activity. The Internet seems to be playing a role to some degree in this embrace of what would have been seen as excessive fandom less than a decade ago:

Storytelling has not been killed by TV, but in fact has inspired lots of amateur fiction, which you could say is storytelling "of the people." In the 1960s it was a struggle to get fan stories to other fans. But with the advance of the Internet, storytelling is at an all time high. (Loretta)

Of course, if "the people" are committed to *shared* ownership of their texts, this means the industry gets to play with fans as much as (and likely more than) this means that fans get to play with the industry. While changes among viewers involving attitudes towards fandom and fan activities are significant, it is also important to consider in what ways the *industry*'s changing attitudes have impacted the uses made of cult, fan, fandom, etc. – especially in the domains of creative production, conceptual ownership, and marketing.

I would like to end this chapter by pointing out an element of Lauren's quote above that has played a key role in how the industry has begun to shift in its orientation towards fandom: the pleasures of having a "voice" – whether that be a voice heard by fellow fans, a voice heard by detractors, or a voice heard by producers and writers and marketers. Regardless of what motivates any person's desire to be heard, the pleasures of speaking and being heard are near universal across my audience reception research. The Internet appears to be correlated with an increasing sense among viewers that they *can*, in fact, be heard – and the history of *Buffy*'s executive producer Joss Whedon attesting that he was listening online has become the stuff of legend among later TV fans.

Debates exist among my respondents and among industry professionals as to whether or not viewers being heard and heeded is a right, but the *pleasures* of being heard are not up for question. After *Buffy* and *Xena* and other cult shows of their era, the pleasures involved have been noted by more than Joss Whedon – witness programs such as the decidedly non-cult *American Idol* or *The O.C.* As Cheryl Harris (1998) notes, higher involvement in a TV show correlates with a higher enjoyment of the TV text and of TV more generally; in short, a sense of tele-participation can translate to the kind of attention that producers of most any television program in the US desire strongly, given that paying attention bodes well for the desires of advertisers. In the following chapter I will explore these notions of "paying attention" and "being heard" and what this means for viewers, producers, network executives, and marketers in the age of the Internet.

Notes

1   Unless noted otherwise, the viewer quotes in this chapter come from my work on fans of *Xena* and *Buffy* and the answers they provided to survey questions about these shows; the surveys were distributed and collected from 1999 to 2001.
2   The show became additionally famous in its fourth season for portraying an open lesbian relationship between lead characters Willow and Tara, both witches.
3   The books and articles in print are too numerous to lay out here; the best-known conference is called Slayage Conference, and began in 2004.
4   After five successful years on the WB, Buffy was optioned for renewal by UPN and UPN won the bid. The reaction of fans to this change will be discussed further later in this chapter.
5   Polly Baigent also was a body double for Lucy Lawless, the actress who plays Xena, in two episodes.

6   It was also during the final season that producers of the show asked an online fanfic writer, Melissa Good, to write two episodes. "Coming Home" was the actual season premiere, and "Legacy" was the middle episode in a trilogy featuring Gabrielle – an episode that famously opens with a nude bath. (The bath featured partial on-screen nudity in initial airings of the episode in some areas of the country; the scene was edited by the time other stations offering the show in later time slots aired.)

7   A similar reaction occurred with a Season 4 episode in which Buffy and Spike – an enemy vampire – decide to get married while under a spell unwittingly cast by Willow (by then a Wicca); much online slash fiction involved exactly this sexual pairing. Marianne Cantwell (2004) also argues that Season 7's "Storyteller," in which a minor character is used to self-consciously mock Buffy, could be correlated to an increase of online fan criticism of her character throughout that season; however, given the show's production schedule, it is not likely that writers would have been aware of such criticism in time to work it into a script to such a degree.

8   See Zweerink and Gatson (2004), also Larbalestier (2002).

9   For example, in the sixth season of the show, Buffy's "Big Bad" (the evil force of the season) is actually a trio of humans – Warren, Andrew, and Jonathan – who are mutually bonded via their shared love of cult media texts (specifically, science-fiction/fantasy comic books and films).

10 See Gwenllian-Jones (2003, 2004); Hills (2002); Jenkins (1992); Lancaster (2001); LeGuern (2004).

11 See also Gwenllian-Jones and Pearson (2004).

12 See, for example, Allen (1992); Brown (1990, 1991); Brunsdon (1981).

13 Indeed, as I alluded to earlier, *Buffy* in particular became academically respected as a series by the end of its run; in no small part this is due to the fact that the Internet began to make *researching* the show and its fans easier.

14 Pullen sees *Xena's* online fan base as more representative of the typical TV viewer in the late 1990s and early twenty-first century than I do, arguing that by early 2000 "the web had mainstreamed fandom" (56). Interestingly, she also paints a picture of *Xena* fandom similar to my own, suggesting that she sees the dynamics of tele-participation at work with this fan base as normative (she in fact makes comparisons to the fan base for the Top Ten show *E.R.*) and to a degree predictive. The fact that we describe similar dynamics among *Xena* fans, yet I see these dynamics as less continuous with the later shows I examine in this book (particularly those that are non-fantastic in origin), indicates the importance of historicization in such studies. Doubtless by the time this book is published, another scholar will see what I have and be able to provide a different perspective on this!

15 See Hills (2002); Jancovich and Hunt (2004); LeGuern (2004); Zweerink and Gatson (2004).
16 Both shows have been nominated for some awards. *Xena* was nominated for an Emmy in musical composition in both 2001 and 2002; *Buffy* was nominated for writing in 2000, musical direction in 2002, and several years for makeup. Sarah Michelle Gellar of *Buffy* was nominated for best actress by the Golden Globe committee in 2000 and the show was nominated for best drama by the American Film Institute in 2001. With *Buffy* especially, fans became convinced that the "industry" was determined not to snub the show, particularly in 2002 when the episode "Once More, With Feeling" was left off the Emmy ballot accidentally.
17 For an excellent discussion of similar boundary-setting among female fans of the sometimes-labeled cult *The X-Files*, see Bury (2005).
18 See Benjamin (1968).
19 The remainder of the book references quotes from this later round of research; respondents replied to a survey about TV watching and the Internet (as well as follow-up queries) from 2005 to 2006.

References

Acosta, B. (2002) Fandemonium! Cult Television Shows and the Power of Positive Letter-Writing. *Austin Chronicle* (February 15) pp. 40–2.

Allen, R. (1992) Audience-Oriented Criticism and Television. In Allen, R. (ed.) *Channels of Discourse, Reassembled: Television and Contemporary Criticism*. University of North Carolina Press, Chapel Hill, pp. 101–37.

Baym, N. (2000) *Tune In, Log On: Soaps, Fandom, and Online Community*. Sage, Thousand Oaks, CA.

Benjamin, W. (1968) *Illuminations*. Ed. H. Arendt, trans. H. Zohn. Schocken Books, New York (orig. pub. 1955).

Bird, S. E. (2003) *The Audience in Everyday Life: Living in a Media World*. Routledge, New York.

Bourdieu, P. (1984) *Distinction: A Social Critique of the Judgement of Taste*. Trans. Richard Nice. Harvard University Press, Cambridge, MA.

Brown, M. (1991) Knowledge and Power: An Ethnography of Soap-Opera Viewers. In Vande Berg, L. and Wenner, L. (eds.) *Television Criticism: Approaches and Applications*. Langman, New York, pp. 178–98.

Brown, M. (1990) Motley Moments: Soap Operas, Carnival, Gossip and the Power of the Utterance. In Brown, M. (ed.) *Television and Women's Culture: The Politics of the Popular*. Sage, London, pp. 183–98.

Brunsdon, C. (1981) Crossroads: Notes on Soap Opera. *Screen* 22, no. 4: 32–7.

Brunsdon, C. (1997) *Screen Tastes: Soap Opera to Satellite Dishes.* Routledge, New York.

Bury, R. (2005) *Cyberspaces of Their Own: Female Fandoms Online.* Peter Lang, New York.

Cantwell, M. (2004) Collapsing the Extra/Textual: Passions and Intensities of Knowledge in *Buffy the Vampire Slayer* Online Communities. *Refractory: A Journal of Entertainment Media* 2 (vol. 5), available at www.refractory. unimelb.edu.au/journalissues/vol5/cantwell.html. Accessed July 8, 2007.

Ellis, J. (2000) *Seeing Things: Television in the Age of Uncertainty.* I. B. Tauris, New York.

Fiske, J. (1987) *Television Culture.* Methuen, New York.

Gwenllian-Jones, S. (2004) Virtual Reality and Cult Television. In Gwenllian-Jones, S. and Pearson, R. (eds.) *Cult Television.* University of Minnesota Press, Minneapolis, pp. 83–97.

Gwenllian-Jones, S. (2003) Web Wars: Online Fandom and Studio Censorship. In Jancovich, M. and Lyons, J. (eds.) *Quality Popular Television: Cult TV, the Industry and Fans.* BFI, London, pp. 163–77.

Gwenllian-Jones, S. and Pearson, R. (eds.) (2004) *Cult Television.* University of Minnesota Press, Minneapolis

Harris, C. (1998) A Sociology of Television Fandom. In Harris, C. and Alexander, A. (ed.) *Theorizing Fandom: Fans, Subculture and Identity.* Hampton Press, Cresskill, NJ, pp. 41–54.

Hills, M. (2002) *Fan Cultures.* Routledge, New York.

Holloway, D. (2001) Trekkies Rejoice: UPN Coming Back to Time Warner. *Austin American Statesman* (June 20), p. B3.

Jancovich, M. and Hunt, N. (2004) The Mainstream, Distinction, and Cult TV. In Gwenllian-Jones, S. and Pearson, R. (eds.) *Cult Television.* University of Minnesota Press, Minneapolis, pp. 27–44.

Jenkins, H. (1992) *Textual Poachers: Television Fans and Participatory Cultures.* Routledge, New York.

Kuhn, A. (1992) Women's Genres. In Caughie, J. and Kuhn, A. (eds.) *The Sexual Subject: A Screen Reader in Sexuality.* Comp. Mandy Merck. Routledge, New York, pp. 301–11 (orig. pub. in *Screen* vol. 25, no.1, Winter 1984: 18–28).

Lancaster, K. (2001) *Interacting with Babylon 5: Fan Performances in a Media Universe.* University of Texas Press, Austin.

Larbalestier, J. (2002) *Buffy*'s Mary Sue is Jonathan: *Buffy* Acknowledges the Fans. In Wilcox, R. and Lavery, D. (eds.) *Fighting the Forces: What's at Stake in Buffy the Vampire Slayer.* Rowman Littlefield, New York, pp. 227–38.

LeGuern, P. (2004) Toward a Constructivist Approach to Media Cults. In Gwenllian-Jones, S. and Pearson, R. (eds.) *Cult Television.* University of Minnesota Press, Minneapolis, pp. 3–25.

Murphy, D. (2006) "Almost Two-thirds of US Homes Have an Online Computer." www.insiderreporst.com/storypage.asp_Q_ChanID_E_HU_A_StoryID_E_20012775. Accessed March 8, 2006.

Pullen, K. (2000) I-love-Xena.com: Creating Online Fan Communities. In Gauntlett, D. (ed.) *Web.Studies: Rewiring Media Studies for the Digital Age*. Oxford University Press, New York, pp. 52–61.

Radway, J. (1984) *Reading the Romance: Women, Patriarchy, and Popular Literature*. University of North Carolina Press, Chapel Hill.

Ross, S. (2002) Super (Natural) Women: Female Heroes, Their Friends, and Their Fans. Dissertation, University of Texas at Austin.

Rust, L. (2003) Welcome to the House of Fun: *Buffy* Fanfiction as a Hall of Mirrors. *Refractory: A Journal of Entertainment Media* 2 (March) available at www.refractory.unimelb.edu.au/journalissues/vol2/lindarust.html. Accessed March 8, 2006.

Staiger, J. (2000) Writing the History of American Film Reception. In *Perverse Spectators: The Practices of Film Reception*. New York University Press, New York, pp. 43–57.

Wen, H. (1999) "*Buffy* Fans Distribute Postponed Finale Online." (May 28th) available at www.archivesalon.com/tech/log/1999/05/28/buffy_tapes/. Accessed March 8, 2006.

Zweerink, A. and Gatson, S. (2004) *Interpersonal Culture on the Internet: Television, the Internet, and the Making of a Community*. Edwin Mellen Press, Lewiston, NY.

2

Power to the People, or the Industry? *American Idol* Voting, Adult Swim Bumping, and Viral Video-ing

It doesn't take much for someone to be a fan of a TV show. I think that simply making an appointment to watch a particular show is enough. The "interaction" with the show ... is another level of fandom that comes later. (PanPan)

Any show that inspires discussion will definitely have an Internet site devoted to it. This includes controversial discussions, "ooohhh he's so hot" discussions, and "did you see that?" discussions. If people are in any way entertained by a show, they want to talk about it and read about it. (Samantha)

Those who receive television have little or no possibility of becoming producers of television utterances. (Ellis 2004: 276)

Introduction

In this chapter I begin to explore more specifically television viewers' experiences with and thoughts about tele-participation, focusing on TV texts that offer what I describe as overt invitations. Texts that offer overt invitations clearly and concretely urge viewers to become active in their reception, from suggestions to visit a website for more information, to suggestions to call a phone number and vote so as to register an opinion. Such overt appeals towards tele-participation have become increasingly common since the late 1990s, with the possibility that this "normalization" of becoming involved with a text can be linked to changes surrounding television that include the Internet.

As the quotes above from PanPan and Samantha indicate, some viewers at least seem to be aware of a broader understanding of how viewers engage with TV (that requires refinement of the concept of fandom in terms of "levels"), and also an awareness of a growing universalization of the Internet as a site to which people gravitate "naturally" when they wish to discuss a show. It is, I believe, no coincidence that understandings of both forms of media are shifting concurrently.

Earlier I argued that some television shows' prompting of viewers to become involved beyond the experience of sitting down and watching an episode can also be linked to fans feeling a sense of shared ownership of their text. In this chapter I wish to explore related notions of power more thoroughly. What do we even mean when we speak of the term "power": Does this translate to absolute power *over* some group or entity, or with television is it appropriate to think also of power as the opportunity *to do* something in relation to the text? And if we are thinking of "power to," what might the range of related activities be and to what ends?

As John Ellis notes, viewers are still, in the end, on the receiving end of television that is offered to them by industry professionals who, in very real ways, have much more power when it comes to determining how viewers can interact with television. However, what happens when it serves the industry to, in fact, allow viewers to "produce television utterances?" I will argue in the pages ahead that the Internet has played a significant role in prompting the television industry to begin seeking viewer tele-participation. This is not to say that the Internet has been the only – or even the primary – impetus; but the rise of Internet sites related to television and created by fans has slowly revealed to industry research analysts the appeal of tele-participation for viewers. Producerly texts such as I argued *Buffy* and *Xena* to be (among other series of the mid-to-late 1990s) demonstrated to an industry battling DVDs, video games, and eventually the iPod and TIVO that viewers possibly fleeing TV might be brought back through an overt call to tele-participation that offers, at the very least, a *sense* of power.

In the pages ahead I will delve into this "delicate eco-system" of industry-viewer relations, focusing on *American Idol* (2002–), *Family Guy* (1999–2003, 2005–), and the Cartoon Network's Adult Swim lineup (2001–). These three texts offer a fruitful place from which to move past the discussion of smaller cult series offered in the previous chapter. *American Idol* has been a stunning hit in the US – as has been its predecessor in Britain, *Pop Idol* – inspiring a fervent following among viewers who more and more often can turn to the Internet to expand their experience with the series. *Family Guy*'s history is a narrative of failure and success that brings together other narratives, including a transition from cult to mainstream categorization that traverses several networks as well as the realm of DVD sales. And Adult Swim (including *Family Guy*, which airs in syndication in that lineup) reveals a narrative about the young male audience, and also the rise of viewer/user-generated content as an increasingly popular form of visual entertainment for younger viewers.

These three texts are also useful to examine given their tenuous cultural capital standing within mainstream society (Bourdieu 1984). Critics and viewers regularly dismiss reality television series such as *American Idol* and animated programming aimed at young men such as *Family Guy* and Adult Swim's lineup. Even among my own sample of viewers, it was not unusual to find science-fiction fans telling me that *American Idol* was "garbage" or "distasteful" and "manipulative," and anime fans explaining that non-anime animation was "light weight" or "childish." Such distinctions can be rooted to some degree in animation's strong association with children's cartoons, as well as the general shifts across history in how viewers thought about the genre of animation – including the cult value of anime beginning in the US in the early 1990s (see Mittell 2004).

Such criticisms are also in line with my discussion of taste in the previous chapter: specific genres of television fall at the bottom of the ladder of cultural TV capital – with television itself already residing at the bottom of the general ladder of cultural capital. As John Fiske (1992) explains, referring to the work of Pierre Bourdieu, fans produce their own "shadow cultural econom[ies]" that mirror to some degree the workings of formal cultural industries (the arts industries of film, music, television, etc.) (30). Within the field of fandom – and then further within fields of specific kinds of fandom – individuals and groups compete for power, working to accumulate symbolic capital (as opposed to literal economic capital). For fans, their symbolic capital is cultural in nature: how much does one know about a given genre or show; what kinds of things does one know about a given genre or show; how creative can one be with regards to a genre or show? While Bourdieu limits cultural capital to that accepted by the dominant spheres of society, Fiske argues that the cultural capital of fan cultures operates similarly. And, given the typically historical isolation of fan cultures from the official culture industries, I would argue that fans' cultural capital takes on heightened value for participants. Nevertheless, because these are "shadow economies," the dynamics of power within fan cultures operate similarly to those within dominant society – they rest on hierarchies and classifications, resulting in a sort of "my genre is better than your genre" mode of classification.[1]

To a considerable degree, then, what brings these different social audiences together *conceptually* is ironically part of what keeps them apart: for viewers of denigrated genres, the opportunity to explain the value – or cultural capital – of their text's appeal to someone who will listen (be it a researcher or a fellow fan) is a point of pleasure that allows them to demonstrate the cultural capital they hold. As John Ellis explains about the draw of niche television, we share a "deep human need for association and personal fulfillment ... [that drives] like-minded individuals [to] try to find each other" (2000, 64). The Internet can provide a pipeline to these like-minded individuals.

Yet, among those I surveyed most recently, few discussed going online in these terms, particularly in comparison to those involved with online fan sites for *Buffy* and *Xena* in the mid-to-late 1990s. While the pleasure of engaging with like-minded individuals was important, these viewers spoke less often of the Internet being a "safe space" for them as fans of denigrated shows. More often, viewers spoke of going online because of the additional pleasures of tele-participation with which the Internet could provide them – including the opportunity to be heard by individuals and groups within the television industry. This shift accompanies a necessary shift in the conceptualization of Fiske's shadow economy of fan cultures: not only does this field reflect dominant society's tendency towards hierarchies and classifications, it now also is closer in nature to the dominant field of culture industries in society – and thus translatable to literal economic capital.

Thus, on the one hand, what *some* viewers of shows as widely different as *American Idol* and *Family Guy* have in common is a desire to be heard in some way with regards to their programs.[2] As Henry Jenkins (2002) points out, there are distinct pleasures involved in collecting (and, I would add, creating) knowledge and circulating that as cultural capital and making it available to a group one finds online. This sharing involves a reciprocity of listening, allowing for an awareness among spectators of being part of a collective – a social audience – which brings its own pleasures. While this description of social audience tele-participation is exciting, such experiences are in fact not necessarily normative. But, on the other hand, what *all* of the viewers I discuss in this chapter have in common is that sectors of the television industry do, in fact, want to listen to them – and that these professionals structure their texts with this desire at work, in the hopes of translating fans' circulation of cultural capital into economic capital. *American Idol* asks viewers to call in with their votes – and increasingly has encouraged viewers to visit their website as well, so as to voice more opinions. Once there, fans are encouraged to engage in other activities that are rooted in economic capital. Adult Swim asks its viewers to use their website to send questions, comments, and increasingly photos and videos and even suggestions for other entertainment sites that Adult Swim fans might enjoy. Again, other activities more economic in nature are encouraged once the viewer reaches the site.

Mindful of the tendency for cultural studies reception researchers to ignore dynamics of interpellation and favor a vision of the viewer as the ultimate arbiter of meaning, in this chapter I will examine the industrial discourses "which structure the interaction of people with texts" (Nightingale 1996: 69). Yet, as both industry professionals and academics (not to mention viewers) have learned, audience members do not always follow the "guidelines" that television lays out for them. This is even more so the case when the industry offers an overt invitation to participate in the dynamics of a series. What emerges are processes of negotiation – between viewers and industry, among groups of viewers, and even internally for a single viewer (Gledhill 1988). At times these processes of negotiation are conscious, as viewers work to create meanings via texts that are immersed in any number of arenas; as is evident in the following sections, the Internet has assisted an industrial move to make negotiation itself a concrete part of the viewing experience.

A key goal of this chapter, then, will be to explore how the television industry in the United States has been working to manage tele-participation, and the role the Internet plays in both this management and viewers' disruptions of the same. As I described in the introduction to this book, media industries have long played the game of managing fans' tendencies towards extending media text experiences, seeking to convert cultural capital to economic capital; there is a lineage reaching back from websites, blogs, and viewer-generated content to industry magazines, fanzines, and conventions. Corresponding tensions exist between industry-created sites for interactivity, and viewer-created sites focused more "purely" on cultural capital – with the Internet today providing an interesting wrench in this history in that the Internet has been a difficult domain for the television industry to corral.

While attempts to achieve synergy through cross-marketing have become *de rigueur* (watch Hannah Montana's sitcom, then buy her CD and a book novelizing the series), the media industry has been slower to fully incorporate the Internet into its broader corporate framework – choosing instead a "wait and see" approach that only recently has segued into moments of distinct action (e.g., Rupert Murdoch's 2006 purchase of MySpace.com). The resulting synergistic lag is important in two key ways. It allowed the television branches of the media to observe the trial and errors of other branches, notably the music industry's alienation of younger consumers using Napster.[3] It also allowed fans of smaller shows (cult shows, to be more precise) to demonstrate to industry professionals the value of opening up two-way communication with fans. During this "observational" period, television experimented with strategies of overt invitation sustaining tele-participation that was more one-way in nature, such as emails and sites focused on episode recaps and buying opportunities for fans.

By early 2006, the television industry had begun to appreciate the synergistic potentials of the Internet, as evidenced by the emergence of new job positions – indeed, new departments entirely – focused on the Internet and digital platforms more generally. This was not an over-night shift, and that is precisely the point: television executives, pro-ducers, writers, and marketers took some time to study the Internet, from its technology to its content. At the 2006 conference for the National Association of Television Program Executives (NATPE), dig-ital platform discussions were present as a topic at the majority of panels (with tremendous attendance numbers) as industry professionals came together *en masse* in an attempt to unravel and manage knowledge that was emerging from research conducted from the late 1990s into the 2000s.[4]

On one panel examining market research, Stacey Koerner of Global Research Integration and Ken Papagan of Rentrak Corps. discussed the importance of television executives paying greater attention to *why* people were watching specific series (what Papagan referred to as "granular data"), and to *how* viewers were engaging with these shows (as opposed to an exclusive focus on how many people were tuned into a show).[5] Both Koerner and Papagan stressed that such information can assist the television industry to better target viewers, and Koerner in particular emphasized that online fandom was an important source of such information. Pointing to what she called a "fan culture perspective," Koerner noted what several television reception scholars have emphasized in the more closed world of academia: viewers who participate with their television beyond the confines of watching a specific episode demonstrate a high level of loyalty to their text – a loyalty that often includes purchasing products related to that text. Koerner also noted that people who watch television with others tend to have better ad recall (including the appearance of product placement) and switch channels less often while watching. In short, fans *can* be "ideal viewers" from a marketing perspective, if executives reach out to these viewers in the right way. As Koerner notes, "our challenge is to create brand experiences that move with them [viewers] in ways that *heighten their engagement rather than disrupt* it" (quoted in Creamer 2006; my emphasis).

What Koerner is describing is the management of tele-participation, observing astutely that fan engagement can include an engagement with products and brands. Thus, management of tele-participation translates in this scenario to television and advertising executives being able to convert the cultural and relational capital (the value fans accord to the bonds among fans) into economic capital. Koerner also notes the importance of being non-disruptive: while fans can take great pleasure in being heard, marketers are rarely at the top of their list of preferred listeners. Yet, viewers are increasingly aware of the fact that the survival of shows they enjoy depends on being heard by advertisers – particularly when the show in question is at risk (as is the case with many cult shows, for example).

In the following sections I will explore viewers' desires to be heard on a variety of levels and the ways in which these desires can mesh (or clash) with industry professionals' strategies for "listening in." One overarching strategy at work with the texts that I examine in this chapter is the promotion of the viewer as a storyteller: the "conclusion" of *American Idol* is determined by how viewers vote; the "continuation" of *Family Guy* was determined by viewers buying the DVD and watching the show in syndication in record numbers; and Adult Swim's flow of programming is "chaptered" by viewer comments pulled from a corresponding website. Such strategies work to convince/remind us that we have stories worth telling – although the stories to be told are guided in very specific ways. A driving dynamic that brings viewers and producers together around these texts is the struggle to define and maintain authenticity in the storytelling experience. For that reason, I also explore the rise of entertainment websites such as YouTube.com that promote themselves – and indeed, are often promoted by their users – as the "voice of the people." What are the connections and discordances between the corporate-driven authenticity of *American Idol*, the "indie cred" of (initially) *Family Guy* and Adult Swim, and the consumer/citizen driven authenticity of YouTube and similar websites?

"You vote, you decide": *American Idol* and Choice

As difficult as this is to comprehend, in 2001 every major US TV network turned down the chance to have *American Idol* as part of its lineup (Carter 2006). This may have to do with the fact that *Pop Idol*, even though a smash in Britain, was understood to be, and indeed pitched as, a soap opera – a genre that has traditionally been accorded higher esteem in the UK than in the United States (Carter 2006: 179). It may have to do with the fact that the show's distinctive element (when compared to then-current reality hit *Survivor*, on CBS) involved expectations that viewers would become engaged enough with the program's contest of dueling singers to phone in and cast votes for their favorites. In the end, it took a daughter telling her father (Rupert Murdoch) that the show was destined to be a hit to get the show on US TV (Carter 2006). Her reason? The meanness of the lead guest judge, Simon Fuller, when evaluating contestants – perhaps because this offered conflict with authenticity.

As Bill Carter (2006) observes, desperation breeds experimentation. FOX took on the series at a time when a new hit was needed; the network had lost *Ally McBeal* and *The X-Files*, and with those shows key audiences of adult professional women and loyal fans. *American Idol* was expected to be a modest hit with teen girls during its initial summer 2002 run – and some extra insurance was added with the contingency that the show come on board with full sponsorship. By the end of the summer, it was clear that FOX had a juggernaut on its hands and *Idol* began airing during the regular TV season – and has been airing every January through May since 2003.

Many have speculated as to the causes that can explain why this relatively simply premised series has captured the ever-growing audience it has. What was it about this show that drew so many viewers – specifically, viewers willing to make repeated phone calls, to pay for repeated text message votes, and to purchase CDs and concert tickets? While some explanations will be offered in the following pages, I am less concerned with what makes the show a ratings success than I am with how the program has positioned itself successfully as an overtly producerly text, tapping into viewers' desires to become a part of the storytelling process. *American Idol* is a model for the argument that many viewers see tele-participation as pleasurable work, as well as being an example of the continued cultural value to many of having a shared storytelling experience that extends beyond "niche" or "cult."

An overarching dynamic of this series has been its ability to anticipate viewers' responses to the form of the show – the success of the series, that is, has as much to do with how the story of the contest is structured as it does with the results of that story (i.e., who wins). The choice to propel plot via viewer votes is a crucial part of a larger aesthetics of multiplicity that guides the structure of the series, allowing for slight mutations each season. I describe the dynamics of this program as quilt-like in its multiplicity; the show itself is the fabric, and the phone voting system is the thread. Patches emerge via the show's complicated web of associations: the judges and the relationships among them and between them and the performers, the relationships among the performers, the links and disconnects set in motion by the performances themselves, and a swirl of opinions about a variety of program-related elements. With the Internet well established as a forum for entertainment information and elaboration by the time *Idol* developed as a solid hit, the emergence of additional patches in the form of online discussion topics was no big surprise – and indeed, by the third season of the show, producers began encouraging viewers (the "stitching mechanism," if you will) to "do more" than vote and to go online to discuss the show's weekly results with others (and ostensibly to share opinions with the producers and the network).

Thus, *Idol* quickly came to be *about* this web of associations, *about* how this quilt was stitched, unstitched and sewn back together season after season. While results were important, the appeal of the show ultimately lies in the processes that lead to the results, with the Internet allowing for elaboration of these processes. As the official site for the series became more sophisticated in this regard – in other words, as it became less about basic information and more about viewers discussing contestants, the judges, the structure of the show, etc. – the text of *American Idol* expanded exponentially to include chatrooms, games, and contests. By the fifth season of the show, television ads began to appear for the show's website, emphasizing the many different ways in which viewers could interact with the show – including the ability to stay in touch with the storytelling process during the summer off-season when auditions take place in cities across the country.

In short, the producers of the show began emphasizing the essential seriality of the program: the story, if viewers so choose, will never truly end. As one season is ending on the TV set, it nevertheless continues via a concert tour and stream of CD releases; and as well, the next season begins before we can see it on TV – viewers can see the new version of the basic story begin by watching auditions online. Henry Jenkins (2006) notes that such synergistic marketing creates an environment of "more" – more sharing of knowledge among viewers (and perhaps from producers to viewers) that sustains watching (86–7). Thus, an aesthetics of multiplicity serves viewers, which in turn serves the show.

As Jennifer Hayward (1997) explains, serial storytelling for viewers taps into the "delights of repetition with a difference," rooting pleasure in the observation of the nuances that can occur as the same basic story is retold (1997: 136). While the story proper of *American Idol* remains the same, the "patches" of that quilt alter as new contestants prompt new webs of associations for viewers to stitch together. This patchwork of storytelling is in line with the codes of soap opera, television's most strongly serialized form; as season builds upon season, episode upon episode, and website upon website, viewers oscillate radically among any number of storytelling elements – sustaining a much richer textual experience than many critics realize.

Indeed, when examining the codes of soap opera and much of current reality television, considerable overlap emerges when considering the experience of the viewer – in ways particularly evident in *American Idol*. Information is repeated in order to fill in viewers who may have missed a moment or an entire episode; producers rely heavily on sound to italicize for viewers who may be "half-watching" when something key is about to occur; and of course, the narrative is constantly interrupted in serial fashion, with producers using commercial breaks and episodic breaks to draw out suspense. In fact, one particularly amusing example of the recognizability of the interrupted narrative as a distinct strategy unfolds during *American Idol*'s result show episodes: host Ryan Seacrest will whittle down remaining contestants until there are two to three, then turn to the studio audience and say: "You'll find out the results …" Without fail, the audience calls out in response, "After the break!"

This collective literal response to a specific storytelling strategy – while something that would never happen on a soap opera proper – resonates nonetheless with that genre. As Hayward notes, seriality brings together people who might have no common bond otherwise: we can all recognize the "tricks" at work in *American Idol* as the producers cut to commercial breaks, find new ways to reveal results of voting, etc. All viewers are capable of hazarding a guess about who will stay and who will go, and can savor the pleasure of never knowing for sure what might happen – as well as the pleasure of trying to do more than guess and actually "figure out the game" (Hayward 1997: 153–4). With *Idol*, as with soap operas, the Internet increasingly offers viewers opportunities to move from guessing to "figuring," as viewers seek out extra-textual information (which contestants have garnered the most web searches, for example) and as they engage in speculation and prediction with other viewers.

As Nancy Baym (1998, 2000) discusses with regards to online forums devoted to soap talk, several key practices emerge among viewers: sharing information, with great cultural capital accorded to those who can offer knowledge that might enhance the pleasures of figuring things out; speculation – being able to offer reasons behind one's predictions; criticizing; and reworking, including suggestions for improving the text.

For many soap fans, then, talking about a show with others is more important than watching the show itself, to the extent that "such discussion increases the meanings, and hence the pleasures" of watching in the first place (Baym 1998: 126). Henry Jenkins (2006) argues that the producing strategies of *Idol* encourage discussion that is akin to gossip; the focus for many viewers is on using the show to maintain social ties with other viewers. And as Lorraine Code (1995) argues, gossip is a form of knowledge-building associated with women, and correspondingly belittled. In fact, a recent poll offers the information that 35 percent of workers discuss *American Idol* with co-workers; and, as with soaps, women are more likely than men to admit that they take pleasure in discussing the show with others (Keveney 2006).[6]

Yet, some of the most popular websites related (but not affiliated) with *American Idol* are run by male fans of the show, suggesting that – as with soaps – male viewers have become increasingly invested in serial stories on television. One such site is DialIdol.com, created by Jim Hellriegel in 2005, towards the end of the show's fourth season. As Hellriegel relates his story:

> I was doing the laundry one day, and I was trying to dial the phone to vote for – whoever ... and it just got frustrating hitting redial, and hanging up the phone and hitting redial ... So as I'm standing there in the laundry room redialing, I'm trying to think how the computer can do this for me. You know? It's such a repetitive, manual task and that's what computers are supposed to do ... So that day in the laundry room, it all just kind of came together. I had this idea: Could you really measure the busy signals? (Interview, July 8, 2006)

By the fifth season of the show, DialIdol was up and running and becoming increasingly popular online. There is a unique twist to the information that the result of measuring the busy signals offers to viewers: Hellriegel's program tells him who is receiving a lot of votes (long periods of busy signals) and who is not (easy to ring through), and the website tells viewers who is most likely to go home – rather than who is most likely to stay. Hellriegel suggests that the fact that his site runs "contrary to the show" by listing those contestants most likely to lose has been part of the appeal, as it suggests another way to look at the story of the series. I would also venture to say that the high accuracy of the site in "figuring out" who is going home has much to do with the pleasures of the site, as well. Fans can take this knowledge back to discussions they might be having with others, increasing their cultural capital. This in fact seems to be how the site's success spread, as word-of-mouth online and eventually in the press led more and more people to download the site's software, allowing the main server to collect more and more data on busy signals:

> It was kind of overnight. The first three weeks ... it was just me out there on message boards and in chatrooms [telling people I had this

site]. And then I actually paid Yahoo and Google advertisements to have them – so like when you searched *American Idol*, DialIdol would come up. But really, this was one of those word-of-mouth things, and then a couple of weeks had gone by and it gained a little momentum.[7]

Hellriegel sees his minimalist site as part of a larger viewing experience for fans of the show, arguing that with a series that emphasizes interaction through voting, viewers will be prone to want even more interaction – particularly because *American Idol* ends each episode with questions (i.e., with a cliffhanger). The Internet allows for this furthered interaction – and then prompts more voting to occur as information becomes available to viewers via sites such as DialIdol. As Hellriegel describes the appeal of the show (including its online appeal), the show invites viewers to become a part of the story:

> When the show is over, and you've really enjoyed yourself, you almost want more. And you do – you get to vote. I think that's the primary factor in *American Idol*'s success – it's the interaction. So you can vote after the show, and now DialIdol adds the element of "oh my gosh, I can see how my favorites are doing, and I have three or four favorites, so now I can figure out which one I really want to vote for the most." … It's kind of like living that dream [of stardom] with them [the contestants], in a weird way. It's almost like you're helping them become the star, because you get to vote … So it [DialIdol] can help you make your vote count even more – it's an extension of the show.

A personal investment has been made on the part of the viewer who votes, encouraging a sense of shared ownership. Beyond this, Hellriegel adds, the relationships present on the show – especially those involving the judges and the host – are key to the show's success and a significant aspect of people's online discussions. In fact, Hellriegel believes that were the show to "mess with" the judges and the host, the show would begin to lose its appeal. The more there is – the deeper the aesthetics of multiplicity – the more, and deeper, the viewer becomes enmeshed in the show.

Much as a soap fan might, then, Hellriegel highlights the core of the story's appeal in its paradigmatic structure – in the web of relationships and associations that emerge via the story and via discussion of it. Interest lies not only in who will win, but in who will lose – and in why, and in what will happen next *because* of who will win and lose. Interest lies in the dynamics that occur between judges and contestants, and among the judges and among the contestants; how do they play into the trajectory of the narrative? No moment, no episode, and increasingly no season is viewed in isolation from what has come before and what might come next, resonating with Horace Newcomb's description of soap aesthetics as rooted in intimacy, history, and continuity (1974: 245). One can see these aesthetics at work in online discussions, blending with the soap codes I discussed above; in this exchange between Karla and Sally during Season 4, one can see the pleasures (and displeasures!) of "figuring out," and the role that history and continuity plays in this process:

> Currently watching AI [*American Idol*]. Bummed about Aloha. Can't believe she was the one to go, but was pretty sure it was going to be her and Vonzell. (Karla)

> Yes, Aloha should have stayed longer. I told you there was no way Constantine was going out. There are too many hot-to-trot 40-something white chicks who are madly in love with him ... Is "I didn't get much air time" going to be the new excuse when people go out? It seemed to work with the chick last week ... Interesting that they dropped the offer to sing after you've been booted. Did everyone do that last season, or was it just the top 12? The format last season had people at this point coming from larger groups ... Was that the way it was done in the first two seasons? (Sally)

Here Sally especially reveals several key pleasures of soap, and increasingly reality, viewing. First and foremost, there is the pleasure of discussing the show with others. Karla, a "veteran" fan, has the potential to bring Sally further into the fold by explaining the history of the show's structured seriality ("Did everyone do that last season? Was that the way it was done in the first two seasons?"). Simultaneously, Sally moves to establish her value in the discussion via her ability to predict accurately through speculation (knowing *why* Constantine stayed) and via her awareness of the importance of continuity (predicting that contestants will now use an excuse that they didn't get enough air time to explain getting fewer votes). One could even argue that the contestants themselves are demonstrating awareness that this competition is very much about relationships – between them and the audience: not getting enough air time – interviews, bio reels, etc. – means the audience doesn't know you intimately enough to keep you in the game.

The point I mean to make here is not that the Internet *causes* such discussions to take place, or that *Idol* might not be successful without the availability of the Internet to facilitate discussion. Rather, I simply wish to note that this hit reality series, in a manner similar to soaps, appears to prompt discussion of much more than the plot proper; and I do believe that the Internet makes such discussion easier, feeding back into the success of the show. I also believe that, by inviting the viewer overtly to be a part of the storytelling process, the producers have also invited viewers to feel a sense of shared ownership of that story, and to feel a sense of power with regards to how that story progresses. While Karla expresses disappointment that a singer she likes ended up in the bottom two, she also notes that she "saw it coming"; even as her power to vote did not translate to desired results, her ability to figure things out offers some amelioration of that effect.[8] The ameliorating effect, in tandem with the ways in which an aesthetics of multiplicity enmeshes the viewer in the show, demonstrates that any representation via voting comes at the "cost" of the viewer's intense loyalty, even in the face of disappointment – an advertiser's dream (see Jenkins 2006).

Such pleasures and displeasures ultimately take us beyond the realm of soap opera; in other words, while *Idol* uses soap codes and triggers activities among fans that resonate with those of soap fans, it is not sufficient to label this series a soap opera. The dynamics at work with the show and the viewers and the industry resonate as well with descriptions of cult fans, science-fiction and fantasy fans, and (importantly, given their higher "taste" value) with sports fans. Jim Hellriegel explained how he had to repeatedly emphasize to many of the betting website professionals who approached him that he had created DialIdol for entertainment purposes, and that he did not want people to use the site in quite the way that some people use sports statistics sites, for example (i.e., for accurate scientific data, useful for betting). The fact that he was even approached suggests that some people interact with *Idol* in ways that they might with the "series" of NFL or NBA games. Hellriegel himself would like to layer his site with more statistics: how a contestant does week-to-week, detailed voting statistics after the season is complete – if the show would release them, etc.

Indeed, the world of televised sports has become one of the fastest growing domains on the Internet, with network executives building up connections between watching a game on TV, watching a game online, receiving statistical updates on your desktop and mobile phone, etc. – sports programming executives are working busily with overt invitations. Successful initiatives such as CBS's Larry Kramer's offering of the March Madness NCAA games online in 2006 are an extension of longer-standing online interactive efforts such as fantasy leagues. They are also an extension of growing industry awareness that viewers of particular types of TV shows will watch more, as part of a "looped" experience linking TV to the Internet to TV:

> We need to be cognizant of platforms – all the different platforms that exist now. We have researchers going online to see what people respond to … With March Madness, they could see everything – and they did that and were still watching on TV, also. That's a great way to build an audience, because the marketers are there in both places, pulling viewers in while we move them from TV to the Internet and back. (Interview, June 28, 2006)

Much as soaps have offered female viewers texts around which to communicate with other women in a social audience, sports have traditionally offered the same to men – and as Hellriegel notes, "the Internet is the way to communicate [today]." In literally all of my interviews with television industry professionals, sports was a genre listed over and over as "good for the Internet" because of the importance to viewers of extra-textual elements (players' contracts, statistics, lineup decisions, and coaching strategies) and because of the discussions sports prompt among viewers. Speculation and prediction reign here – with cultural capital again accorded to those who can demonstrate and share sports knowledge.

The relationship between competitive reality series such as *American Idol* and televised sports is striking when viewed from the perspective of viewer engagement. Viewer comments about how they engage with *Idol* are noticeably sports-like in nature, with viewers repeatedly examining the rules of not just the competition, but of the show itself. Consider how football fans debate the value of allowing instant replay, for example – and compare this to how *Idol* fans have debated rules of having gender-blind competition rankings shift to "boys vs. girls"; consider how sports viewers will discuss un-sportsman-like conduct calls – and compare this to how *Idol* fans will discuss what they sometimes see as unfair antics by contestants attempting to gain a voting edge over others. Majiklmoon enjoys "rooting for the underdog" – on

American Idol – and Sally enjoys "analyzing the odds." The series has spawned drinking games online, fan-created video games, betting odds on betmaker.com, and office pools approximating those used for football and March Madness.

In addition, Samantha reveals that she becomes invested in watching *Idol* contestants survive the "trial by fire" moments on the show, as singers are forced to make strategic choices as the season progresses and the field narrows. Particular moments in the show emerge as "event moments" which fans dissect and re-dissect online, much as sports fans will revisit critical plays or critical games that seem to decide if a team or specific athlete will move on to the next level of play – approximating the activities of sports fans during playoffs. Jim Hellriegel notes the appeal as well:

> Still to this day, by far my favorite *American Idol* moment is Bo Bice singing a capella. I have that on my iPod ... So I think there are those moments where – people just love that feeling of their favorite just doing really well.

As *American Idol* moves inexorably towards its finals, episodes take on the mantle of what Daniel Dayan and Elihu Katz (1992) describe as "media events," with the emotional appeal of the contest dominating online discussions. While Dayan and Katz classify entertainment television moments as being on the brink of the festive viewing that they see at work with media events (focusing primarily instead on one-time events in the news, such as the Kennedy assassination, and, importantly and somewhat inexplicably, allowing sports into this category), elements of their description of festive viewing would sound familiar to most viewers of *American Idol*. They emphasize that a media event begins with an invitation to participate – either from another viewer or from a larger source, such as a network or public official. Viewers then prepare for the event, gathering together so that the experience can be shared with others – with an understanding that attention will be focused on the presentation of the event. Participants will be ready to take on roles – which can include taking sides in a contest, judging, and examining rules of the event.

In terms of the televised event itself, the authors' description is telling:

> Media events are rituals of coming and going. The principals make ritual entries into a sacred space, and if fortune smiles on them they make

ritual returns. The elementary process underlying these dramatic forms is the *rite de passage*, consisting of a ritual of separation, of entry into a liminal period of trials and teachings, and of return to normal society, often in a newly assumed role. (Dayan and Katz 1992: 119)

I am intrigued by the fact that sporting events emerge in Dayan and Katz's overview of media events, and wonder if they might now include *American Idol* (or *The Amazing Race* or *Survivor*), given that they were writing before these shows emerged. Certainly *Idol* revolves around the ritual coming and going of contestants who endure "trials and teachings." And most of my respondents who discussed their involvement with this show emphasized that – especially as the season enters its final weeks – they gather to watch with others (or at the very least, to discuss immediately afterwards online what they have just seen). Further, one of Dayan and Katz's main points is that such events "evoke the subjunctive – thoughts of what might be, or what should be," triggering a heightened emotional state and emotionally laden discussions with other participants (119). In other words, media events encourage participants to speculate and make associations, while also "permitting" viewers to embrace and express emotions with others present.

Such a description is strongly in line with my respondents' descriptions of revisiting key moments from *American Idol* that have high emotional resonance; viewers discussed particular performances with each other that they found moving, or the unexpected departure of a performer who they felt should have remained in the contest – and many of these discussions occurred online. In addition, Stacey Koerner (2005b) notes in her research on groups of TV fans that family-friendly shows, among which she includes *Idol*, bring family members together and allow them to express emotions through discussions of "characters" and their relationships. Children and their parents share their thoughts and opinions, and celebrate the emotional moments of an episode as they are watching – something that Majiklmoon describes when she explains how her family discusses the show and then decides how to vote after the competition episodes end each week. Henry Jenkins's description of *Idol* as trading in "affective economics" provides a useful framework for understanding the importance of such emotional connections among viewers: marketers and producers are discovering that emotional investment translates into more tangible financial investments – though professionals' attempts to quantify such investments have had mixed results (2006: 61).

When Dayan and Katz describe the viewers of media events, they are describing a unique social audience – one that, for them, is "temporary" in the sense that, after the singular event has concluded, the participants disperse. For the television industry that creates such events attached to a *series*, however, a more permanent social audience is key to success. *American Idol* offers a glimpse into how the television industry seeks to manage the tele-participation on which the show relies. To this end, at the most basic level, by providing viewers with the opportunity to discuss how and why they tele-participate through online forums, producers have their own opportunity to monitor those discussions. As well (and as their website specifies), producers can use elements of those discussions for promotional purposes. At a more thematic level, by emphasizing the active participation of the viewer ("*You* vote, *you* decide … *You* discuss"), the show positions itself and its network as "benevolent" (for lack of a better term) – graciously inviting the viewer to be producerly.

For viewers I worked with, this aura of authentic participation was a key component in viewing pleasure that kept them returning to the show. Competitors had to be seen as authentic (i.e., as amateurs) and the show's voting system had to be seen as authentic (i.e., fair in terms of access and counting). Website forums often focus on this trait of authenticity – with producers encouraging discussions of authenticity when it appears to be threatened. For example, in the 2005 season, one of the earliest mentions of *American Idol* even having a website with discussion forums occurred when the phone numbers listed on screen for several contestants were listed incorrectly – meaning that if viewers used the numbers as listed, they would actually be voting for a different contestant than they thought they were. Because voting had begun before producers were made aware of this, the results had to be thrown out. The following evening, at the top of what would have been a typical results show, host Ryan Seacrest made fun of the show for its blunder, and carefully explained how the snafu was to be fixed so that voting would remain authentic. The producers re-aired the previous night's performances and had voting start all over again. He then added that viewers should visit the show's website to discuss what they thought of this series of events, emphasizing that "he" understood the importance of tele-participation being authentic over and above the importance of the show needing to air as scheduled.

In the following season, the show began airing its television ads for the website, which over the summer had been considerably revamped to allow for more discussion and interactivity. Once *Idol* opened these doors, however, they also invited participation in a realm over which they had little control – the Internet as a whole. During the same 2005 season, successful and popular fan-created sites began emerging; by the 2006 season, battle lines were being drawn between some of these sites and the official domain of the series. Jim Hellriegel's DialIdol.com emerged soon after the voting fiasco, and gained traction the following season. Achieving 20,000 downloads of the software in less than one season and averaging 2.5 million hits on voting nights (Lauer 2006), Hellriegel was hit with a cease and desist order from FOX that claimed he was infringing copyright and implied that the site was potentially interfering with the authenticity of results.

An information technology expert who had created the site as a fan, Hellriegel was stunned:

> When *American Idol* sent a cease and desist letter, it [my site] became a much bigger story and the media was interested in a different way … From then on, I didn't need to advertise … Maybe they figured I would just run and hide. And I was very nervous about it. I mean, I was scared, I had to go get a lawyer to put it [the site] back up … I wanted to make sure I wasn't going to lose my house and all my savings. And there was a point, actually, where it didn't sound like I was going to be able, actually, to put it back up, even knowing that I wasn't doing anything wrong, because of the legal costs.

Thus, Hellriegel temporarily shut down the site while consulting with lawyers who offered their services for free, receiving guidance in particular from the Electronic Frontier Foundation – an organization that has developed in response to the increasing number of such cease and desist orders in relation to fan sites.

Ironically, a FOX owned and operated TV station picked up the story and garnered the site considerable national attention, focusing on the theme of authenticity. Viewers became upset that an authentic fan – someone who had taken time to create a non-profit website – was being punished by FOX. The idea of curtailing tele-participation seemed contrary to the very thrust of how *American Idol* worked. As Derek Johnson (2007) argues, the intense investments that viewers make in shows involving participation tend to create conflict that producers must learn to manage. Learning, apparently, more quickly than FOX studios had from shutting down FOX TV fan sites of the 1990s and alienating those viewers, the motion was dropped and Hellriegel's site gained even more popularity.

A year earlier, FOX and *Idol* producers had also criticized another growing website – though not from a legal perspective. Dave Della Tarza had created VotefortheWorst.com in Season 3 and by the following season the site had gained a strong following revolving around its humorous focus on authenticity. The site encourages viewers to vote for the worst contestant as a strategy to "ruin" the show by having the least talented singer win, a sort of backhanded attempt to highlight that having talent be judged through an open vote might not yield the most authentic results. The site's notoriety exploded when they kept encouraging viewers to vote for one particular singer – someone most people chatting online agreed was truly horrible (and additionally undeserving because he had an arrest record for domestic violence). The judges did not seem to like him either … yet week after week, this contestant remained in the game while contestants loved by viewers and judges got sent home. Producers of the show kept insisting publicly that VotefortheWorst.com had no impact on keeping the hated singer in the game – that core fans were too respectful of the series to vote for the worst.

Unsurprisingly, the website flourished the more the producers and network insisted that it was an inconsequential domain. As Hellriegel notes, there is something authentic about voting for the worst – and this authenticity can be traced to the series itself. Every season opens with large-scale auditions that feature the best and the worst try-outs; the show has even aired specials and released DVDs of horrible auditions. In addition, by emphasizing that the contest features "typical" people with "atypical" talent, the producers open this claim to investigation. In the fifth season, one of the judges' favorites, Kellie Pickler, was highlighted repeatedly in interview bits and bio reels as a naive Southern gal who had never heard of salmon or spinach, had never sung outside of her shower, and had trouble finding love. VotefortheWorst.com, however, dubbed her inauthentic – and therefore capable of ruining the show if she won:

> VFTW [VotefortheWorst] has received many (many, many …) letters asking us how we can pick poor little Kellie Pickler as the worst

American Idol. We've heard from people that they love Kellie's naiveté
and that she's just a charming North Carolina girl who doesn't know
any better ... To us at Votefortheworst.com, it's obvious that Kellie is
playing up her "oh, I'm just an ignorant country girl" routine to get
votes ... Following are some of the lies and half-truths that Kellie has
been shown telling us ... We think Kellie Pickler deserves the VFTW
crown for putting on such a desperate and ridiculous act, and we hope
we can help her last well into the competition ... Read on and weep.
Oh, and Vote for the Worst, too. (www.votefortheworst.com, April
18, 2006)

Thus, this site, in line with the show, stresses authenticity. Yet, this is
obviously not the vein within which producers of *American Idol* would
wish viewers to process the show. Therefore, producers made their
public statement that the site has no impact on voting – the site may
stress authenticity, but it also discourages authenticity in voting
(in tele-participation) by asking viewers to *ruin* the show's results.
Of course, one might surmise that viewers who *do* want the show to
work might be visiting VotefortheWorst.com in order to see who is
inauthentic – and then *not* voting for that contestant.

The varying definitions of authenticity that circulate between the
show and this website demonstrate the problem with authenticity
being a central draw of competitive reality series, according to Mark
Andrejevic (2004): viewers are "supposed to" root for the most authentic participants, but this can remove all dramatic conflict from the program – resulting in a non-appealing entertainment experience for most
viewers. This was especially apparent in the 2007 season of *Idol*, when
a contestant named Sanjaya, if nearly all comment boards and mainstream critics' columns were to be believed, was one of the worst singers
to ever make it through the initial weeding out process in the series.
Sanjaya was the VotefortheWorst.com choice, and kept getting through
week after week; critics and viewers began speculating that producers
were working to keep him on the show because he was the only interesting performer – and also because keeping on someone so horrible
raised interest. One particularly odd moment raised questions: a young
female fan in the studio audience began sobbing like a Beatles fan when
Sanjaya sang one night, and viewers began asking online – how was it
that this girl managed to be in exactly the right place for the camera to
catch her "spontaneous" meltdown? Most viewers and critics decided
that she was a "plant" to explain Sanjaya's continued presence on

the show – producers were trying to convince them that young pre-adolescent girls were voting Sanjaya on.

Annette Hill (2005) argues that such discussions of authenticity and manipulation with regards to reality series are an indication that some form of learning occurs for viewers of reality programming via critical viewing. In other words, viewers are aware that such shows are rarely authentic in terms of being direct reflections of some objective reality, and they are aware that a degree of manipulation occurs. I am less certain that this is learning per se, as I envision learning as coming to understand something new, and it appears from both Hill's research and my own that viewers come to reality programming already aware that it is not "real" in any objective sense. I am more inclined to agree with Henry Jenkins's (2006) assessment of the double-edged manner in which viewers watch reality programming like *Idol* and engage in analysis – not necessarily accompanied by any *evaluation* of the program as "problematic" or "not problematic." In fact, as Mark Andrejevic (2004) points out about the competition series *Big Brother*, successful reality series are quick to co-opt any critique that begins to emerge about authenticity, emphasizing the "reality of an illusion" at work in such shows (133).

Indeed, an interesting corollary to VotefortheWorst.com developed on the *American Idol* official website during the Kellie Pickler season which suggests that some professionals attached to the series recognized the appeal of a cynical attitude towards the show's claims to authenticity. The website offered a running blog by "Jaded Journalist." This "official fan" offers running commentary during episodes that other online fans can read and respond to, and the tone of the blog is remarkably similar to VotefortheWorst.com's:

> Time for more from Puck and Pickler. Or Puckler, if you will. Congratulations to Kellie for inventing a new pronunciation of Shanghai. Actual knowledge is useless to Kellie. She feels with her gut and that's good enough, as one Stephen Colbert artfully put it … Let's go girls! Let's sing a saucy montage for America! Big shirts and short skirts? Wouldn't those big shirts hang past the short skirts and create the dreaded, "I just went out to get the newspaper with only a t-shirt on and here are my thighs" effect? I can't wait until Lisa Tucker turns 18 and learns not to use blue mascara. That'll be nice. So who looked tougher during their montage? Kellie Pickler or Kevin Corvais? Judgment call. (May 30, 2006)

This blog suggests that those seeking to manage the tele-participation at work with *American Idol* recognize the appeal of the show's paradigmatic structure, as Jaded offers a running commentary focused on webs of associations. It also reveals an awareness that authenticity is a key discussion point, with the blogger giving permission to other fans to poke fun at contestants who may or may not be faking and to also poke fun at the strategies the show engages in that appear to be misguided in terms of authenticity (such as "big shirts with short skirts"). Such co-optations resonate with Jonathan Gray's (2005) description of "anti-fans" as a component of a show's audience who evaluate the show from a moral and/or realist stance, often tempered by humor. Using TWOP.com as his primary example, Gray describes what the Jaded Journalist blog reveals – anti-fandom can exist within "legitimate" fandom.

Professionals associated with designing the website's development skillfully demonstrate to fans that "we know why you like this" – a move that Stacey Koerner (2005a) points out is key to maintaining a healthy relationship with the viewer. Earlier in the show's history, Koerner's research firm conducted studies for *American Idol* and their sponsors, seeking to see which attempts at prompting tele-participation worked and which did not. Their case studies revealed the importance to viewers of authenticity and of a narrative experience focused on the relationships among the show's participants. When AT&T moved in the second season to encourage more viewers to pay and use their AT&T cell phones for voting, they overlooked these key components of viewing pleasure: their campaign consisted of filmed segments showing a ditzy and perky blonde harassing contestants, judges, and host Ryan Seacrest about texting in votes – and they in turn expressing annoyance with her. Viewers in Koerner's case studies found this campaign offensive; for them, the perky blonde was an inauthentic representation of the *Idol* viewer (2005a: 12). She was silly, and viewers felt that she was overly focused on the results of voting rather than on the true pleasures of the show – the webs of associations.

Thus, sponsors who wish their brand to be successfully associated with the show must find ways to provide the viewer with something that is helpful to the most pleasurable aspects of the viewing experience – as DialIdol.com and VotefortheWorst.com have managed to do, without seeking profit, ironically. As Koerner points out, for sponsors this is a tricky terrain to negotiate. How does a company make product placement seem authentic? Koerner points to the success with which Coke and Ford have managed to do this – returning to advertising strategies common in the 1950s, when corporate sponsors for individual series would become a part of the show, positioning themselves as a polite guest in the audience's home viewing experience (interview, 2006). Thus, Coke and Ford appear as "creators" of entertaining segments within the program (music videos, skits) – segments that are not a part of the contest proper, but rather that work to expand the web of associations already at work in the show. These sponsors also do not attempt to disguise their presence *as* corporate sponsors, heeding the importance of authenticity: viewers are well-aware that they are a market and do not take kindly to sponsors pretending that the audience does not know this.

As the website for *American Idol* developed, professionals and corporate sponsors working in that domain followed this mantra of authenticity. Cingular/AT&T sponsored a trivia game rooted in questions about contestants and judges (and their relationships), and by offering questions about past seasons they demonstrated that they "got" that viewers saw any given season as but one part of the overall textual experience. Progressive Auto Insurance sponsored clips from previous episodes so that fans could see "event" performances again. By the fifth season, web managers had upped the ante for participation, offering "American Idol Underground," in which authentic bands could submit an original song recording (for $25) – which web users could then listen to and vote on; web users could also submit and vote for fan videos. Thirty dollars will now get the online fan access to the "VIP Lounge," a chatroom where they can ask contestants questions live. "Fantasy Idol" allows web users to enter contests in which they can predict the order in which contestants will be voted off. "American Idol Messenger" allows online visitors to chat instantly with a group of fellow fans through AIM, MSN, or Yahoo!, receiving updates from *Idol* without their chat experiences being interrupted. Chatters can even download Meca's Translator, which allows fans who speak different languages to communicate with each other.

Collectively, then, the brands associated with Idol.com and the show itself are working to extend an already tele-participatory experience further, emphasizing the full experience of the show as an authentic one in terms of viewers' opportunities to become storytellers. The proliferation of related tele-participation (new contests for viewers, chatrooms, games, etc.) is "anchored" via the connecting emphasis on authenticity, working to keep the aesthetics of multiplicity that has developed from spinning out of control. Alex Chisholm of MIT, a colleague of Stacey Koerner's, emphasizes that the key anchoring element is bonding – a sort of loose social networking between viewers, the show, and the sponsors:

> You have to create a relationship. You're looking at a space where the more currency that exists – the more touchpoints that this content is floating across – the more appreciative a fan or an audience will be, because they're going to be ravenous … It's like a puppy … Brands that are –
> (Stacey Koerner): Feeding the puppy –
> (Alex): Brands that are feeding the puppy are going to be the ones that audiences and fans are going to remember. (Interview, August 15, 2006)

Thus, this is a democracy that requires management. The emotion that swirls through the aesthetics of multiplicity needs to be tapped and tamed, and then encouraged further.[9] As John Ellis notes, modern viewers are already living in a TV era of plenty, in which there is increasing awareness that each choice about what to watch entails leaving behind some other (potentially better) option (2000: 165). *American Idol* as a solitary text revolves around this potential anxiety: every week, the host and judges emphasize that if viewers do not take advantage of the opportunity to vote, they may have "caused" their favorite person to lose. Websites, both official and not, provide voters with information to help them manage their choice-making. However, the radical oscillation that can emerge via a simple visit to the main site for the show threatens to reinvoke the anxieties attendant with choice (perhaps explaining why, of those respondents participating in this study, less than half reported regularly visiting the website).[10]

However, enough people visiting the official site appear to be anxiety-free when faced with the array of tele-participation choices. Towards the end of the 2006 *Idol* season, I was able to find over 3,000 *pages* of discussion forums active on the website with an average of 20 forums per page. These ranged from the to-be-expected forums for discussing particular contestants, to forums centered on specific social audiences such as Baby Boomers, Gay Friendly Heterosexuals, "Straights Only,"

GLB only, etc. Some forum topics were difficult to link easily to the originating text, other than that the "discuss anything" environment fits the show's rhetoric of choice and authenticity. Such forum topics included racism in promotions of winners, religion's role in how contestants engage with the public, and whether or not the FOX series *24* was better than *Idol*.

One possible explanation for viewers' ability to manage this aesthetics of multiplicity is that the plentitude is not *necessary* to the core experience of watching; viewers do not *have* to go online in order to make an informed voting decision and the potential radical oscillation does not intrude. But, for those who do want a fuller tele-participatory experience, that *choice* exists. It is important to keep in mind here the historical-industrial context of *American Idol*; this show came of age during not just the "Age of the Internet," but what market researchers refer to as the "Age of Lifestyle Media." In 2006, PricewaterhouseCoopers released a report to those television executives attending NATPE titled "The Rise of Lifestyle Media: Achieving Success in the Digital Convergence Era," emphasizing the need for entertainment providers to help consumers manage their media experience options so as to corner as much of that consumer market as possible – a market that is a different beast from "pre-Internet" days:

> Today's media consumer is very different from the consumer of even a decade ago. Rather than passively viewing content produced for a singular audience, consumers now can participate in a highly interactive, socially networked community focused on particular content. *They feel a sense of ownership in that content, and they are not satisfied with mass or segmented media.* (PricewaterhouseCoopers 2006: 16; my emphasis)

American Idol, both televisually and online, expertly emphasizes viewer ownership of the story; and with the development of their website, producers have created an environment that is somewhere between mass media (democratic voting, record numbers) and segmented media (forums for increasingly specific social audiences surrounding increasingly specific discussion topics).

PricewaterhouseCoopers also notes that the TV genres leading the way in Lifestyle Media include two emphasized in this chapter – sports and reality (the third being news). The report says specifically about

Idol that "the viewer does not passively consume packaged content as much as he or she *dwells inside the event* as it is happening, almost like a video game" (17–18, my emphasis). This sense of belonging – of ownership as naturalized – suits an American rhetoric of choice rooted in voting; and the additional tele-participation offered online serves to suture the viewer more deeply into the fabric of the show. As Stacey Koerner describes it, the Internet site (and its sponsors) becomes a "touchpoint" for users that enables fans to extend the text and the experience of watching it (interview, 2006). For Koerner, this strategy approaches the "something useful" that Walter Benjamin seeks in storytelling: it helps fulfill a "core need, human need, to make it [the story] your own" (interview, 2006).

Of course, one must consider the possibility that this human need may be amplified in a country in which 35 percent of *Idol* voters see their show voting as "equal to or greater than" in terms of making a difference when compared with voting in a presidential election (de Moraes 2006).[11] In other words, it is possible the show eases the frustrations of feeling powerless in more important areas of life. This is a significant point to consider, given that in 2005, 28.1 million people tuned in to watch the final vote's outcome being revealed live, with 10 percent of the entire US population (not just the viewing population) voting (de Moraes 2006); in 2007, 29.5 million viewers tuned in (Reuters 2007). John Ellis (2000) argues that television in the 2000s is being viewed in "the age of uncertainty," with viewers witnessing events on television with a sense of "separation and powerlessness: the events unfold, like it or not" (11). *American Idol* certainly to some degree stems sensations of powerlessness in terms of events unfolding without the witness being able to have an effect – and indeed emphasizes this element of viewing pleasure. As Mark Andrejevic (2004) argues, it is possible that in an increasingly commodified world that relies on digital forms of communication, "true experience" shrinks, with citizens accepting entertainment television's version of true experience as "true enough."

Still, a cursory examination of topics being discussed on the official website demonstrates that something more than diversion might be operating for some viewers. In particular, issues of sexuality and race emerge repeatedly. For example, in 2006, a favorite contestant (Mandisa) spoke on the *Idol* blog about her personal idol, author Beth Moore – a proponent of the concept that through Christianity, gay people can be "cured." That evening, Mandisa had sung a gospel tune preceded by a dedication to people struggling with addiction and problematic lifestyles – and the boards quickly lit up with debates about what her beliefs might be, and also about if an "anti-gay" advocate should be an American Idol. (Mandisa got voted off.) Viewers online also have debated how African American winners have been promoted in comparison to White winners. One female African American winner, Fantasia, continues to evoke discussions of race, class, and gender; during the show viewers came to know that she was a single mother who had struggled to make ends meet until she auditioned successfully for the show, and after winning she revealed that she was illiterate and had had to memorize song lyrics by listening rather than reading and memorizing. (Fantasia went on to star in a made-for-TV movie based on her struggles.)

I point out such examples because of the tendency for many viewers, critics, and scholars to dismiss both the show and its viewers as having little value in the larger scheme of things. As Henry Jenkins (2006) points out, *Idol* fans who go online to extend their experience are exposed to competing points of view, particularly surrounding ethical issues; such exposure can provide varying examples of how the personal and private aspects of life intersect with the public and potentially political, as viewers use their own experiences to make points that support their own point of view. Likewise, while I evidenced some disagreement earlier with Annette Hill's (2005) contention that real critical viewing and learning is occurring via such exposure, I do agree that reality programming tends to promote communication about everyday issues within a framework of tele-participation that overtly encourages socializing surrounding a given show. The end results of such exposure can be variable, including a tendency for a consensus to form around any given issue, ultimately shutting down debate (Jenkins 2006); however, exposure itself can teach that one's own point of view is not the dominant or not the only point of view that exists. I am less concerned here, though, with whether or not viewers are learning anything per se. I am more concerned with the ways in which overt invitations can reach out to "dismissible" viewers via "dismissible" genres, at times relying on that very dismissibility to cement viewers to their product. In the following section I will examine this dynamic with young adult male fans of animation.

Sink Or Swim: Adult Animation And Young Males Who Want To Be Heard

Many viewers in my sample who were dismissive of *American Idol* found fault with the show because it was a hit; as I discussed earlier, scholars have noted the relationship between the concept of "tasteful" and "elite" and correspondingly between "distasteful" and "mass" in Western European cultures (Bourdieu 1984; Stallybrass and White 1986). While the *Family Guy* and Adult Swim viewers I corresponded with were not necessarily dismissive of this other program, many stressed the importance to them of following a show/lineup that was not mainstream in terms of ratings – there is a sense of pride (apparent in my discussion of *Buffy* and *Xena* fans in chapter one) in being members of a select social audience, even as these viewers fervently seek critical and audience approval of the texts. In particular, there is a sense of pride as well in being fans of adult content.

Stacey Koerner's (2005b) marketing research of television fans reveals that adult viewers do indeed engage differently with shows they are fans of when compared to family oriented viewers. Adult fans focus on the construction of plots and the craft of visual aesthetics (including especially acting and writing); they also see the shows they are fans of as uniquely suited to their individual personalities and viewing preferences. Among the fans of *Family Guy* and Adult Swim with whom I worked, these trends are evident:

> It's [*Family Guy*] good. It's funny without being dumb. The jokes are good enough that you appreciate them differently over time. (GrinfilledCelt)

> [I like to discuss] the quality of the production (whether it's animation or live-action) [on Adult Swim programs], the writing, the video quality, the shot composition, and the hilariousness or seriousness or deepening of the story and the show itself. (Kendall)

> In thinking of the shows I have consistently been a fan of, I see three common factors: intelligence, availability, and personal connection. Now, *I don't expect every show I watch to be "cerebral" (I watch American Idol, for God's sake), but I don't like it when a show insults my intelligence (i.e., Family Guy).* (PanPan, my emphasis)

> Adult Swim (or at least most of its programming) works as a very nice buffer against the age-old "cartoons are for kids" mentality. Not only

are these shows set up to appeal to my age demographic [19], they are also not something I would show to children. (Caleb)

I have been to the AS [Adult Swim] forums. I registered there once and even posted a few comments, but it's too big, too chaotic with too many children, morons and trolls for my taste. There is a very large AS community and it is much larger than the AS forums. (GrinfilledCelt)

As GrinfilledCelt's comments demonstrate, the importance to adult TV fans of their shows being "for" adults extends also to Internet fan activity. A common complaint among fans of Adult Swim in particular was that official sites quickly became "juvenile" in their tone and style – and that this was evident to some degree in the "bumps" (or interstitials) that appear regularly during Adult Swim programming. In Adult Swim parlance, a "bump" is a title card that appears in-between program segments; Adult Swim bumps offer comments from people working at Adult Swim, or from viewers who have written comments online which they want to appear in bumps. Essentially, the bumps become part of the program content for viewers, as they are distinct from television ads. This demonstrates further an aesthetics of multiplicity: the individual programs are embedded within a larger Adult Swim "program" and "chaptered" by bumps that offer viewer commentary and questions, along with Adult Swim "producers'" responses and commentary. These bumps are pulled from a specific forum within Adult Swim's official online site.

Among *Family Guy* viewers, there was less discussion and concern surrounding that show's official website; in fact, approximately one third of *Family Guy* fans reported visiting the website regularly compared with half of the Adult Swim viewers. This might be traced to the very different trajectories at work with these programs – as well as the fact that Adult Swim is an amorphous entity. (It is not a network, but rather a named lineup of constantly shifting programs that, significantly, includes repeat episodes of *Family Guy*.) Original Adult Swim programs are 15 minutes long, and at first were predominantly re-purposed versions of old Hanna-Barbera cartoons. As the Cartoon Network and its Adult Swim lineup grew (both in terms of programs and in terms of availability via cable), the lineup expanded to include anime, original cartoons, and stop-action animation.

Family Guy, however, had a rocky trajectory on FOX, emerging in 1999 only to be cancelled twice (2000 and 2002). Upon its "final" cancellation, fans utilized the Internet to develop an online petition that simultaneously encouraged fans to watch the show on Adult Swim – the "network" that had picked up the series due to its fit with their other programs.[12] On Adult Swim, fans could see episodes that had never aired on FOX; they could also use the Adult Swim online forums to continue pushing for further development of the show. Within a year of having been dropped by FOX and picked up by Adult Swim, a DVD of the show's first season was released – and almost overnight this DVD set became the most profitable television show on DVD in the history of this technology. In the same year, *Family Guy* was the top-rated basic cable series; while airing new episodes and repeats on Adult Swim, syndicated repeats were running on WTBS (Sanderson 2004). Approximately two years later, FOX revisited their decision to cancel the series and the network struck a deal with Adult Swim: FOX would begin airing new episodes on their network, and Adult Swim would retain exclusive syndication rights during the "new," third run of the series.

Thus, for *Family Guy* fans, their relationship with this show was rooted in having a cause – and the Internet was primarily a tool they used to achieve the goal of keeping the show alive. The varying history of the show also resulted in a somewhat uncohesive fan base: some viewers watched the show through its entire run, but more came to the show via DVD or via a combination of DVD and Adult Swim and/or WTBS viewings. As GrinfilledCelt explains, "I didn't watch FG [*Family Guy*] when it first aired much, maybe an episode or two ... I started watching it when it came on Adult Swim. *By then I had heard online about how good it was*" (my emphasis). While products related to the show sell well, once the series reemerged on FOX, online activity surrounding the program diminished (as evidenced in the Adult Swim forums).

It was as if a momentary cult following had developed, seeking the continuation of the show – and once the show became "mainstreamed" (i.e., was thriving with a larger audience base on a "Big Four" network), the cult following dissolved. On the main website for *Family Guy*, in fact, attempts by participants to engage in adult discussion of the show (in the manner described by Koerner) are quickly shot down as "elitist." For example, after one user complained that no one was actually discussing the show in the forums, several regular users asked this new user to "lighten up or leave." This led to another user to chime in:

> This forum does have a lot of people coming in with stupid, nonsensical opinions, mostly stupid little 12 year olds who watch *Family Guy* because

it is a cartoon. This forum does have some true fans but this forum doesn't have enough people coming in with worthwhile opinions and most only want to come in with asinine subjects like porn links and [comments like] "Does anyone eat jam here?" I came on this *Family Guy* forum to interact with other family guy [*sic*] fans, but most of the "fans" here are just stupid idiots that have found a site for just talking about sh't because they've got nothing else to do. (SG)

SG was also asked to "lighten up or leave," and in fact the discussion did return to topics that had little or nothing to do with *Family Guy*.

While similar complaints about nonsensical content emerge in Adult Swim forums, to a certain degree the "chaos" of the Adult Swim online opportunities provides for such disagreements. Much as with the multi-layered television experience of Adult Swim, one can travel to the Cartoon Network site to find directions to the Adult Swim mainpage, where forums emerge within forums – within forums. Those who wish to discuss specific shows can do so in designated areas; those who wish to discuss Adult Swim as an entity can also do so. In addition, fans can "simply" post on the boards of Williams Street (the programming and production arm of Adult Swim) – which is the venue for those who are hoping that something they write or post will make it onto television in a bump. Viewers can even choose to discuss the website itself. As if anticipating the kinds of debates that can emerge within fan cultures that center on typically disparaged genres such as animation, the boards at AdultSwim.com also offer a "Noise" section, with individualized forums labeled "Babbling (general discussion about life, music and video games), Incoherent Babbling (babbling minus intelligence), and Rants (tirades from angry people)" (www.boards. adultswim.com/).

For Adult Swim fans who go online, a heavy emphasis on "being heard" emerges that does not dissipate upon being heard (i.e., via someone involved with Adult Swim or AdultSwim.com acknowledging what a fan has said or asked about). Both the television bumps and the website offer overt invitations that are as explicit as anything involved with *American Idol*; indeed, there is a place within the online forums where people can submit original music and short films – and at times the TV bumps have encouraged viewers to visit the website (and sometimes to visit other websites) in order to sample fellow fans' creative work. A contest in fall 2006 also bridged the TV lineup to the website: a bump running during Adult Swim informed viewers that they could submit a few sentences at AdultSwim.com explaining why they should win custody of an Adult Swim shot glass. The winning entry was: "If I won the glass, I'd take my shot and send it to another [as {Adult Swim}] fan. They would do the same. It would be like that stupid traveling gnome. Only better and stuff. (duzitickle)" (www.boards.adultswim.com/adultswim/board?board.id=3 [duzitickle-shot glass winner!!!]).

Thus, what seems to have developed between Adult Swim and its viewers is a relationship that rests to a considerable degree on a website rooted in overt invitations. This practice suggests that tele-participation on the viewers' part will help them to be a full-fledged member of the social audience – something that became apparent when an online academic article about Adult Swim offered explanations for the success of the lineup (Heinricy, Payne, and McManaman 2005). One scholar suggested that the use of the bumps creates an "imagined 'we'" of programmers and viewers that builds and sustains a sense of intimacy. Many Adult Swim fans who had found the article felt the "imaginary" descriptive suggested that fans were either naively believing that they had an actual relationship (in the traditional sense of that term) with industry professionals at Adult Swim, or that the relationships that existed among Adult Swim online users were somehow frivolous or inconsequential. Thus, Kevin responded to the authors of the article: "This community is not 'imagined.' ... You should visit the boards before you speak." Other fans then joined in with gentle chastisement, seeking to explain to these scholars from a fan's perspective what the appeal of the boards and the bumps was:

> I don't watch AS [Adult Swim]; I participate in it ... AS has a personality I can interact with. (Herb)

> No other network allows this much input from its loyal viewers. (Allison)

> It's all part of the fun! The promos bring us into the show and make us feel like we're in on the production. (Lindsay)

Some viewers, however, felt that the bumps created by the producers and programmers at Adult Swim could be bullying, in much the same way that some *Buffy* fans trying to enter The Bronze website (as I discussed in chapter one) complained that elitist hierarchies existed among select fan groups. One anonymous respondent to the academic article suggested that the bumps serve to subtly alienate those viewers who have not immersed themselves in the online culture of the show, pressuring them to go online and also to watch more of the TV lineup so that they can understand the jokes in the bumps. Two of the respondents I interacted with had issues with the tone of the boards as well:

> Adult Swim tends to be very against their fan base. Some of their bumpers seem to strictly blame them for any and all of the mistakes they make. They think their [*sic*] being funny, but they just sound angry. (Phil)

> I think their willingness to listen is too tuned into the reach of their personal forums ... The members of the Adult Swim boards are more than happy to take what is given them at any turn, but many viewers outside those forums are in an uproar. (Caleb)

> [At AS] they only seem to pay attention to their own forums full of ... chattering children. Thus they keep producing these ugly, vulgar monstrosities they call "comedies." (GrinfilledCelt)

Such complaints and inner battlings could be a result of the unique historical trajectory of the animation genre as manifested in the development of the Cartoon Network. Kevin Sandler (2003) traces the shift in cable networks adopting animation in the mid-1980s through the 1990s to solidify their brand images in an era during which network/channel branding became increasingly important as a means of supporting synergy (90). Cartoon Network attempted to bring together the kid-oriented leanings of the genre with a new emphasis on adult orientation, particularly by offering the Adult Swim lineup and its corresponding web forums. Sandler notes the importance of the website in situating the "personality" of the network, but what occurs when the core audience disagrees as to what that personality should suggest or reflect? Looking at the opinions offered here, it is not so easy for viewers to let go of animation's association with children and (via that association) animation's association with low quality.

As Jason Mittell (2004) argues, "genres can be seen as key ways that our media experiences are classified and organized into categories that have specific links to particular concepts like cultural value, assumed audience, and social function" (xii). Cartoon Network's attempt to shift the genre understanding of animation from kid oriented to adult oriented seems to have resulted in a disagreement with some viewers as to what is "adult" when it comes to the content and style of not just individual programs, but of the Adult Swim "show" as a whole – including its website. Is it "childlike" to listen primarily to those who blindly accept what is offered, as Caleb and GrinfilledCelt suggest in the above quotes? Is it childish to make fun of your fan base, as Phil's quote suggests? Or is it childish to expect animated programming and its promotional environment to be more serious about its aesthetics and cultural value, as Adult Swim bumps suggest? Here, it matters less what the answers are to such questions than the fact that the overt invitations to tele-participation that Adult Swim puts out open the door to a battle over what Adult Swim should "be" if it wishes to succeed with its market.

GrinfilledCelt alludes to the important marketing potential of the Adult Swim forums, regardless of any one fan's pleasure or displeasure in the site itself, suggesting that, bottom line, programmers and producers will court the tele-participation of fans when its suits their interests. Indeed, it is likely that, as one respondent argued, the TV bumps themselves emerged originally to take up ad space that early on could not be filled rather than through any concrete pre-design of tele-participation. Few fans, though, believed that advertisers, sponsors, or marketers were paying attention to online discussions, noting astutely that advertisers might worry about alienating the majority of the viewing audience if they were to heed online voices as representative of the whole. Thus, battle or not, the power to define animation for Adult Swimmers appears to reside in the hands of the network; and the fact that unhappy viewers remain attached to the lineup to some degree suggests that the tele-participation may serve to maintain the connection over and above the content itself. As one fan put it, the bumps that emerge on Adult Swim serve to hold together both the programs in the lineup and the viewers *with* the lineup, threading these elements together via a "sarcastic male personality" (Heinricy, Payne, and McManaman 2005).

Nevertheless, it is likely that marketers and advertisers are indeed paying attention – or that they will be soon. The PricewaterhouseCoopers (2006) report notes that, increasingly, those media users in the key 18–34 years of age demographic are willing to provide data about themselves online – data that marketers can use to design ads tailored to small groups (such as fans of Adult Swim). The report specifies that, while such groups might be small, they are growing in terms of their influence as trend-setters – and the best way to capture their attention is through "the combination of a personalized media experience with a social context for participation" (2). Thus, unhappy viewers may be able to make their desires known with some result if they are valuable enough to the network's sponsors in the end.

The report recommends further that TV networks consider the value of branding themselves, so that the viewer/consumer considers the network in a personalized manner – much as Adult Swim fans conceptualize the lineup on the Cartoon Network as an entity with a distinct personality. As Peter Sanderson (2004) notes in his examination of the "network within a network," Adult Swim in fact pulls in more 18–24 year old viewers than competing networks in that time slot – and in particular more men in that demographic are watching Adult Swim. The young adult male demographic is one that TV has been attempting to capture since the mid-1990s, when the TV industry began noticing a decrease in that group watching broadcast television. Cartoon Network executive John Friend describes Adult Swim viewers as "inclined to want to get deeper. If they love a show, they want the extra stuff" (quoted in Lafayette 2006). This "extra stuff" encompasses the obvious, literal "stuff" (videos and DVDs, tee-shirts, collectibles) but also increasingly the less obvious, intangible "stuff" of the Adult Swim forums. In the end, it may be the "extra stuff," which is linked to tele-participation, that keeps viewers coming back for more. And if the network's goal is to extend their overt invitations primarily to the 18–24 year old male, the initial participants will somewhat quickly age out of the party, perhaps finding what they once considered to be entertaining now "too childish" for their tastes.

As recently as fall 2006, the Cartoon Network began a full-fledged campaign to anchor this intangible arena of tele-participation with the launch of a new series that they are marketing to both *younger* viewers *and* to Adult Swim viewers. In the press release for *Class of 3000*, Cartoon Network executive Jim Samples states: "From exclusive behind-the-scenes footage of the show to streaming full-length episodes, not to mention downloadable songs, ring tones and podcasts, we're making sure that *Class of 3000* has compelling offerings on every available platform." Taking a page right out of the PricewaterhouseCoopers report, the Cartoon Network is aggressively developing the strength of their cross-platforming – a move that PricewaterhouseCoopers stresses serves both the viewer (allowing them options and a sense of control) and creators (helping them collect more thorough data about the kinds of activities in which their key viewers are most invested). However, doing so may come at the cost of alienating those "old-guard" viewers who RSVP'd first and who may see younger viewers as "crashers" and/ or the network as a bad host.

The press release emphasized as well that viewers will be able to share their own creations with other viewers – what Pricewaterhouse-Coopers refers to as "convergence-native content" (2006: 7). With convergence-native content, the user can "share their experience *in a social context* across a network with other users" (7, my emphasis). Tapping into what many of the viewers I discussed in this chapter spoke of when describing their online experiences, media producers are finding that users wish to share their media experiences with others in their social audience. While I will examine in the following chapter the phenomenon of online social networking and its association in the early 2000s with younger viewers, in this chapter's concluding section I examine a corresponding desire developing among media consumers: the wish to create their own media to share with others.

Conclusion: Out With The Old... "Authentic Television" is on the Internet

I began this chapter with the proposition that the Internet has become an increasingly important element in TV's ability to build tele-participation, and that a key aspect of what emerges from this are processes of negotiation. On one level, the rise of Internet sites related to TV programs, but not attached to them officially, has led to tension-filled negotiations between the industry and site creators over the issue of ownership. On another level, industry professionals have been encouraging viewers to claim a sense of ownership in their programs by overtly calling out to viewers to go online and voice opinions. In both of these scenarios, and in the cases I have raised so far in this chapter, the balance of power lies inevitably with an industry that has the resources to shut down sites over copyright, with an industry that is responsible ultimately for the texts around which tele-participation develops, and therefore with an industry that seeks to incorporate the work of tele-participation into its own logic of capitalization. As Mark Andrejevic (2004) puts it, "the invitation to viewers is not to seize control but rather to participate in the rationalization of their own viewing experience" (152).

What sorts of negotiations emerge, though, when it is the viewer who is responsible ultimately for the content in question? Since the turn of the century, media companies have been developing Internet sites that allow consumers to generate their own content – what some in the industry refer to as UGC (user-generated content) or VGC (viewer-generated content). Chris Anderson (2006) calls the new millennium the "age of peer production … [resulting in] a shared culture of fandom, community, and camaraderie" that has developed out of an increased availability of the tools people need to create and alter video and sound (137). Indeed, viral videos reached epic proportions in terms of industry and popular culture topics of conversation in 2005/2006, as myriad sites independent of TV companies gained millions of users ostensibly overnight; one user would post a short video (typically, humorous in nature) and soon scores of people would have viewed it as one person passed it along to another.

Some people's ability to download video to their computers, edit content, and then upload the results to websites that were popping up for expressly this reason indicates a changing relationship to entertainment – and this change extends to the TV industry. As Ryan Magnussen of Ripe TV (a company that produces video content specifically for the Internet) points out, "the value of NBC in the past was their distribution platform, which was incredibly powerful. But that's now starting to break down'" (quoted in Kirsner 2006). TV companies now find themselves in the position of having to negotiate with "TV" on the Internet – in the sense that people are watching short-form narratives on their computers, and in the sense that people have been finding clips from broadcast television programs online also.

Five significant points of negotiation seem to be pertinent. First, key demographics of viewers are becoming accustomed to the idea that they can be the "taste-makers" when it comes to determining what will circulate as viable entertainment. Second, these viewers are becoming accustomed to the process of sharing with their friends that entertainment which they enjoy most – immediately. Thus, the industry will have to learn to negotiate these two new sets of expectations developing among viewers. Third, the TV industry will need to begin negotiating directly with the many independent websites that allow users to offer, watch, and share content, following the "viruses" to consider if there is content online that might also work offline (i.e., on TV). Fourth, the TV industry will also have to negotiate directly with sites that wish to show clips from TV shows, rather than risk the wrath of viewers who will then see the TV industry networks as both retrograde and as not in a position to claim ownership in a new media environment that promotes sharing.[13] And fifth, the TV industry will have to negotiate internally issues of rights and pay for professionals creating additional online content related to television shows.

I will be addressing several of these points of negotiation in future chapters. For now, I would like to examine briefly the negotiations that began occurring between the TV industry and online sites as both broadcast and cable networks scrambled to offset a slide of viewers from key demographics to the Internet. Unsurprisingly, smaller networks were the first to forge online relationships, with Comedy Central developing Motherlode, Nickelodeon developing TurboNick, and MTV developing MTV Overdrive – all sites that rely on external servers to generate the capability for users to view original content (some UGC but most created in-house). As Anne Becker (2006b) notes, networks already reaching out to niche audiences have been quick to use their own sites as a sort of "minor league where executives roam the sidelines scouting for talent to jump to the majors." Contests online related to TV have now become commonplace, also as a breeding ground for new talent. The New York TV Festival in 2006 developed a deal with msn.com, the Independent Film Channel, and Rainbow Media: festival contestants submit pitches for shows online and eventually viewers online vote to result in ten finalists who can then pitch their series ideas in person to TV executives (a process that festival head Terence Gray describes as "an *American Idol*-like format") (quoted in Learmonth 2006). FX since 2005 has used the Internet to have viewers vote on which short-form narrative they think should be developed into an actual sitcom for the network – which to date has used the contest to develop successfully the series *It's Always Sunny in Philadelphia*.[14]

One of the more publicized sets of negotiations occurred in 2006, as one particular website, YouTube.com, gained immense popularity. In early 2005, YouTube.com emerged as a site where users could upload personal video clips and people could watch, make comments, and send the videos along for friends to watch. In a little over a year, owners Steve Chen and Chad Hurley had a massive hit on their hands – it was almost as if YouTube.com was its own program, akin to how Adult Swim fans sometimes conceptualize that lineup of programs as its own show. The site gained fame as more and more people found it; it gained notoriety in 2006 when a popular skit from NBC's *Saturday Night Live* ("Lazy Sunday") was uploaded by a user and spread rapidly across the Internet. A public battle developed as users began berating NBC for having YouTube pull the clip – and NBC took note of two things: the potential bad PR if they held firm, and the potential good PR (and attending profits) if they could find a way to work with YouTube.[15] NBC quickly struck a deal with the site that developed into ways for NBC to promote their own content while still maintaining an environment of shared ownership. For example, in the summer of 2006, NBC used YouTube for a UGC contest in which YouTubers could create and upload promotions for the NBC comedy *The Office*; the winner had their promo aired on NBC.

With more viewers and industry professionals paying attention than ever before, it is small surprise that Bill Lawrence turned to YouTube when NBC passed on a sitcom pilot he had produced (with Warner Brothers Studios) and that *Family Guy* writers Garrett Donovan and Neil Goldman had created. Ironically titled *Nobody's Watching*, the show posted on YouTube and soon gained a tremendous number of viewers. YouTube then officially featured the show and soon after NBC was back in talks with Bill Lawrence to develop the series for television. Less than three months later, as multiple networks began making deals with YouTube for access to clips from network shows, Google, an online search site and server, purchased YouTube for $1.65 billion, demonstrating both the might of the site (Google had developed its own UGC-oriented site, Google Video) and its future potential.

"Suddenly," everyone was talking about UGC and the role that sites like YouTube might come to play in how people understand visual entertainment and storytelling: Will the experiences users find via UGC prompt expectations concerning corporate-created content? There has also been considerable discussion over the ephemeral notion of ownership: As major corporations buy independent sites, will they lose their ability to appeal to the users that generate their content? Will consumers worry about their creations falling into the hands of corporate entities concerned more with profit than storytelling? Will sites be overrun by network or film studio content? As of this writing it is too soon to tell. However, in interviews I had with creators of two UGC-centered sites, both professionals emphasized the importance to them of maintaining a sense of independence on behalf of their consumer clients that would allow authenticity.

Mika Salmi of Atom.com, which specializes in short-form animation and films, as well as games, explained that when he was developing his site in the late 1990s, Hollywood had not been able to understand that there was an art to short-form storytelling.[16] But media *users* "got it" and were able to create short, funny bits that played well online:

> It was clear that people were not only looking for an alternative form [of entertainment] … It had to be on demand and short form … Within a year we got interest from Hollywood. But they came at it from, you know, Hollywood talent would create this stuff … The problem with that was, they didn't really have the sensibility, they didn't really understand the idea of on demand and short form, and the way the audience reacted to it … I think they were trying to bring their movie or TV business kind of mindset and saying, "we'll just shorten it! We'll just make it five minutes!" (Interview, July 20, 2006)

Thus, Atom hired artists to create content for their site and recruited others based on work they sampled from outside traditional industry channels. Users can submit online and they get paid a percentage of advertising revenue attached to the site – based on how many hits their work gets from people visiting the site.

Simon Assad of Heavy.com, which specializes in short-form animation as well, believes that the TV industry, in line with Salmi's observations, will have to start green-lighting more projects from independent artists (rather than developing work in-house) in order to retain viewers now accustomed to a greater sense of cultural power (interview, August 11, 2006). In his experience, artists delivering to the key youth demographic enjoy the creative freedom that online sites offer. Viewers enjoy the ability to provide feedback and to be the arbiters of the tastes that drive culture – as opposed to relying on the TV industry to choose what is "taste-worthy":

> The euphoria you feel when you make something and then you get an immediate response, and then translating that into millions of dollars – it's hard to describe how liberating that is when it's not attached to the bullshit of the industry … There was an element of a very small niche

group of people driving culture for about twenty or thirty years. And, you know, it was that group of people who were television executives, development executives, and those types of industry that bought and sold media companies – those were the guys that determined what you're going to watch on television ... Well, obviously that's all changed.

Salmi agrees that a significant appeal for creators is the "now" element of interaction with consumers that is difficult to achieve in traditional television:

> There's instant communication between the creator and the audience. Direct, one-to-one communication, which never existed on TV. So the creator gets instant feedback – not the next day or the next week ... It can be numbers, or comments like "I hated that!" or "Why did the character do that?" (Interview, 2006)

The cautions about corporate ownership and the traditional TV industry routes of obtaining and circulating content do not seem unfounded. In the summer of 2006, Warner Brothers Studios made a deal with Guba.com, a moderately popular UGC site. "Guba sees less of its future tied to video content generated from the public" and more tied to studio-created content from WB – a marked shift for a site that had prided itself on its independent online status as a UGC-oriented site (Kehaulani 2006). Television critic Rob Owen, TV editor of the *Pittsburgh Post-Gazette*, warns that "there's definitely going to be more crossover [between the Internet and TV]. It may very much be the way there was the whole Internet boom and then bust, where ultimately all the popular viral video sites end up being owned by the five corporations" (interview, September 4, 2006). Still, such sites are a lot of work to maintain and copyright risks abound with users able to upload any content they wish. Partnering with a larger corporate entity reduces risk and provides financial resources as well; for the larger corporate company, the website can become a source of free advertising and marketing for related entities, as well as a source of demographic data.

This tension between a desire for UGC sites to maintain their independence from larger entertainment industry companies and their own need to remain economically viable results in interesting conundrums surrounding the monetization of viewers' cultural capital. The rhetoric surrounding UGC focuses on how it is more authentic because it is untainted by economics, but clearly this is not the case – entrepreneurs such as Chen and Hurley, Salmi, and Assad are not in this for simply the freedom and fun of it:

> The audience is, as people, we are all voracious consumers of stuff that we find entertaining. It's kind of like the all-you-can-eat buffet that you never get sick at. Right? You just keep consuming and consuming, and now on the Internet you get into this place where ... part of the entertainment is distributing it to your friends ... who think you're smart, funny, in touch, whatever it is, because you're the one that sent them this stuff ... We call it an ancillary and nobody's really worked out how to monetize it yet. But the fact of the matter is, the more of that ancillary, the larger your distribution network is, and the more loyalty you have. (Simon Assad, interview, 2006)

> [The networks are] hearing from their advertisers, they're hearing from their sales people: "Hey! Business is booming over here [on the Internet]!" And they're seeing their audience eroding, especially the under thirty crowd. The shift is dramatic. It's different than it was five years ago – now there's actual money there and an actual audience there. (Mika Salmi, interview, 2006)

> Marketers are really concerned with getting their message through. This [the Internet] is actually an even better environment [for advertising] than TV ever was, because you're so engaged with your screen that you're not going anywhere ... In a way, I think the networks have been prompted by the advertising community [to engage with Internet sites], to be more creative about how they approach this stuff. Marketers were the first on that train – they really got it when "Subservient Chicken" went haywire and "Lazy Sunday." When something goes so viral and gets so explosive, and people are participating – that's what you want. And I think definitely the generation behind you and me is way more on board with that than us cynical Gen-Xers. They're totally happy to pass on that link or clip or funny game – there's not as much of a "oh no – I'm doing The Man's marketing" there. (Maureen Ryan, TV critic *Chicago Tribune*, interview, September 13, 2006)[17]

Thus, sites that position themselves as independent of the mainstream TV industry are not necessarily by default independent of mainstream industry economics – and perhaps do not want to be. And the mainstream TV industry, as much as it is often positioned as losing power in the 2000s, has considerably more money and clout with marketers and advertisers than do Internet entertainment sites. While UGC sites may position themselves against the TV industry and industry-sponsored sites, the distance separating them may not be very much more than that between something like VotefortheWorst.com and *American Idol*. In fact, one primary connecting thread across the texts I have examined in this chapter – be they programs or websites – is that each positions itself against another, supposedly more main-stream, more distasteful, and less authentic "other" text. Each attempts, on a surface level, to emphasize its authenticity via its overt invitation to tele-participation – there are no "tricks" or "men behind the curtains" here.

Intriguingly, it is in the arena of politics that television's most overt attempt to encourage tele-participation has developed – a good year before people were talking about UGC and YouTube and viral videos. Current.TV is a digital cable network developed by former US Vice President Al Gore and aimed at young adults, with the goal of providing their generation with a forum in which they can present their point of view on news and entertainment – but with a heavy emphasis on news. David Neuman, president of programming at the network, explains: "We're the place that you go for the highest and best form of … user-generated pieces. If you have a video of your kid's second birth-day, go to YouTube. But if you want to see somebody in the middle of the conflict in Haifa, to show you what it's like to have bombs raining down over your head, you come to Current" (quoted in Littlejohn 2006). Thus, Current.TV is situated against YouTube as offering more important authentic moments for young adults in today's world.

Because Current.TV online is tied to its cable network, it has nowhere near the cultural cache that YouTube does. However, given the trend towards corporate buyouts that is occurring with other UGC sites, it may be its "lowly" status that keeps it afloat.[18] Viewers can upload original pieces to the network's website (content referred to as VC^2 – for viewer-content squared); then online viewers vote on which pieces they would like to see aired on *television*. In my interview with David Neuman, he explained that Al Gore's vision for Current was to maintain a focus on TV as a medium that belongs to the viewers – but to acknowledge that for the current youth market, the Internet is their medium of choice:

> The digital revolution gave people the means to create; the Internet gives people a way to distribute and participate in a dialogue of democracy. Much like the printing press removed barriers for people, and then

TV helped remove some geographical barriers, now the Internet can remove even more. By using the Internet to give some power to the TV viewer, you are democratizing the process – and you can potentially transform the viewer and society. (Interview, July 17, 2006)

With a more concrete and literal understanding of democracy than *American Idol*, Current nevertheless relies on overt invitations, depending on younger viewers to respond online to what they see on television and to offer their own stories for sharing. The site, through its voting system, encourages users to converse about what they are seeing and hearing – on TV, in politics, in their lives – a move that Neuman sees as fundamental to democratic decision-making:

> Current.TV believes that conversation is fundamental to democracy and progress. And kids today want to talk about things. It's too easy to say that kids aren't interested, they're apathetic – and if you keep saying that they have nothing to offer, then that's going to become a self-fulfilling prophecy. So Current.TV *is* conversation – you talk by offering things for viewers to vote on; you talk when you make your decisions about what gets on TV; and you talk when you send something of your own in when you think something that made it onto TV wasn't good enough.

Through a process of epistemic negotiation (Code 1995), younger viewers are pushed to examine competing points of view before taking a stand on any issue. This occurs in an environment that actively combats what Neuman describes as the "deeply flawed stereotype" that young adults are unable to make informed decisions (interview, 2006). Current.TV sees itself as an advocate for young adults who want a more authentic representation of their generation's point of view, positioning itself against other, more mainstream venues for news (and to some degree entertainment). In response to Current, even CNN has gotten in on the act. In August 2006 the 24 hour news network launched CNN.com/Exchange, allowing users to upload video and text in a section tagged "I-Reports." For CNN, the resonance of UGC with the young professional demographic has the potential to pull in viewers who might not see the network as "cutting edge" – who in fact may be getting their news from *The Daily Show* on Comedy Central. As executive Mitch Gelman put it: "What we're doing with the Exchange, and I-Reports in particular, is creating a single vehicle, *a simple branded environment in which people are going to be able to more consistently and easily participate in the news*" (quoted in Becker 2006a; my emphasis).[19]

Right in line with the PricewaterhouseCoopers' report on Lifestyle Media, CNN is seeking to associate their entire network with the notion of tele-participation. While CNN and Current.TV's programming content is as far removed from *American Idol*'s, Adult Swim's, and for the most part YouTube's as one might imagine, their shared emphasis on ownership and authenticity unites them. All of the texts discussed in this chapter succeed because they overtly encourage viewers to either literally create/generate their own stories or to actively navigate the directions another person's/entity's story takes. Each claims to be offering something more authentic than some other choice that exists – and in fact to *offer* more choice through tele-participation.

These venues offering overt invitations are well known; they are front-and-center topics in newspapers and magazines outside of the industry proper. What the full impact of this turn towards the Internet might be remains to be seen at this early stage of media shift. Certainly, the industry is watching online activity now more than ever; where there were once a few well-known sites for UGC, there are now countless "official network sites" such as NBC's IVillage.com, CBS's InnerTube.com, and Nickelodeon's TurboNick. com. As Larry Kramer (President of Digital Media at CBS) notes, the Internet is proving to be a useful forum in which to test riskier story ideas (and in fact, several shows launched at such sites have been developed for television after doing well online) (interview, June 28, 2006). And as the work by market researchers such as Stacey Koerner reveals, advertisers are heeding the trends and patterns developing online as well.

The themes of choice, authenticity, and shared ownership raised in this chapter "harken back" to the original vision of the Internet as a source of information abundance that would democratically allow anyone access to any number of perspectives, theoretically leading to an expectation of shared ownership and participation in the realm of culture (Neuman 1991). As John Hartley (2004) notes, however, a primary goal of this expanded choice is to teach viewers (and users) to keep watching (and using) – thus maintaining a profitable cultural marketplace. The Internet has become a powerful tool for TV executives seeking to maintain loyal viewership, and the most successful attempts are rooted firmly in PricewaterhouseCoopers' description of "lifestyle media" – emphasizing how the complex interweaving of media can operate to create a sense of community belonging.

In the following chapter, I will examine how programs aimed at teenaged viewers are very much in the vanguard of building the Internet into viewers' environment of reception, informing how this target social audience relates to media texts. In my interviews with David Neuman of Current, Simon Assad of Heavy.com, and Mika Salmie of Atom, each emphasized the emerging importance of the Internet's relationship with television and film for consumers under the age of thirty. As Simon Assad succinctly put it: "They don't know a world without the Internet. For them it's not emerging media – it *is* media." In addition, each underscored the importance of scholars and entertainment professionals understanding the value to younger consumers of social networking sites such as MySpace.com and FaceBook.com, and how these sites interact with teens' and young adults' understanding of entertainment. What patterns of reception are developing for this key group of viewers? How are they defining television and television watching? And in what ways is the industry managing this group's set of expectations for entertainment and community?

Notes

1 For a full discussion of the dynamics described here, see Bourdieu (1977, 1984) and Bourdieu and Wacquant (1992).

2 My overall sample involved 78 viewers. This included 18 who listed *American Idol* as a show they watched regularly, and 24 who listed *Family Guy* and 16 Adult Swim. Of these groups, only 5 individuals watched all three.

3 A key exception here is FOX's tendency as discussed in the previous chapter to follow in the music industry's footsteps by shutting down fan sites centered on Twentieth Century Fox produced series such as *Buffy* and *The X-Files*.

4 NATPE is an annual convention held in Las Vegas, featuring producers, writers, programmers, and research and development professionals. The conference also serves as a marketplace for syndicated programming, both original and pre-aired. In 2006, the conference took place in late January.

5   Stacey Koerner at the time was executive vice president for Global Research Integration, Initiative – a marketing firm division that has developed a variety of software tools and research projects measuring audience engagement (e.g., how much online "buzz" a new show is gathering). Shortly thereafter, she became president of a new research division called "The Consumer Experience Practice," which examined online involvement with television texts in more detail; some of these projects were conducted in conjunction with the Massachusetts Institute of Technology. In 2007, she left Global Research Integration, Initiative, beginning work as a freelance consultant. Ken Papagan is the executive vice president of Strategic Planning and Business Development for Rentrak, a company that researches business information and strategies for the entertainment industry.

6   Spherion Workplace Snapshot Survey (cited in Keveney 2006).

7   The software program is free; users download it to their computer, allowing their computer to measure how many busy signals their phone-line receives as they dial in for their favorite. The fact that this program cannot measure phones separate from the computer (cell, landline in a broadband house) makes the accuracy of the results even more intriguing – and also suggests that viewers with dial-up Internet offer a fairly solid sampling of the audience of voters.

8   One cannot help but draw a parallel here to the voting process in the US, especially after the 2000 election, when so many people for the first time fully understood that aggregate voting counts more than the individual vote. Further on I will discuss the connection this series makes with the American voting mindset.

9   Henry Jenkins (2006) discusses how sponsors now wish to position themselves as bringing "love" to the viewer by becoming more firmly entrenched in a text that viewers love. The goal for such sponsors is to become a "lovemark" for the viewer (68–70).

10 In European versions of *Idol*, voters must pay for every call they make; one might imagine this would serve to curtail the democratic process, but the success of the show globally seems to belie this assumption.

11 Pursuant Inc. poll (cited in de Moraes 2006).

12 The show was also a success in Canada (where it aired before landing on Adult Swim) on Canada's Teletoon network.

13 According to the Online Publishers' Association, UGC videos are viewed by 25 percent of those who surf the Internet (Vascellaro 2006).

14 In 2006, FX used the Internet social network MySpace.com, at that point owned by Rupert Murdoch – who also owns FX.

15 Amusingly, when the clip was first pulled, two YouTube users created a spoof called "Hazy Sunday" that became almost as popular.

16 Salmi has since gone on to work as president of Global Digital Media for MTV Networks.

17 "Subservient Chicken" was a 2004 viral marketing campaign for Burger King's chicken sandwiches that emphasized UGC and interactivity: people could visit a website of a person in a chicken suit reacting to directives that users were sending to it over the Internet (you can "have your chicken your way"). The campaign was a huge success for Burger King and took place entirely online.

18 The network's channel reached only 20 million homes in 2006 (Reuters 2006).

19 The "success" of this approach can be seen in the widely circulated I-Reporter cell phone footage of the shooting spree at Virginia Tech University in the spring of 2007; a student captured activity closer than any network was able to, and all the major networks used CNN's footage in their initial coverage of this tragedy.

References

Anderson, C. (2006) People Power. *Wired* (July), p. 137.

Andrejevic, M. (2004) *Reality TV: The Work of Being Watched*. Rowman and Littlefield, Lanham, MD.

Baym, N. (2000) *Tune In, Log On: Soaps, Fandom, and Online Community*. Sage, Thousand Oaks, CA.

Baym, N. (1998) Talking About Soaps: Communicative Practices in a Computer-Mediated Fan Culture. In Harris, C. and Alexander, A. (eds.) *Theorizing Fandom: Fans, Subculture and Identity*. Hampton Press, Cresskill, NJ, pp. 111–29.

Becker, A. (2006a) CNN Enlists Citizen Journalists. *Broadcasting and Cable* (July 31). www.broadcastingcable.com/. Accessed August 1, 2006.

Becker, A. (2006b) TV's New Greenhouse. *Broadcasting and Cable* (August 21). www.broadcastingcable.com/. Accessed August 25, 2006.

Bourdieu, P. (1984) *Distinction: A Social Critique of the Judgement of Taste*. Trans. Richard Nice. Harvard University Press, Cambridge, MA.

Bourdieu, P. (1977) *Outline of a Theory of Practice*. Cambridge University Press, Cambridge.

Bourdieu, P. and Wacquant, L. J. D. (1992) *An Invitation to Reflexive Sociology*. University of Chicago Press, Chicago.

Carter, B. (2006) *Desperate Networks*. Doubleday, New York.

Code, L. (1995) *Rhetorical Spaces: Essays on Gendered Locations*. Routledge, New York.

Creamer, M. (2006) Interpublic Opens Consumer-Focused Unit. *AdAge* (February 24). www.adage.com/mediaworks/article?article_id=48651. Accessed July 19, 2006.

Dayan, D. and Katz, E. (1992) *Media Events: The Live Broadcasting of History*. Harvard University Press, Cambridge, MA.

De Moraes, L. (2006) Survey Gives "Idol" a Vote of Confidence. *Chicago Tribune*, section 5, p. 12 (Thursday, May 4) (reprinted with permission from the *Washington Post*).

Ellis, J. (2004) Television Production. In Allen, R. and Hill, A. (eds.) *The Television Studies Reader*. Routledge, New York, pp. 275–92.

Ellis, J. (2000) *Seeing Things: Television in the Age of Uncertainty*. I. B. Tauris, New York.

Fiske, J. (1992) Cultural Economy of Fandom. In L. Lewis (ed.) *The Adoring Audience: Fan Culture and Popular Media*. Routledge, New York, pp. 30–49.

Gledhill, C. (1988) Pleasurable Negotiations. In Pribram, E. D. (ed.) *Female Spectators: Looking at Film and Television*. Verso, London, pp. 64–89.

Gray, J. (2005) Antifandom and the Moral Text: Television Without Pity and Textual Dislike. *American Behavioral Science* 48, issue 7 (March 1): 840.

Gripsrud, J. (2004) Broadcast Television: The Chances of Its Survival in a Digital Age. In Spigel, L. and Olsson, J. (eds.) *Television After TV: Essays on a Media in Transition*. Duke University Press, Durham, NC, pp. 210–23.

Hartley, J. (2004) Democratainment. In Allen, R. and Hill, A. (eds.) *The Television Studies Reader*. Routledge, New York, pp. 524–33.

Hayward, J. (1997) *Consuming Pleasures: Active Audiences and Serial Fictions from Dickens to Soap Opera*. University Press of Kentucky, Lexington.

Heinricy, S., Payne, M. and McManaman, A. (2005) Pass the Remote: Adult Swim. *FLOW: A Critical Forum on Television and Media* 2 (issue 2). www.jot.communication.utexas.edu/flow/?jot=view&id=700.

Hill, A. (2005) *Reality TV: Audiences and Popular Factual Television*. Routledge, New York.

Jenkins, H. (2006) *Convergence Culture: Where Old and New Media Collide*. NYU Press, New York.

Jenkins, H. (2002) Interactive Audience? In Harries, D. (ed.) *The New Media Book*. BFI, London, pp. 157–70.

Johnson, D. (2007) Inviting Audiences In: The Spatial Reorganization of Production and Consumption in "TV III." *New Review of Film and Television Studies* 5, no. 1 (April): 61–80.

Kehaulani, S. (2006) NBC Taps Popularity of Online Video Site. *Washington Post* (June 28), D1.

Keveney, B. (2006) "Idol" Contest is a Numbers Game, Too. *USAToday.com* (May 22). www.usatoday.printthis.clickability.com. Accessed June 27, 2006.

Kirsner, S. (2006) Low-budget Viral Videos Attract TV-sized Audiences. *Boston Globe* (July 30). www.boston.com/business/personaltech/articles/2006/07/30/low_budget_viral-video. Accessed July 31, 2006.

Koerner, S. (2005a) Insight from the Inside Out. *The Hub* (May 2), 10–13. www.hubmagazine.com/?p=26. Accessed July 19, 2006.

Koerner, S. (2005b) Listening to Fan Voices. Family Friendly Programming Forum, presentation.

Lafayette, J. (2006) Net Brings Licensing In-House. *Television Week* 25, 9 (February 27), 3.

Lauer, K. (2006) Web Sites Adding to "Idol" Craziness. *Allentown, PA Morning Call* (May 13). www.tmcnet.com/scripts. Accessed July 5, 2006.

Learmonth, M. (2006) New York TV Fest Gives Pitchers Their Chance. *Variety* (July 16). www.variety.com/7/19/06. Accessed July 19, 2006.

Littlejohn, J. (2006) Surprise! Current TV is Generating Electricity. *Chicago Tribune Online Edition* (July 31). www.chicagotribune.com/entertainment/tv/chi. Accessed July 31, 2006.

Mittell, J. (2004) *Genre and Television: From Cop Shows to Cartoons in American Culture.* Routledge, New York.

Neuman, W. R. (1991) *The Future of the Mass Audience.* Cambridge University Press, New York.

Newcomb, H. (1974) *TV: The Most Popular Art.* Anchor Press, Garden City, NJ.

Nightingale, V. (1996) *Studying Audiences: The Shock of the Real.* Routledge, New York.

PricewaterhouseCoopers (2006) The Rise of Lifestyle Media: Achieving Success in the Digital Convergence Era.

Reiss, S. and Wiltz, J. (2004) Fascination with Fame Attracts Reality TV Viewers. In Balkin, K. (ed.) *Reality TV.* Greenhaven Press, Farmington Hills, MI, pp. 25–7 (orig. pub. 2001).

Reuters (2007) American Idol Finale Audience off from Last Year (May 24). www.reuters.com/article/televisionNews/idUSN2436759820070524. Accessed August 13, 2007.

Reuters (2006) Gore Wants TV to Welcome More Users Internet-Style. *New York Times.com* (August 27). www.nytimes.com/reuters/washington/politics-media-gore-tv.html. Accessed September 1, 2006.

Sanderson, P. (2004) Adult Swim Upfront 2004 (April 1). www.filmforce.ign.com/articles/503/503483pl.html. Accessed July 19, 2006.

Sandler, K. (2003) Synergy Nirvana: Brand Equity, Television Animation, and Cartoon Network. In Stabile, C. and Harrison, M. (eds.) *Prime Time*

Animation: Television Animation and American Culture. Routledge, New York, pp. 89–109.

Stallybrass, P. and White, A. (1986) *The Poetics and Politics of Transgression*. Harvard University Press, Cambridge, MA.

Vascellaro, J. (2006) Making a Buck Off Your Pet-Trick Videos. *Wall Street Journal Online* (July 12). www.onlinewsj.com/public/article_print. Accessed July 19, 2006.

3

Managing Millennials: Teen Expectations of Tele-Participation

Buffy *definitely has a strong fan base online, with Lost following close behind. As for why, I think it's because* they have a strong following with young people, and it's them who populate the Internet, more than their parents. (*Seffy (40-year-old male), my emphasis*)

I think that any show can have a website, but there are certain shows that are better suited to Internet sites. Teen shows work very well, especially if it is a teen soap with a lot of characters. Had the Internet been as huge in 1990 as it is now, Beverly Hills 90210 would have had about as much of a net following as The O.C. (*PanPan (28-year-old male), my emphasis*)

Seffy and PanPan might appear to be odd choices as representative voices of "Millennials" – those coming of age in the early 2000s, avid consumers of media of a wide variety. Older men by industry accounts, they nevertheless speak to three provocative themes relevant in this chapter. First, both make clear a series of assumptions at work within popular culture, mainstream society, and the television industry: younger people today "just are" active online – and for programs aiming to capture this audience, a "natural" relationship with the Internet is crucial to success. In this chapter, I will explore this mindset and its realities, focusing on how television programs and indeed, entire networks, work to organically invite in viewers, working off an assumption that their core market is always already online. How deliberate are producers, writers, and marketers with their efforts to meld together viewers' television and Internet experiences?

The second theme at work in Seffy's and PanPan's responses is, of course, the fact that they do not fit within the demographic group for organic invitation. As adult men, they fall far away from the demographics of those that producers of shows such as *The O.C.* and *Degrassi: The Next Generation* target. Yet, considerable research is beginning to reveal that many adult viewers are fans of "teen TV," especially those who grew up as members of Generation X (born from the mid-1960s through the mid-1970s), posing questions as to what teen TV is. Is the organic inviting at work in recent teen series an outgrowth of earlier marketing strategies that older viewers are familiar with? Is organic inviting evident in texts and online today serving to situate new trends beyond the Millennial demographic?

Third, as PanPan notes, Internet or not, the style and content of programming is ultimately the primary draw. As he later elaborated:

> Personal connection does tend to be one of the more defining characteristics of a particular genre of shows – the teenage drama. I was a fan of *My So-Called Life* when it first aired in 1994 because it was a show that spoke to me as a teenager. I was in high school at the time and up until then, only had *Beverly Hills 90210* and *Saved By the Bell* to go by (*Degrassi High* had long since faded away). *MSCL* presented pretty realistic characters and situations and I found it to be engaging because in my narcissistic, ego-driven teenage world, I was looking for characters I could relate to.

Here, PanPan implies that teens expect something "more" when watching television than adults do – a series of elements that speak more directly to their personal experiences. I will examine in the pages ahead what these elements might be – and how programs that highlight such elements are well suited to an online presence. In particular, the serial structure of much of teen TV encourages discussion among viewers at a time in adolescent development when informal conversation dominates social life. The power of conversation – especially for females – is significant given the Internet's ability to facilitate this. If the media industries can tap into this dynamic of storytelling, and extend the televisual experience beyond the originating text, they can often strike gold in profoundly significant ways.

The Teen Market

Gen-X. Gen-Next. Gen-Y. Gen-Y-Not? Millennials. Since the 1980s, media industries have worked diligently to classify viewers so as to better reach out to and capture whatever the current teen and young adult market is that dominates the demographics of consumers. Of course, reaching out to teens has been a strategy within television since its earliest days, but monikers such as "Gen-X" and "Millennials" are a more recent phenomenon in keeping with cultural notions of a generation gap that marks teens and young adults as culturally unique in comparison to their parents.

TV offers a prime venue for tapping into this notion of a unique market, with its ever-increasing strategy of niche marketing – a move that snowballed in the 1980s in the United States as cable began to pose real threats to the broadcast networks. Capturing this market (whatever its moniker might be) requires increasingly that television is able to demonstrate to teens and young adults that professionals understand their distinct cultural attributes and that programs are being developed with corresponding sensibilities in mind. This trend of concentrated effort makes my own audience results somewhat remarkable, then, in that over 50 percent of those responding to my surveys indicated that they watched a teen show regularly – and that the age range of these respondents stretched from 13 to 64. Clearly, something beyond "being a teen" is at work with shows ostensibly labeled "teen" by the industry.

What might capture industry attention are the demographics behind the demographics, so to speak. The majority of people responding to my survey and who watched some teen programming also reported the following: ownership of multiple TV sets; digital cable or satellite subscriptions (although, intriguingly, a *minority* reported paying extra for pay channels such as HBO); and ownership of cell phones (with a minority reporting ownership of cell phones with video capacity). I am sure that it would be significant to the industry as well that, among my respondents, the highest concentration of iPod and MP3 ownership occurred among those under the age of 25. Across the board, the majority of these respondents also reported regular use of the Internet in relation to the teen shows they watched, with concentrated activity occurring in the following realms (in order from most reported to least): finding information about episode content; finding information about cast members; purchasing DVDs of the show; chatting with other fans about the show; watching clips related to the show; and purchasing music from the show.

Also significant is the reporting by 80 percent of those who watched some teen TV that they spend time online visiting general TV entertainment sites such as TVGuide.com and E!s Ask Kristin, suggesting that these are viewers who watch a wide variety of TV – and who rely on the Internet to stay informed (and perhaps connected to others) in relation to the shows they watch. These findings from my own small-scale surveying are in line with trends noted by the PricewaterhouseCoopers report I discussed in the previous chapter: media consumers increasingly have the *capacity* to engage in multi-mediated experiences, and the media industries would be wise to appeal to that capacity. It is no surprise that programs I have highlighted in earlier chapters appealing to viewers in this regard are also programs that have had significant teen and young adult viewer bases (*American Idol*, *Buffy the Vampire Slayer*, Adult Swim); today, with increased competition for media consumers, it is more important than ever that the TV industry is able to capture viewer loyalty at ages when patterns of consumption are being solidified.

A key tool in this game is cross-platforming – creating TV products that can thrive in different media forms, most crucially television and the Internet, and via the Internet, the cell phone, and the iPod/MP3 player. Corresponding to cross-platforming is the strategy of integrated ancillary products – the cell phone ring-tone, for example, or the musical soundtrack. Among viewers of teen shows, such extensions of the original viewing experience are key elements of appeal:

> The music was great in *Roswell*: adult alternative, soothing, and different. The "now" shows play annoying punk music that gets old or are just played to advertise the next new hit and don't really fit the show/scene. (Anon19, 19 years old)

> The ideal viewer for this show [*Roswell*] is a woman – of any age. Rich, poor, any race, color or creed from any walk of life. She will like romance and sci-fi. She will be the kind that buys iPods, computers, DVDs, music CDs, goes to Sci-Fi/Fantasy movies like *Lord of the Rings*, *Harry Potter* and *Star Wars* and will encourage (and pay for) her kids or grandkids to enjoy the same. (Thanette, 57)

Thanette's response in particular reveals the advantage of creating a teen series that appeals to older viewers – older demographics may very well have kids or grandkids who they will spread the word to, and when "the word" includes multiple media products, the industry makes out nicely. Her response also reveals an interesting (and for the industry, instructive) assumption: *Roswell* is for "any woman" and "any woman" would have an iPod and an up-to-date computer and money to spend on DVDs and music. Part of the success of cross-platforming and multimedia approaches to TV programming involves the naturalization of such approaches, such that they seem to be inclusive (rather than exclusive of those who may not have the financial means). Ironically, for Anon19, such inclusivity must be balanced with a sense of distinction. For her, the music of *Roswell* is not like that in the "now" shows available to the teen and young adult market: it suits the show – it is aesthetically motivated – and therefore this approach appears "naturalized."

Roswell emerged often in my survey responses as a favorite show among viewers – in no small part due to the fact that this show has become a cult hit among Internet fans. In the concluding chapter I will address the efforts to save this show (which continue today) that ran from 1999–2001 on the WB and then from 2001–2 on UPN. Here I examine the program within the context of understanding organic invitations; this series was one of the earliest to demonstrate to the industry that the Internet could serve as a formidable marketing tool for teen shows in particular. Importantly, this came about "after the fact": outside of the fan base online, few in the industry realized fully the potential that existed all along with this show, especially in the arena of social networking. I would venture to say that if MySpace and YouTube had been phenomena during the original run of this series (or if the PricewaterhouseCoopers report had come out seven or eight years earlier), the show might have had a different fate. With little prodding from its writers, producers, or networks, *Roswell* fans developed strong social networks online, to the point that this experience of tele-participation has outlasted the text itself:

> *The show was cancelled almost four years ago and yet*, people write fan-fics every day, make artwork, etc. ... I watch the show and discuss it with people in the boards right away through the Internet. We have built a strong base, *almost like a family through Internet only*. (Mariella, 26, my emphasis)

> I belong to the "OTOs ... Over Thirty and Obsessed," and we go on trips together that started with *Roswell* (fan events). *Now we've developed a deeper relationship that goes beyond Roswell*. We care about one another. We share about our families, our kids, health, joys, sorrows, etc. We go on trips non-*Roswell* related, but always find something *Roswell* in

whatever we do. *Roswell brought us together, but our friendships have lasted beyond the show*. (Lori, 44, my emphasis)

I've gotten together with online *Roswell* friends – for gatherings, parties and just small get-togethers – all around the country and once in England. We have charity auctions, do raffles of items connected with the show, sometimes have cast members as guests who do Q&As *and/or sometimes we just talk*. (Jass, 56, my emphasis)

Remarkably, a considerable number of women (some who were teens and young adults during the show's initial run, some older) created their own social network around this series, foreshadowing the emergence of social networking and sharing sites that would explode within five years after the show expired. Today, social networking around a teen TV series is starting to emerge as par for the course because such environments are primed for media marketing, indicating how shifts in genre can include more than textual elements (see Mittell 2004). This element of "chat" and social bonding taps into longstanding modes of communication among women, a lineage that has included chat as varied as teen girls exchanging classroom notes and adult women gossiping about soap operas. Production companies and networks have slowly begun to acknowledge such forms of communication, particularly when dealing with texts aiming to reach young women.

Still, not just any show is conducive to social networking. *Roswell* fans emphasized repeatedly that this show was rife with specific elements that encouraged them to find other people with whom to share their experience of the text. One can recognize quickly, I think, a resonance among the appealing elements of this teen science fiction story of aliens living among humans and shows I have discussed in earlier chapters:

I enjoy how the characters in the show relate to each other and go through some of the same problems most of us do. I mean I don't have special alien powers, but the show is also about friendship, love, family and finding yourself. When *Roswell* first started I was in 10th grade and very confused. High school is hard on teenagers in general. Trying to deal with everything and trying to find who you really are. By relating to *Roswell*, it gave me at least a new view on life. (Kim)

Who hasn't felt alone or out of place in a certain environment, be it school, work, etc.? I think anyone can relate to *Roswell* if they don't let the "teen" labeling deter them. I've found that Roswellians (*Roswell* fans) come from all walks of life, different races, etc. (Rhoda)

As with *American Idol, Buffy,* and even to some degree Adult Swim, *Roswell* prompted viewers to relate to varying viewpoints and perspectives; therefore, it is hardly surprising that many fans took to the Internet to discuss these varying viewpoints and perspectives. A heavily serialized series with an ensemble cast, *Roswell* tapped into storytelling elements that I have argued promote radical oscillation as Jennifer Hayward (1997) describes this concept. Viewers can take great pleasure in the ability to take up with ease multiple points of identification, and serial stories tend to promote exactly this.

Scholars such as Lorraine Code (1995) and Carol Gilligan (1982) argue that such storytelling strategies can prompt among listeners processes of second-person knowing and epistemic negotiation – attempts to understand an event from another (second) person's point of view and then to negotiate about competing points of view until consensus is reached. Both scholars in their work focus on issues of gender, arguing that these processes occur more often among women than men, due in part to centuries of women being excluded from "legitimate" modes of decision-making. Gilligan further concentrates on teen girls, examining how their development in Western cultures focuses on taking others' feelings into consideration (at times requiring them to ignore their own), resulting in a moral code that places context above rules.

In the years following Gilligan's work in particular, many feminist scholars have paid special attention to the phenomenon among teen girls in the United States of "losing their voices" – of feeling silenced in schools and in popular culture as well.[1] While I have no doubt that this can occur in perhaps different ways for young boys as well, there certainly appears to be some resonance when considering such sociological and philosophical observations about gender and communication on the one hand, and the preponderance from the 1990s on of teen shows marketed primarily to females. That is, those teen shows that have appealed most strongly to their core demographic have been strongly serial, featuring ensemble casts, and focusing narratively on a constant presence of multiple points of view and the difficulties of ever determining that only one of those points of view or "voices" is correct.

As Jennifer Hayward (1997) describes the standard soap opera, such texts suggest to readers "that we must seek knowledge of all points of view before making judgments" – we must allow typically silenced voices to be heard (4). For teen viewers (and perhaps especially for teen girls) this thematic could hold tremendous appeal:

> There are so many different types of people that watch *Buffy* and get something out of it. That is another reason I love the show. So many people can relate to it in so many different ways, and I wouldn't have it any other way because eventually I get to hear those different perspectives. (Emma, 18)

Thus, a primary component of successfully reaching out to a teen market (particularly females) appears to be the creation of a show that prompts different perspectives. A second key element that may explain the pervasiveness of both fantasy elements and serial structure in teen shows is the ability for change to occur among major characters. As Hayward explains with regards to soap operas, all characters can become heroes (and, I would add, villains). This narrative inscription of constant change and experimentation with pre-set identities may resonate strongly with teen viewers exploring their own identities.

Victor Turner's explanation of the concept of liminality best encapsulates this state of change (1967, 1969, 1982). In pre-literate societies, Turner argues, formal rites of passage often involved adolescents entering a formally organized liminal state – undergoing rituals of transformation that allowed an individual to experiment with issues of identity and relationship to their community. Upon exiting the state of liminality, the individual has solidified their identity and relationship to the community and is prepared to enter a new phase of existence informed by their liminal experimentations. This concept of a "moment" of experimentation, as an individual moves into adulthood, sounds remarkably like modern Western notions of adolescence as a time where those who are in a state of "in-between-ness" (no longer children, not yet adults) are expected to experiment with boundaries laid out for them by friends, family, and society.

Turner argues further that in post-industrial societies, the arts have come to function as a stand-in of sorts for liminality; theater, for example, allows the audience to momentarily enter a liminal state where boundaries of identity and reality can be played with – a sort of cathartic ritual that can periodically renew a community. Other scholars specializing in the study of fandom have made similar claims about the power of media to fulfill psychological functions.[2] Danah Boyd's (forthcoming) work on teens' use of the social networking site MySpace, for example, stresses that teens experiment with the content and design of their profile pages, performing identity several times over as they deal with the liminal status of their identity and create their own social dramas online – away from the world of their parents.

Given the pervasiveness of media in many teens' and young adults' lives, it is not unreasonable to suppose that narratives immersed thematically in the concept of liminality would resonate with viewers experiencing liminality themselves:

> I remember reading on the Internet how *Buffy* had helped some people get through their teenage years, and I remember thinking it was ridiculous when I read it, but looking back, *Buffy* did help me get through high school. I remember reading an interview with Joss Whedon in which he said the show ... ultimately said, "Anyone who got through adolescence is a hero." (Genevieve, 18)

> I thought *Roswell* was a well thought out series about high school students. It was about aliens but it was not necessarily the aliens from outer space but how a teenager can feel like an outsider in the middle of a crowd. (Laura, 30)

Again, it is significant that females respond so strongly (and openly) to these narrative elements of feeling a sense of outsiderness in adolescence and to the narrative structuring of multiple perspectives. Correspondingly, it is also significant that shows featuring elements of the fantastic dominate so many of the teen shows that inspire viewer loyalty. If, as Sigmund Freud argues, we are all essentially beings whose identities are rooted in a sense of loss that draws us to explorations of the unknown, the genres of science-fiction, fantasy, horror, and gothic romance certainly provide easy fodder.[3]

Still, the history of television's appeals to teen viewers suggests that genres which fall within the domain of the fantastic, while well suited to adolescence, are not the only genres that can speak to teen viewers. Examining the responses offered so far in this chapter, it is clear that an aesthetics of multiplicity becomes paramount – narratives that allow for multiple points of view, and that can prompt an expansive experience of that narrative that includes the perspectives of other viewers. Hayward (1997) suggests that ultimately it is a serial narrative structure that allows for this experiencing of a "polyphony of voices" (51).

Over the history of teen TV, the television industry has become increasingly successful at targeting teen viewers with narratives that have become increasingly polyphonic. In the 2000s in particular, the industry has done so by increasingly incorporating the Internet and its ability to accentuate the liminality of teen experiences, as well as to ease any anxiety that liminality might provoke.

Building an Aesthetics of Multiplicity for Teen Viewers

As I have discussed elsewhere with Louisa Stein, the roots of today's teen TV strategies can be found in the earliest days of TV's history in the United States (Ross and Stein forthcoming). From the musical songs incorporated into *The Adventures of Ozzie and Harriet*, to the pop music choices of *American Bandstand* in the 1950s and 1960s, to the emergence of MTV in the 1980s, the use of television to market other media has been a tradition in attempts to appeal to younger viewers. The incorporation of teen and young adult perspectives has also been a longstanding tradition in the development of teen narratives, from local market programs featuring "real teens talking" in the 1940s and 1950s to the "seven strangers ... [who] start getting real" in MTV's *The Real World* of the 1990s. From an industrial perspective, such programming offered inexpensive ways to fill up a TV schedule in early years, and relatively inexpensive ways to jump-start new network ventures in later years.

While trends in programming are fascinating and worthy of study in terms of what such patterns reveal about industry conceptualizations of teen and young adult viewers, to a considerable degree the variations are more about the industry imperative to first replicate what works and then break with the mold in order to stand out. In the 1950s, ABC targeted younger viewers as a way to stand out from longer-established competitors NBC and CBS; in the 1980s MTV would do the same, focusing explicitly on teens and young adults. In the 1990s, both FOX and then WB went after an African American market and then abandoned this niche in favor of (White) teens and young adults; UPN attempted to follow suit, only to find that the market could not sustain both UPN and WB – resulting in the 2006 merger of these two networks into the teen and young-adult oriented

CW. Along the way, digital cable emerged to offer The N (affiliated with Nickelodeon, which falls under the same corporate umbrella that MTV does), seeking to establish itself as the more cutting-edge and diverse teen network, while MTV has developed MTV-U for exclusive transmission on college campuses.

What has remained a constant across these networks and their competing programming trends are: an increasing emphasis on incorporating a teen and young adult perspective (in the sense that characters in that demographic are the narrative voices for their series); an increasing emphasis on multiple perspectives within narratives (in the sense that series feature ensemble casts – albeit predominantly White); an increasing use of serial plotting; and an increasing expansion of the TV experience – first through cross-marketing that resonates with early teen TV strategies (characters singing their actor's hit songs, cameos from young actors about to launch a teen film) and then through cross-platforming that prompts tele-participation.

To a degree, then, the current state of what Anna Everett (2002) refers to as a viewing environment of "digitextuality" is but another step in the "natural" progression of media aimed at teens and young adults – an ever-increasing incorporation of an aesthetics of multiplicity, both within the narratives proper and across the wide variety of media texts offered. Industry understandings of youth culture have been primed for the opportunities that new technologies now offer: teens and young adults are conceptualized as watching TV in groups – with friends rather than with family – and as seeking a sense of participation in their overall media experiences. Before (and still coexisting with) the Internet, a standard teen TV experience might include talking with friends while a program is on, or calling a friend up during a commercial break, or college dorm mates playing a drinking game.

In short, social networking has long been a part of teen and youth media culture – be it in the malt shop, the basement, the dorm room, the bedroom, or via discussions at school or on the phone. With popular culture as a source of conversation fodder, and popular culture aimed at younger viewers increasingly invoking a range of media texts, the incorporation of the Internet into teen TV viewing culture is "natural" – something Rupert Murdoch must have been thinking about when News Corps (FOX's parent company) purchased the social networking site MySpace.com. As Danah Boyd's (forthcoming) research with 14–18 year olds suggests, "everyone" knows about MySpace even if they are not involved with it directly. With the Millennials, in fact, there is a general consensus that boundaries between the Internet and television and film have become non-existent compared to previous generations – which is not to peg this generation as unable to make medium distinctions, but rather to acknowledge that Millennials with the means do not find it "eventful" to visit a website for a show, or to text friends during an episode, or to look up a song they hear on a favorite series so as to purchase it, or find product placement jarring ... This is a generation of viewers who grew up immersed in a multimedia *and* multi-*medium* culture.

From the perspective of writers, producers, and executives hoping to find this market then, it is key that they create narratives that organically invite viewers – that they demonstrate an awareness that viewers should be able to take certain things for granted when it comes to their media experience. Paramount among these things is "a common faith in freedom of movement and choice" and what Margaret Morse (1998) describes as a "sites" mindset that sees the world's "elsewheres" as connected to the listener's here-and-now moment, and experiences and stories as things that can be "visited" (118). This mindset needs to be evident on (at least) two interconnected fronts: the narrative proper (plots that address the role of media in teens' lives and plot structures that emphasize multiplicity and thus some degree of choice thematically), and the extension of that narrative into other realms, with multiplying narratives that continue the thematic of choice and movement.

Thus, networks seeking out this market have found success via demonstrating an awareness of this environment of digitextuality as much as via their development of entertaining programming. For example, MTV2 has created an awards show that allows people to vote online for "all that rocks" (the name of the show) in pop culture; once online, voters are encouraged to upload videos of themselves voicing support for their choice – videos that might air on MTV2 as promos (Riddell 2006). At FLUX – a British MTV network – executives created a means online for viewers to select video lineups and upload their own clips, and also incorporated cell phone texting of messages to friends that could be aired onscreen during the broadcast of a video. In line with everything that *American Idol* and Adult Swim (and even MTV's sister network, The N) have been demonstrating since their inceptions, " 'MTV is challenging the status quo in TV programming and transferring control directly to its audience,' " according to Angel Gambino, vice president of commercial strategy and digital media for MTVUK and MTVIreland (quoted in Goldfarb, 2006).

A key point here, of course, is that such initiatives *are* becoming the status quo among younger viewers: communication through and about media is becoming very much par for the course. In particular, the rising trends include an active refutation of the stereotype of the multimedia savvy individual as a lone, socially isolated and inept person (usually male). Instead, what the mainstream press has dubbed the "digital native" has a desire for constant connectivity – not just to their media, but also to other individuals. In a 2005 Campus Computing Project survey, 29 percent of college campuses reported offering blanket wireless accessibility to their students, with an additional 64 percent reporting that they had developed formal plans for the same as a means of enticing students to choose their campuses (Jayson 2006). By 2006, MySpace.com and FaceBook.com dominated high school and college campuses as a means of chatting with friends and keeping them informed, as well as a means of meeting new people. From the perspective of the TV industry, as the PricewaterhouseCoopers report notes, these "technological ends" are now the means – content providers are *starting* with social networking sites as a way to promote a sense of intimacy and community among potential viewers (2006: 4).

The rise of social networking sites and the surrounding culture of constant connectivity has raised concerns in a number of arenas, contributing to a tradition within the history of teen TV (and indeed youth culture more broadly) of worries about delinquency, violence, rebellion, and general danger. The predominant worries concern overexposure: teens might become "too" immersed in their use of media, and overload in a manner akin to over-dosing, and teens (especially girls) might become vulnerable to predators (both commercial and sexual). While it is beyond the scope of this book to examine the rhetoric of danger surrounding the Internet, it is important to note that such rhetoric does not escape teens and young adults as they surf and chat and IM – particularly females, who use the Internet more for social networking than do boys (Mazzarella 2005: 2). Nor does this rhetoric escape the attention of parents raised without the media Millennials are accustomed to.[4]

And certainly this rhetoric does not escape the attention of the media industries. Television has sought to demonstrate its awareness of online dangers, from *Dateline NBC*'s regular and highly-rated episodes about adult male Internet stalkers of teen girls, to *Degrassi: The Next Generation*'s episodes about the same. Television has alternately sought to offset the anxieties that surround this new medium that it is becoming increasingly reliant on, from NBC series such as *Saturday Night Live, Studio 60*, and *30 Rock* incorporating skits that poke fun at the *Dateline* specials, to *Degrassi*'s incorporation into their plots of students taking mandatory Media Immersion classes. At a broader level, many websites associated with teen and young adult TV networks and programs seek to highlight the more optimistic (some would say utopian) rhetoric that also informs teens' and parents' understanding of new media – in particular the argument that the Internet can promote the importance of younger media consumers developing an awareness of alternative points of view that in turn can prompt "true" learning. A cursory examination of MTVU's website, for example, reveals a "Digital Darfur Activist" video game (from a contest jointly conducted with Reebok Human Rights Foundation and International Crisis Group Darfur aid workers), a forum for discussing depression in college ("Half of Us"), a blog detailing the experiences of female Israeli and Palestinian Rutgers students sharing a dorm ("The Middle East Co-Existence House"), and "Chat the Planet," a digital satellite venue for conversation between students from literally around the world.

This complex environment is an integral part of the television experience for viewers; attitudes about teen media use and about the role that media play in teen lives cannot be escaped as younger viewers and their families make decisions about when and how to engage with teen TV texts. As David Morley (2004) eloquently describes it, "the modern home can itself be said to be a phantasmagoric place to the extent that electronic media of various kinds allow the radical intrusion of distant events into the space of domesticity" (304). This notion of "intrusion" pervades experiences of watching TV and using the Internet, as do more positive notions of learning and exploring. As Morley notes, media technology in the home (or classroom, library, or dorm room) holds symbolic meanings that become part of the media experience.

With TV and the Internet especially, converging symbolic themes sustain a tension between freedom (mobility, choice, communication) and restriction (personal danger, concerns about regulation, limits of technology, cost). This tension plays a key role when TV series and networks reaching out to teens aim for organic invitation, naturalizing expectations that teens and young adults are willing (and able) to take the experience of viewing an episode beyond the TV set and into the world of the Internet. The strategies at work in organic invitations, in order to succeed, must on the one hand promote Pricewaterhouse Coopers' call for an "untethered, participatory, dynamic and hyperlinked" media experience, and on the other hand must be able to control an aesthetics of multiplicity that raises concerns about the dangers and disadvantages of tele-participation (2006: 16). In the following sections, I will examine two teen series and two teen networks that have staked their success on organic invitations to teens and young adults, emphasizing an aesthetics of multiplicity that reverberates within and beyond the television narrative proper.

Beyond TV: Experiencing Teen Stories in the Twenty-First Century

The two programs I have chosen to study in this chapter are perhaps as different as possible. *The O.C.* began airing in the US in the summer of 2002 on FOX, emerging as a surprise hit for the network. A serial dramedy, the series' narrative revolves around a young male delinquent, Ryan, whose court-appointed legal counsel adopts the troubled teen into his Jewish-Christian family when his mother proves unable to take care of him herself. "The boy from the wrong side of the tracks" finds himself thrust into an Orange County California community of extreme wealth and all its *Dallas*-like complications, including a romantic relationship with the leading teen female socialite, Marissa (prone to much drinking and drug-taking). The series distinguished itself from previous teen series in the US via its cynical view of wealth, its incorporation of adult storylines and characters, and its pop culture driven sense of humor (often located within Ryan's new adoptive same-age brother, the socially inept Seth).[5]

In the summer of 2005, *The O.C.*, seen as *the* teen series of choice, found itself competing against the increased attention that critics and fans were giving to *Degrassi: The Next Generation*, which had been airing on The N – a digital cable network – since the network's inception in 2002. This half-hour serial drama is produced and set in Toronto, Canada, and revolves around the lives of junior and high school students attending a community school.[6] While certainly replete with personal dramas comparable at times to those found in *The O.C.*, *Degrassi*'s primary narrative thematics differ considerably from *The O.C.*'s, using a large ensemble culturally diverse cast to address issues of gender, sexuality, family, education, and socioeconomic class on a regular basis. In the States this series is a minor hit, given its digital cable status; in Canada it is a bona fide hit for a wide age range of viewers. The show has also achieved a "special" status via its lineage; not only is the series "non-LA," it is "non-industry" in that an elementary school teacher (Linda Schuyler) devised the concept of *Degrassi*'s community school setting in the 1980s as a way to continue the story of elementary school children learning to make a film about their neighborhood (*Ida Makes a Movie*, 1980). The resulting trajectory went from *The Kids of Degrassi Street* (1980–6), to *Degrassi Junior High* (1987–9) – which aired on some PBS stations in the US, lending it an additional cultural legitimacy beyond that available to *The O.C.*[7]

As different as these programs are, both achieved legitimacy among teen and young adult viewers in terms of speaking to their desires and experiences. Both offer serialized storylines featuring teen girls, teen boys, and adults. Both have also had to contend with a changing viewing environment, emerging on air as Millennials *became* "Millennials," with their accompanying environment of digitextuality. I find it useful to examine these two programs in light of their different industrial and cultural situations, and in this section I will focus on how each has approached offering organic invitations to their target audiences in ways both unique and similar, as well as how the creative professionals for each series have learned to grapple with the Millennial mindset.

"California, here we come": The O.C.*'s cultural cache*

If you ask, I'll tell you that I still watch The O.C., *dip in quality be damned, and hell, I'll even tell you that I like Marissa … If one of my shows is horrible, I'll usually know it, and I'll defend it anyway. (Llamacran)*

If you think of [a fan] of a show like The O.C., *[you think of] the Tiger-Beat-reading, poster-on-the-wall, crazed thirteen-year-old mall denizen. (PanPan)*

These quotes from Llamacran and PanPan demonstrate the formidable battle facing the producers of *The O.C.* when they brought their project to FOX – as well as the best possible routes to success. As PanPan (an admitted fan of many teen shows) describes it, teen hits exist culturally in an environment predisposed to dismiss the audience as immature and shallow, with viewers indiscriminately latching on to whatever the current cultural phenomenon in TV might be. Yet as Llamacran notes, if a series ostensibly aimed at teens can capture initial viewer loyalty – particularly via its characters and its "smartness" – that loyalty will often persist through the roughest of times. These dual challenges can conflict with each other at times, and for the professionals behind this series, the role of the Internet especially brought these (and other challenges) to light (creator and executive producer Josh Schwartz and co-executive producer Stephanie Savage, interview, July 14, 2006).

The O.C. developed an online following quickly, with teen viewers creating their own web pages, and TV forums such as MediaBoulevard. com and TelevisionWithoutPity.com devoting considerable space to the series. Producers Stephanie Savage and Josh Schwartz believe that a number of factors contributed to the show being an online hit, a key one being the timing of the show airing just as the Internet was becoming solidly integrated into younger people's everyday lives:

> *Savage:* We understand now the culture of writing on boards – the degree to which the Internet has been integrated into life. Now you don't just watch the show – you watch the show, you read the boards, you post.

> *Schwartz:* It seems like people are live blogging. They're watching the show while they're posting. It's a crazy way to watch TV, but that's the trend.

While not every viewer may follow these practices, some younger viewers responding to my survey described this Millennial way of watching:

> I watch *The O.C.* by myself and sometimes, the next day, I will discuss the show with my friends. Sometimes I will write about *The O.C.* in my online journal and sometimes I will go to the *O.C.* forums and chat about the show there. I like to discuss what is going to happen next and who is the hottest on the show. ☺ ... *The O.C.* definitely has a strong fan base online because the major demographic for *The O.C.* is teenagers and teenagers spend the majority of their free time online. (Ashley, 16)

> I watch *The O.C.* alone and discuss it with friends immediately afterwards. I then go on the Internet and post my opinion on message boards and view other people's opinions ... People from other countries who

enjoy the show are able to talk with people from all over the world to share information. I like to discuss the clothes, the music, info on cast members, fan fiction, and spoilers. (Elizabeth, 13)

For Ashley, visiting websites for shows she watches regularly is not unusual; she reports as well that she will go online at times to visit sites associated with *Buffy* and Adult Swim (though interestingly, while a regular viewer of *Degrassi*, she does not report visiting websites for that series). Elizabeth, on the other hand, speaks exclusively to *The O.C.* in her responses. This variation is likely due to the primary pull of the series for these viewers (as well as their ages), with Ashley representing a more typical viewer – and Elizabeth ironically representing an almost "impossibly" ideal viewer:

> I enjoy getting lost in the show and wishing that I was [*sic*] the characters and that I was doing the things they were doing. I have been watching *The O.C.* since it first came on and I watch it every week, never missing an episode … The ideal viewer for *The O.C.* attends high school and is probably a very bubbly teenage girl. This is not always the case, though, as *The O.C.* I know from going online has a wide range of viewers. I myself am a teenage "rocker." (Ashley)

> Shows like *The O.C.* have characters that you can get attached to very easily and relate to them, and this leads to a kind of addiction especially in fan-fics, which people like myself read … It is filmed where I live, in Palos Verdes, and some of the scenarios are similar to ones people in my community deal with. Their lives, in some ways, are similar to mine, living in an affluent community, going to private school, being involved in those types of social and financial pressures. (Elizabeth)

Ashley and Elizabeth thus prove to offer interesting points of comparison. Both are fans of the show, and both use the Internet to expand their viewing experience. Both identify with the characters, but in dramatically different ways. Ashley voices a sense that these are characters and to some degree situations she would like to experience herself, and she seems to feel a distance from the environment of the series that nevertheless does not impede her viewing pleasure (or, she hypothesizes, the pleasure of other viewers who are more like her than they are like the "ideal viewer"). Ashley reports that, while she has her own TV set and easy access to the Internet, she and her family do not have the money for the many things she sees teens owning on this show, from cars and mansions, to cell phones and iPods. Elizabeth, conversely, identifies more directly with the narrative environment and characters of *The O.C.*; she lives this kind of life, and she is aware of the fact that she and her family are well off financially – reporting that she owns her own TV, computer, video cell phone, and iPod.

Given the preponderance of teen shows focusing on the wealthy, it would certainly be fruitful to examine more closely the impact of such narrative settings on younger viewers of differing socioeconomic backgrounds; here I can only note that it is telling that two young women from such very different circumstances nevertheless share an experience of viewing that takes them beyond the moment of viewing in front of their TV sets. Both also responded to my survey while the series was in its downward ratings slump, yet expressed (in my interpretation) a loyalty to the show because of their unique connections to it.

Stephanie Savage and Josh Schwartz both explained to me their belief that younger fans (i.e., pre-teens and teens) were more traditional in their viewing relationship with the series, identifying with the characters and their universal teen experiences and mindsets – a viewing stance prompted to some degree by serial storytelling:

> *Schwartz:* I think the show is really reflective of being a teen – sort of out of control, making mistakes, partying too hard, staying out too late. I found early on that [they] were responding to the situations characters were in. And I think that's because, especially at the time, there weren't really any night-time serialized dramas on, and there were no teen dramas on. It's not a procedural, where viewers have no control, the problem is solved in the episode, and they just sort of are passive viewers. With this [show] they become engaged in longer ongoing storylines, and the characters and their decisions become more real.

Akin to the manner in which scholars describe the viewing relationship of adult women with daytime soap operas, the melodramatic, serialized exaggeration that is a part of so many soap operas allows for emotional realism: the everyday trials and tribulations of life (for teens – losing a boyfriend or girlfriend, parents whose problems impact their children's lives, being unpopular at school; for adults – relationship problems, problems with children, the challenges of balancing family and career) are accorded the narrative importance in fiction that viewers experience such things as having in their lived reality.

Savage and Schwartz also noted that the serial structure of the show at times caused problems for younger viewers, pointing to letters and online commentary indicating a sense of impatience:

> *Schwartz:* There's tons of times where people weigh in on our characters – especially our new characters. And after one episode they think they're going to reveal unbelievable layers of depth. And we're like, "if you could just wait one more week!" ... I also think we're in a time in our culture where things move faster now for teens. You can watch a show, write about it and go on the message boards, and just consume so much ancillary – and it's side-tracking. There's music! There's clothing! It's so much that after a year, you're now ready for something new.

Indeed, events and character situations, like much in teen culture, become "old" quickly. The network strategy to alleviate this can best be seen in the extension of the TV narrative through the show's fan magazine, *The O.C. Insider*, developed by the second season of the program – a strategy that Savage and Schwartz ironically see as only adding to the problem of teen viewer malaise. FOX and WB (the studio producing the show) created a website for *The O.C.* that emphasized insider information, chat forums, and access to products associated with the characters on the series. Full "insider information," however, requires paid membership of $24.95, and this primarily allows fans to purchase (or enter contests for winning) songs and technological gadgets – and to receive the magazine, in which all the "real" scoop on the show emerges.

In particular, the magazine works to assure viewers that serial developments are indeed "going somewhere," as with this example from an issue at the end of the low-rated third season when the female lead character Marissa, was killed off:

> As the official authority on all things "O.C.," it's our duty to give you the inside scoop on what's happening behind the scenes. But this season's shocking cliffhanger finale left even us asking, "What's next?!" So, in order not to disappoint you guys, we dug up a little dirt via IM from an "O.C." staffer on what to expect for season four ...
> IHEARTOC140124 (1:29:52PM): EVERYONE IS FREAKING OUT OVER THE DEATH SCENE!
> INSIDERQUEEN1210 (1:29:59PM): YEAH, BUT IS SHE REALLY DEAD? ☺

IHEARTOC140124 (1:30:15PM): YEP, RYAN WAS UNABLE TO SAVE HER THIS TIME …

…

INSIDERQUEEN1210 (1:32:05PM): YEAH, LUCKILY KAITLIN IS BACK IN TOWN. YA THINK SHE'LL BE ABLE TO LIVE UP TO THE COOPER NAME?
IHEARTOC140124 (1:32:30PM): DEFINITELY, WAIT TIL YOU SEE.
INSIDERQUEEN1210 (1:32:35PM): WHADDYA MEAN? DO YOU KNOW SOMETHING ALREADY??
IHEARTOC140124 (1:32:51PM): LOL, MY LIPS ARE SEALED. ☺ OH! AND TAYLOR IS A NEW SERIES REGULAR AND YOU WILL BE SURPRISED TO SEE WHO SHE IS ROOMING WITH AT COLLEGE … (*The O.C. Insider* 2006b: 64)

This simple exchange demonstrates key elements of organic invitation. First, it speaks to the impatience viewers might be feeling concerning this storyline, and also reassures those who may have been invested in the character of Marissa that new characters will emerge to offer equally enticing points of identification – *all within the context of an Instant Message on a computer or cell phone*. Taking what might have been a standard text interview in the pages of any other magazine, *The O.C. Insider* assumes its readers will recognize this IM format (replete with its abbreviated language and spelling); the IM approach also marks the series' means of communicating with fans as distinctly youth-oriented in both content and style. This is a conversation, not an interview. (Or, this is not your parents' interview?)

As Rhiannon Bury (2005) notes with her research of online groups, language use can be one of the practices members engage in to set the boundaries of their community, necessarily excluding those who cannot "master the language." Bury describes this dynamic as creating linguistic capital as a form of cultural capital; in the case of *The O.C. Insider*, then, the magazine is demonstrating that it has the "correct" form of cultural linguistic capital to fit it with teen viewers. Correspondingly, Savage and Schwartz note that distinct online cultures have developed around the show – cultures that can be distinguished by age:

Savage: We find that different message boards, you can tell if they're teens, just by how they speak with each other, versus those people who seem like they're in college.

Schwartz: Yeah – there's definitely different message board cultures.
Savage: I don't think it is the 16-year-olds who are being mean. I actually think the 16-year-olds are making beautiful collages ... I think the
younger people are more enthusiastic ... It's actually the older viewers
who are more like wanna-be TV critics, wanna-be bloggers, wanna-be
"if this was me, I could do so much better."

The O.C. Insider conversation also demonstrates a recognition of what
viewers are saying online about the show, reinforcing the first strategy
and tapping into the theme of shared ownership that I have discussed
in previous chapters: viewers lay claim to this show, do not hesitate to
use the Internet to demonstrate that claim (especially on TheOC.com,
as it is an "official" forum), and expect to be attended to. Savvily, by
restricting access via cost, the creators of the site and the magazine
attach prestige to membership and guarantee that the majority of those
voicing demands will be loyal fans:

It's not every day a blogger tapping away in her parents' attic attracts the
attention of Hollywood, but that's the story of Emma Loggins ... [who]
has been mistress of a TV fan site since she asked her parents for a computer server back in high school ... When "The O.C." premiered, she dedicated a large portion of her site – and time – to the hot new drama. Loggins'
reward? Her very own column on TheOCInsider.com – and show scoops
straight from the production team. (*The O.C. Insider* 2006a: 18)

Here, the magazine calls attention to the right of fans to speak online
about their favorite series, to the "largesse" of the show and the website
in listening to such fans, and to the "rewards" of loyal fandom. In my
membership letter – complete with a membership card – I was thanked
for "all [my] great suggestions about the show, site and magazine on
TheOCInsider boards" and assured that official people "frequently read
[the boards] and take every post seriously, so keep on posting!"

Of course, this reward system includes the ability to claim ownership
via the purchase of ancillary products as well: fans can purchase clothing, accessories, photos, music, makeup, and even characters' and stars'
iPod lists – via membership. It is important to note here that the purchasing of most of these products works on a logic of traditional interpellation. Members are encouraged especially to buy products that
they see characters wearing and using in the show – especially
technological products – in order to feel that they fit in with the

narrative's tone and environment. For example, in my most recent O.C.Insider letter (they arrive via email), I was informed that in a fourth season episode "we'll see a sleuthing Seth and Summer texting, photographing and catching bad guys in the act on their T-Mobile Sidekick IIs. Don't know what that is? Take a look at the picture – you could have one too. Click here and enter to win it right now!"

This invitation points more directly to the organic inviting that occurs within the series proper. Given the financial direction of the TV industry in general, the notion of product placement such as characters using a T-Mobile Sidekick is nothing unusual – and while this may occur in heightened form in shows aimed at teens, product placement is hardly a specifically teen phenomenon. Organic invitations occur on two fronts here: the placement of a new technological product used for *communication*, and the use of that product by the two characters in the series who are media fans themselves. As Savage and Schwartz explained, Seth (Ryan's adoptive brother) and Summer (Marissa's best friend) are the primary points of identification in the series for the program's comedic thematic of fandom and popular culture. Seth is positioned as a somewhat typical geek within the narrative of the show (it takes some time, a lot of gumption, and Ryan dating Marissa to help Seth and Summer come together); he loves young adult indie rather than teen pop music, enjoys his fantasy-based video games, and eventually creates and sells his own comic book, *Atomic County*.[8] Summer is the avid fan of a teen TV soap opera, *The Valley*, the plots and behind-the-scenes goings-on of which sound "suspiciously" like those of *The O.C.* itself.

Such self-reflexivity in television is not unique to *The O.C.*, and reaches far back into TV's general history in varying ways – but many cult and teen series especially have specialized in the reference of pop culture texts in ways that allow them to comment upon their own pop cultural status. Indeed, *The O.C.*'s most immediate predecessor, *Dawson's Creek*, featured a title character who was obsessed with Steven Spielberg, and who ultimately abandoned the world of film to become a producer of a teen TV series, *The Creek*. What is different about *The O.C.*'s "shout-outs" to fandom is the depth to which it operates, and, frankly, its timing. References to comic book fandom and teen TV fandom brought the world of the actors into the world of the series, with the actor playing Seth (Adam Brody) becoming a comic book writer and touring the comic book convention circuit with his series

Red Menace. The artist (Eric Wight) who provided illustrations for *Atomic County* (never made into an actual comic, but with "issues" available via Verizon Wireless) also received offers of further work and began illustrating the manga *My Dead Girlfriend*. References to the TV show *The Valley* included discussion of the romantic leads on the show dating each other, calling upon the fact that the actors playing Seth and Summer in *The O.C.* were also dating each other.

These complicated, interwoven references occurred on a regular basis throughout the series, establishing a pattern of organically inviting in viewers – of assuming and naturalizing the assumption that fans of *The O.C.* were, in general, fans of many different kinds of media that existed across many different mediums. Further, *The O.C.* truly was the first hit teen series in the US that grew along with the development of a digital communication culture among its core audience; the studio, network, marketers, and producers for this series had to learn along the way about how to acknowledge and speak to this changing viewing environment.

Savage and Schwartz emphasized that they were unaware that a culture of Internet fandom and commentary existed for mainstream shows when the show first began – the rise of Internet commentary surrounding the series was something to be caught up with. They noted that trying to follow what viewers said on the boards could be "like a disease," especially for younger staff writers; they stressed that commentary – especially negative commentary – had a stifling impact:

> *Schwartz:* When the show started, I had no idea …
> *Savage:* It's narcissistic and masochistic to read about yourself and also to be insulted … I'm way more, "let's just stay off the message boards."
> *Schwartz:* Yeah – we'd say we'd cut ourselves off cold turkey, we're not going to look.
> *Savage:* Because all the message board people seemed to believe that the first six episodes were the very best episodes. And those were the episodes that were conceived and executed without message boards … So there is some value in writing without that.
> *Schwartz:* Right! It infects you, *and* the network.

During the second season of the show, FOX began asking for summaries of fan commentary from different boards, ignoring, producers felt, the dynamics of how fan boards operate. While some commentary can be genuinely useful, Savage and Schwartz felt that the most vocal people online were viewers with extreme expectations for the show, who had the power to sway commentary. If a line of commentary was positive coming from a board leader, others online tended to fall in line – and vice versa. The network did not consider such dynamics, and did not understand the mindset of commentary sites such as Television WithoutPity.com, which tend to be dominated by older TV viewers who specialize in a practice called "snarking" – avidly criticizing not just TV series writing, but the writers (often in personal ways) as well. Both Savage and Schwartz felt that FOX at times asked for changes in the writing style and content of the show that were rooted in online commentary that was not necessarily representative of the average viewer – and that at times their vision for characters and the narrative became lost in efforts to please fans (and thus the network) in immediate ways:[9]

> *Schwartz:* I was talking to Chuck Klosterman [a cultural critic], and he said, "why do you always assume that it's the mean critics who are the smart ones?" It's not really a barometer ... It's [online commentary] good, in that it gives you some feedback, and some people have intelligent things to say.
> *Savage:* And anyone who's taking the time to write a 1,500 word essay about an episode of television – that's somebody who's invested in the show, and it's important to have a sense of what their point of view is.
> *Schwartz:* Absolutely! But at the same time, it's drawing from such a narrow pool of people ...
> *Savage:* They're [the networks] sort of interpreting the message boards as fact. And that to me is anecdotal evidence ... Just because it's on the Internet – it's no different than, "I found this girl's journal on the bus, and this is what she wrote about *The O.C.*, so I'm gonna' call a meeting."
> *Schwartz:* And then we found out that the head of the network wanted summaries of the message boards, so it's getting that level of validation.
> *Savage:* And that's *not* market research. It's a discursive formation that's no different from people coming over to the network head's house and having a chat.

The situation with *The O.C.* thus demonstrates the difficulties television professionals face when attempting to balance the "old" dynamics of writing and marketing to youth with the "new" dynamics of Millennial viewing. Broadcast network television in the United States has faced increasing pressure as its economic structure has shifted, with more and more entities (and their different goals) making demands of the primary product. The growth of the Internet and corollary modes of media communication add layers of pressure to bear, as much as they might bring opportunity.

Is it possible that a series emerging from Canada, being aired on a small cable network in the United States, has been able to avoid these pressures to a greater degree? Whether or not *Degrassi*'s success can be traced to a more unfettered industrial and cultural environment is less important than the fact that this program's (and its US network's) approach to reaching out to Millennials has operated more organically and offered a more concentrated aesthetics of multiplicity than *The O.C.* – potentially making a difference in how viewers have experienced the stories of these Canadian teens.

"Oh, Canada! It goes there": Degrassi's *"E-components"*

With the new show, you can buy a ton of things online, that we couldn't have bought say, five years ago, from photographs, to signed scripts, from DVDs of the show to meeting and greeting parties where the cast meets the fans. I truly believe at least for Degrassi, *we owe this to Mark Polger with the help of Pat Mastroiani (Joey Jeremiah). (Audrey[10])*

Characters affect you so that over the seasons, it seems like you're friends with them, you know them so well. It's more realistic. It deals more with our problems. 'The O.C.' is more soap-opera-ish. Not everyone's rich and living in [Orange County] and going to the beach all the time. (Sabrina (quoted in Kronke 2005))

At first, I didn't really like it. I thought it wasn't cool enough. After a while I fell in love with it … It has more of an ability to handle serious stories. On 'The O.C.,' when Marissa … O.D.'d, it was kind of funny instead of serious. (Jenny (quoted in Kronke 2005))

On many levels, *The O.C.* and *Degrassi* offer similar narrative themes, and even (as evidenced by the quote from Audrey) similar marketing appeals in terms of the Internet offering access to ancillary products. However, the quotes above point to key differences as well. Audrey describes a fan commitment rooted in earlier incarnations of *Degrassi* – an almost cult-like devotion, on the part of both an older fan and a star of *Degrassi Junior High*, that helped with the development of an audience in the United States for *The Next Generation*. And Sabrina and Jenny point to a difference in tone; while *Degrassi* certainly has its moments of humor, it does in fact take itself more seriously than *The O.C.* took itself, refraining from self-reflexivity in the content of the show itself (reserving this strategy for its promotions in the United States instead, as I will discuss in the following section). Indeed, when comparing similar story points such as teen drinking and teen drug use, teen pregnancy, and rape, *The O.C.* in every case (except for the rape storyline) at some point introduced humor into these arcs.

This was likely due to the observation made by Jenny – that *The O.C.* was "soap-opera-ish" in its approach to stories. In the US, soap operas are still associated strongly with melodramatic narrative exaggeration, whereas in Canada and England, the soap opera has a tradition of social realism rooted more firmly in a traditionally dramatic vein – lending itself less to comic interpretations. *Degrassi* is more often a drama with elements of humor, than a dramedy proper like *The O.C.* In addition, as noted by Jenny, this series is not quite so immersed in the "cool factor," with its product placements existing at the level of corporate sponsorship rather than at the level of seeking to incorporate consumer products that would appeal to the Millennial market and/or to integrate potential ancillary products.[11]

On one level, this lack of ancillary products may help to minimize the problem of the show "aging" past its "cool factor" too quickly. On a more significant level, socially and culturally, this also allows the writers and producers to introduce cultural products important to Millennials as phenomena to be discussed within the narrative – something that has made the show a hit with teachers and parents. The most consistent integration of consumer products as a point of discussion (as opposed to a point of sale) occurs via what writers James Hurst and Brendon Yorke refer to as the "E-component" – a mandate of sorts that helped sell the Canadian Broadcasting Corporation on the show: *Degrassi* would *naturalize* (make organic) discussions of the rise of electronic media in teens' lives within the narrative framework of the show itself (interview, November 10, 2005).

While I will discuss this E-component in more detail later, it should be clear to most readers that this approach to potentially saleable products (leaving room for criticisms and cautions as much as for more benign examinations) is not typical for a modern teen show airing in the United States. The industrial environment within which *Degrassi* operates is more than different – it effects a different product. For example, funding and tax considerations require that casting efforts first be made from within the city of Toronto, where the show is shot; this "restriction" allows for the multi-ethnic, near-age casting (where the actors are close to the age of the characters they play) that has been part of the show's appeal in the United States:

> We do cast for diversity. We want our cast to be representative of Toronto. There's no hiding the fact that this is a Toronto-based series … Toronto being as multi-ethnic as it is, we obviously try to reflect that. It just makes the show more interesting – it's *real*. It just all goes back to how people say when they see this show, they can relate. They see kids who are from their region … It's in our best interest. I don't think anybody can say that it's patronizing or tokenism. When people come to Canada, there's a lot of support for maintaining their roots, their culture, their history, their craft and art and dance. My impression of the US – I could be wrong – is that that's all left behind. But those things continue to flourish here. It's really celebrated – the diversity is really celebrated. (Stephanie Williams, supervising producer, interview, November 10, 2005)

The series' history is also rooted firmly in literal social realism: the three preceding *Degrassi* programs began and continued with primarily "real" kids participating in acting improv workshops that taught them how to turn their lived experiences into collaborative storytelling for CBC (the equivalent roughly of PBS in Canada). As Williams explains, a strong emphasis in Canada on the need for programming to remain Canadian has contributed to a viewing environment in which audiences expect specificity and authenticity:

> [The CBC set a standard] – TV is meant to be meaningful … We embrace everything American … but we see our television differently. *The O.C.* and *Dawson's Creek* are huge here, but we make sure we're very different. Those are twenty-somethings playing teens, soapy, less social realism.

The writers also believe that the broadcasting environment in Canada has allowed them to delve into topics in a manner different from how

US series featuring teens approach the same issues (if at all). *Degrassi: The Next Generation* airs on CTV, a private commercial network carrying a mix of Canadian produced programming and US based series. Thus, *Degrassi* airs in a prime slot on an "adult" network – as opposed to Canada's YTV, a channel specializing in youth programming. (In 2006, it aired right before NBC's *Medium*.) CTV often asks the producers of the show to push the envelope in terms of topics and content – "pressure" that has allowed The N (the cable network aimed at teens that airs the show in the US) to run with their promotional tagline for the series: "*Degrassi*: It Goes There." This adult framework for the series might account to some degree for the adult following the show has in the US. As seen in these comments, a primary appeal of the series for these two adult viewers is the realism brought about by the issues addressed in the program:

> *Degrassi*, I would say, stands out, because as the phrase is said [*sic*] "It Goes There." And it does. It is by far the most gripping, realistic teen drama out there. (Angie, 27)

> *Degrassi is* a wonderful show, dealing with REAL events that could, and do, happen every day, in schools all across the country and in Canada … There was just a school shooting recently in the US, where the vice principal's life was taken … *Degrassi* can reach parents, students, and adults from all around, the demographics are ENDLESS! (Audrey, 29)

The "offhand" way in which Audrey references a school shooting reveals (in combination with Angie's assessment) that such topics emerge regularly on the series – they are rarely "a very special episode." Indeed, the narrative event alluded to in Audrey's quote developed over two seasons (longer in the US, as The N airs at a different rate), tracing the growing violence of a male character who first engaged in relationship abuse, and who eventually became the targeting of bullying that contributed to him bringing a gun to school, with a hit list. Stephanie Williams explained that the 1999 Columbine High School shooting was a major news story in Canada, but that many Canadians felt that US coverage skimmed over the environment of bullying and more generalized school violence, framing the story as an isolated incident of "two deeply disturbed boys." In Canada, as compared to the United States, she feels there is a greater acceptance of fully exploring social and political issues such as bullying in fictional television.

The writers agreed that a liberal environment in their country has allowed them to examine this and other issues from a variety of perspectives, and in great detail. In much the way that daytime soap operas work in the US, *Degrassi* is allowed (and encouraged) to explore cause and effect and the long-term repercussions of one's actions. Two seasons after the school shooting episode, characters have continued to grapple with the ramifications of this "moment" in their narrative lives, from a major character (Jimmy, who had been a basketball star) being paralyzed from the waist down, struggling with falling behind in classes, having sexual difficulties with his girlfriend, and trying to forgive a friend who had pushed the shooter over the edge in a bullying incident; to another major character who was almost shot (Emma, the "good girl" of the series) dealing with post-traumatic stress disorder and its symptoms, such as sexual permissiveness and eating disorders.[12]

As writer James Hurst describes it:

> We don't bullshit, and we are allowed more leeway. Maybe it's because we're a more liberal country – we don't ever fall into that kind of "family value" stuff, or "oh, it'll all be okay" … We're totally gray … You see everybody's side of things – we're showing all sides of the puzzle. And I think that's probably ultimately what makes the show so successful. There's a real cause and effect – we get teased about the cause-and-effect thing all the time. Nothing's ever random on *Degrassi* – things are *always* linked. I think that's actually appealing to people, especially teens, because it's basically saying that there is a reason for everything. It is kind of comforting: if you only – if you *really* understood your neighbor, if you really understood your classmates, you wouldn't be mad at them or hate them. You'd be able to understand and have sympathy for everybody.

Thus, the show's writers make a conscious effort to expand narrative moments through a loose serial structure that encourages an appreciation for both the value of exploring different perspectives on issues and for the value of considering the complex and long-term consequences of behaviors and decisions. This narrative approach is supported by the series' educational framework. As I mentioned earlier, creator Linda Schuyler is a former teacher, and she has made a practice of having researchers and educators review episodes "to make sure scripts accurately portray *various sides of an issue*" (quoted in Chandross 2005). Schuyler also creates classroom guides for teachers who choose to screen the series in class.[13]

The educational framework also informs the series' approach to the role of new media communications in teens' lives, working with the E-component incorporated into the show's initial production. One of the original contributing partners to the show was the new media company Snap Media, which worked with CTV in Canada to develop a website that emphasizes the show's attention to new technology, and that emphasizes as well the website as a place where viewers can share their reactions to "E-narratives" (Nicks 2004). The writers I spoke with talked about the dual narrative approach related to the E-component that made the show unique: on the one hand, the show features regular episodes that showcase new media technology as an active force that deserves special attention (new media as an issue); and on the other hand, the show represents such technology as a natural part of today's teen culture (new media as an organic part of the environment):

> *Brendon Yorke:* That's how the show was sold initially: kids are communicating in all these new and different ways – the E-component. That was the mandate for the first couple seasons – we had to have an electronic component in almost every episode.
> *James Hurst:* Kids are kids. It's about who likes who? Who's dating who? The fact that they're using cell phones and texting and computers to talk about that stuff is a new wrinkle in teen culture.

A few brief examples make the point. The series' pilot focused on seventh grade Emma, who had found a new friend online through Internet chat; when she sneaks out to meet him, he turns out to be an adult male who has worked to lure her to his hotel room. The episode focuses on a message of caution, with Emma's friends deciding to tell her mother that they are concerned about her new friend, and ends with police removing Emma's computer from her bedroom as evidence – and suggesting to her mother that they keep the computer in the living room. This narrative was updated in the sixth season, when senior Darcy unwittingly attracts an adult male through a "My Page" social networking account, carelessly offering information that allows him to find her at school after the adult man poses as a friend of one of her classmates. Such episodes resonate with Danah Boyd's research on teen users of MySpace; she notes that two of the forum's unique characteristics are its searchability and its "invisible audiences" (forthcoming, 2). Boyd also emphasizes that it is important to the teen users of this arena that this space is meant to be for them, and not adults. The resulting tensions for parents concerned with their children's safety (especially daughters), and teens who want privacy from their parents – but the ability to "[take] social interactions between friends into the public sphere for others to witness" – is ripe for television (7).

A second season episode focused on the cost of new technology, and the friction this can cause; high school student Spinner steals and pawns his best friend Jimmy's new MP3 player, upset that Jimmy's family can afford such products when he cannot. Such narratives occur within an environment that portrays new media more ubiquitously (and generally more benignly), such as when Emma accidentally sends word of an embarrassing secret to everyone via the school's email system; or when Darcy discovers that her boyfriend (Spinner) has cheated on her after she sneaks a peek at his cell phone text messages. As Boyd's work reveals, teens follow their friends socially – and technologically, when socializing is linked to the technology.

This collective new media narrative environment uses the framework of the series itself to organically invite in teen viewers, demonstrating an awareness of the role that such technology plays in this demographic's lives – as well as in the lives of their concerned parents and teachers. In the following section, I will demonstrate how The N, which built itself around the text of *Degrassi*, extended this approach to the network, using its promotions and its website (TheN. com) as its primary tools. I will also explore how the new US broadcast network CW has attempted to follow The N's model with its website as well.

Free to Share: Network Branding

The N as a network emerged via the children's network, Noggin, which began airing on US digital cable in 1999. Noggin is affiliated industrially with Nickelodeon and MTV, falling under Viacom's corporate umbrella – key, given that Nickelodeon and MTV have always been "branded" networks, aiming to develop loyalty to the network as a whole over-and-above loyalty to specific programs. Noggin was likewise expected to exist more as a network than as a site where specific programs could be found, so the extension of this mindset to The N fits a larger company strategy.

The emergence of The N was very much due to Noggin's acquisition of *Degrassi*; Sarah Lindman, head of production and programming at The N, explained that Noggin's emphasis on pre- and elementary school appropriate series offered a branded environment into which *Degrassi* would not easily fit (Lindman and digital media coordinator Kenny Miller, interview, August 14, 2006). Thus, beginning in 2001, The N was born; Noggin's programs air until 5p.m. EST, and then the channel "turns into" The N for evening and late-night programming aimed at teens and young adults.[14] The N's link to Noggin also extends to each entity's approach to their websites; Sarah Lindman recalled (with some amusement) how the Noggin website "wowed" people with its shifting still frames of images from program content (perhaps the earliest version of video grabs). *Degrassi*'s E-components, therefore, fit well with The N's roots in early online digital experimentation.

Like the series, the network sought from its very beginning to establish itself among teens as an entity immersed in new media forms of communication. Together, *Degrassi* and The N established an aesthetics of multiplicity. *Degrassi* itself offered a narrative structured around multiplicity, with a sprawling ensemble cast and a serial structure that could ostensibly go back over 25 years, as well as a narrative that was immersed in multiple forms of media. The network, building itself around this show, worked with accompanying ways of watching such a story, mirroring potential viewing dynamics from two fronts: the network itself, and TheN.com. Lindman describes this holistic approach as a strategy of "pitch and catch": TV content pitches viewers to Internet content, and the website catches the viewers and pitches them back to TV. Lindman stressed that, early on, this approach was difficult due to limited technology. The N.com relied initially on basic "extras" such as chatrooms, interviews with stars, and quizzes rooted in show content. These elements demonstrated to viewers that The N, as a network, understood the Millennial mentality. Fortuitously, with *Degrassi* already narratively emphasizing exactly this, viewers would be primed to visit TheN.com:

> *Lindman:* I think just even in terms of writing your television show, you have to have this kind of [mediated] interaction baked into how your characters are interacting, like on *Degrassi*. But then even beyond that, you have to understand how TV fits into their [Millennials'] overall media usage. TV's just one leg of the octopus, you really can't look at it in isolation. You need to understand this to make your characters real and you need to understand how this fits into your audience's life.

To strengthen further the connection between the series and The N. com, Kenny Miller, digital media coordinator, devised online content that fit with *Degrassi*'s emphasis on education through the development of multiple perspectives. Visitors could find quiz questions about friends and family coming out of the closet, getting one's first period, having an erection in class, or developing an STD – whatever the topics had been on the series, some forum existed online to explore them further, with most providing educational information. Chatrooms offered space for actual discussion, and it was not uncommon for debates to emerge around the more controversial subject matter of the show, with a wide range of opinions and experiences available for viewers to explore. The following exchange (TheN.com, February 2005) is typical of such an occurrence:

> 88faith: *Degrassi* is a great show, but the last season they really have [been] pushing the limit on the whole gay issue. i mean marco is gay I understand but I really dun [*sic*] feel comfortable when they put that on TV when a lot of children watch it ...
>
> fan04: I personally have nothing wrong with *Degrassi* having a gay character. I think it's great. The only thing I don't like is that Marco suddenly became a stereotypical gay guy instead of staying who he was.
>
> Dianachris: Well I think they should talk about the gay issue because *Degrassi* is the type of show that deals with real issues and even if people don't want to talk about gay people doesn't mean it [*sic*] doesn't exist.
>
> Venus525: Well I don't think that it's right. Yea [*sic*] there are gay people in this world but it's morally wrong.
>
> Aesch11: It's morally wrong? I'm gay and I was born this way. How can you tell me that I'm morally wrong when it's just the way that I am? Would you tell someone that they're morally wrong because they were born Hispanic or with a twin sister? ... People are different and any show that embraces diversity is great.

This exchange continued over several days of chat, and was the "hot topic" highlighted on TheN.com's *Degrassi* link for a full week. Much like the show itself, people offered competing perspectives; and also like the show, the debate reappeared as the topic reappeared in the series from season to season. While one cannot examine such exchanges (either in a show or online) and state definitively that any kind of real learning is occurring, at the very least something useful socially is happening as viewers *use the Internet* to revisit an original story, bringing their own lives to bear upon the narrative. Benjamin's (1968) expectations of storytelling thus fit the dynamics of the series itself – *when the series is placed in conjunction with TheN.com*. In other words, the network website for the show is a crucial element in the process of storytelling.

Within the framework of an aesthetics of multiplicity, the network also worked to promote *itself* as a site for diverse perspectives, with executives using the gaps in-between programming – before the network was established enough to fill up more time with actual ad placements. Early network "filler content" offered standard program promotions, but also "ads" celebrating racial diversity and racial issues, such as four Black young adults briefly debating the use of "the N word" in Black culture. Side-by-side with such content, the network also promoted its very self as a personality that understood its audience and their everyday lives, such as a spot in which a teen girl annoyed by her kid brother receives a text message from The N telling her that her parents will leave her everything, or a teen boy in an English class with a domineering teacher opening his textbook to find a cartoon picture from The N telling him his teacher (shown in caricature) lives alone except for a lot of cats.

By far, however, the cleverest promotions centered on the programs the network offered. One of my favorites featured shots of teens on the streets of New York City rapping *The Fresh Prince of Bel Air* opening theme. Another is one in a series focused on helping new viewers catch up with *Degrassi*, consisting of rapid-fire clips from the show and a breathless voiceover from a teen girl explaining character motivations, as in the following *25 second* spot:

> On this show called *Degrassi*, parents kind of suck. There's this hot guy Craig, whose dad beat him all the time, so he's all "I'm out of here," and his dad's like, "Fine!" Then he gets in a car crash and dies. Then this other girl Ashley, who Craig totally hooked up with, her parents are getting a divorce, and she's like, "Mom, are you and dad gonna' get back together?" And mom's all "No!" And then her dad goes, "Ashley, I'm gay." And Ashley's all, "Why didn't you tell me?!" And her dad's like, "You weren't old enough." And she's like, "You suck!" And that's totally why she's Goth. *Degrassi* – It *so* goes there!

While the text above doesn't do justice to the experience of the audio, the key point is that such promotions emphasized viewing The N's programs as a *social* experience, rooted in teen ways of communicating. In a manner akin to the way Nancy Baym describes the development of specific language norms among online soap fans, a sense of community is evident in specific practices of speech (Baym 2000: 21; see also Boyd, forthcoming).

The network also used on-air spots to communicate to viewers that they understood that teens were beginning to use new media technology to speak with each other; one early campaign featured the appearance of text messages (with no sound other than that a computer makes when you send an Instant Message, until the very end) such as the following:

muscKAT13: you there?
Robotfiend17: hello?
Suegirl22: what's up
Zyanara: hey
muscKAT13: hello!
(Animated girl appears and says: "Don't they know *Degrassi*'s coming on?!")

These spots creatively suggest to Millennial fans that The N is well aware of the role of IM in teens' lives – including the fact that teens often chat *about* television, *while* they are watching television.[15]

Such spots also promoted this cultural environment at a time when the website's technological capacities were still being developed, perhaps reassuring viewers that TheN.com would be able to stay up to speed with new technologies as they developed. In fact, once broadband technology became more widespread and allowed for more directly speaking to Millennial expectations, TheN.com developed appropriate online strategies further. Thus, a trip to the website in connection to *Degrassi* now offers *Degrassi* minis – the first example of webisodes in the US (small narratives featuring series characters, often in humorous situations), and viewers can also watch behind-the-scenes videos and short documentaries about actors' lives. These strategies serve also to cement the website to the show to the network, creating a brand image that encompasses all three components:

Lindman: We made a decision. We had seen and understood the importance of Internet video for a while. Actually, it was something that came from the TV side: there are only between 18 to 22 episodes of *Degrassi* supplied, so we were like, "how can we infuse some more *Degrassi* content – how do we serve our *Degrassi* audience – when we're not premiering *Degrassi* episodes?" And that's kind of where we started – "Hey! Can we start to do more stuff online?" – so that they continue to have a relationship with the network, with the channel, with the brand, 52 weeks a year.

Miller: There are sort of three rules to the site. Most people's sites are either brief ads for retails or a marketing brochure for the network. And while we love ad sales and we love to promote the shows, we know that there is more – the Internet is an additional platform that needs its own content and forms *for* that platform. So (1) the video function [of the minis and behind-the-scenes] is huge, and (2) video gaming is huge … Look at MySpace – it's a game of "where are my friends?" … So we have video on demand, gaming, and (3) we have community.

Thus, as digital coordinator Kenny Miller explains, the website is being used to promote a sense of participatory community: "Content was the old 'sticky' [what would make viewers remain loyal to a network], but community is the new 'sticky' … The first thing they [viewers] do [online] is talk about the shows they love, and the second thing they do is talk about themselves" (interview, 2006). Quizzes and chat continue, and now there are games rooted in social exchanges – such as the avatar prom, where visitors simulate planning and going to a prom via their avatars (graphic images that stand in for the user). The avatar prom idea actually came out of the chatrooms; executives from The N visiting the site noticed users chatting about having their own prom online since they did not like or had not been asked to their own, and suggested to them that The N could help them create a great one right on TheN.com.

Miller has also developed "The Click," a sort of site-within-a-site where users can engage in peer-to-peer sharing of video mash-ups – "mashing" together different clips into a new creation – that they create with The Click's video clip/sound/music archive and accompanying editing tools. The possibility exists for the resulting montages to air on The N, with on-air "shout-outs" to the creator by stars of shows on The N. While visiting with Lindman and Miller, I saw mockups for future Click social opportunities, including the development of social network pages where users could post their mash-ups, email their mash-ups to friends outside of the network, upload personal video stories, and chat while a show is airing with other viewers. Such developments serve to entrench the The N and all its constituent parts as a brand that "gets" its audience, much in the same vein – but to a much "thicker" degree – as *The O.C. Insider*:

> *Miller:* I love it when people come to TheN.com, but what I *really* love is when people can touch our content from anywhere in the universe … I was reading some research today, and they were calling these things a "lovemark" instead of a "trademark" – brands that you have an irrational sort of visceral connection with … Our goal is to share TheN.com's content, to share TheN.com …
>
> *Lindman:* In a universe like this, where your brand is going to travel across multiple screens, you *have* to have a meaning for your brand in addition to your shows. The shows have to feed the meaning of the brand … Advertisers are going to pay a premium to advertise on brands that have a strong relationship with their audience, that really understand what they want, and that do customized things with them … The strength of the brand is actually something that comes strongly from this company. ABC, not necessarily a strong brand, but MTV, Nickelodeon – these are really strong brands. And if you talk to people about the shows they watch on these two channels, they will definitely tell you what channel they were watching them on. The corporate trajectory we're on comes from a history of branding.

The rippling impact of pulling viewers into the world – the brand – of a corporate entity has not escaped the attention of the "other" teen network, the CW. This US network is the result of the combining of two "netlets," WB (focused on teen programming from 1995–2005) and UPN (focused on African American programming from 1995–2005). Unable to thrive in a market where they were increasingly competing for the same viewers, in 2006 a new network launched featuring the more successful series from each – a combined effort from Warner Brothers and CBS Corporations specifically reaching out to teens and young adults (with an emphasis on 18–34 year olds).

The CW's launch was preceded by an aggressive marketing campaign through the summer of 2006 in major markets. Stars from teen-friendly series such as *One Tree Hill* toured the country's malls to sign autographs and pose for pictures; billboards and posters with stars' faces could be seen on freeways and on the sides of busses; and local commercials informed viewers where they would be able to find the new network on their channel spectrum. The unifying theme among these campaigns was the CW's philosophy, "Free to Be ..."; in short, the network was encouraging its potential viewers to feel as if this network was a place that would offer them a variety of positions with which to identify. You could be "free to be strong," "free to be soft," free to be fun ..."

As network head Dawn Ostroff explained, the CW's market is the "'we' generation," Millennials who like to socialize with each other through new technology, but who also want the freedom to be unique, constantly changing individuals (Elber 2006). Thus, one of the most important elements of CW marketing has been its website, which, like TheN.com, brands the network as much as any of its individual programs. As the first season prepared to roll out, CW.com held a "Free to be Famous" contest, which involved young adults creating their own promos for their local CW station or specific CW shows and uploading them to the site, where winners would be chosen to appear on air. The network also purchased MySpace.com for one day, so that CW logos appeared everywhere across MySpace; and the network has a dedicated page on MySpace (which at one point was used to accept samples from amateur bands so that online voters could select one to be featured in the series *Supernatural*). As the season began, the CW website expanded, offering a CW lounge where you can chat about shows online, and a CW Lab – where you can, as on TheN.com, create video mash-ups using clips from network series.

These attempts at branding appear to be meeting with some success, at the very least in terms of network ratings. In those markets where the branding campaigns were heaviest, the network's overall share of viewers was higher than the national average, and in markets that received less promotional attention, the shares are below the average – suggesting that the campaign itself might have had an actual impact (Hibberd 2006). One area in which the network appears to be struggling, however, intriguingly involves a new approach to on-air advertising. In an attempt to maintain a sense of community among viewers while they are watching a night's programming, CW worked with sponsors to develop content wraps. Unlike the interstitials found on The N, content wraps are created by a sponsor to advertise their product, but in such a way that product placement is minimal – the focus on the wrap remains instead on the program in progress. TV critic Maureen Ryan, from the *Chicago Tribune*, argued that such an approach could work with Millennials – a demographic less dismissive of marketing campaigns than previous generations have been, and importantly a demographic as savvy and critical about the quality of marketing as they are about all other media (interview, September 13, 2006). In other words, wrapping the content of the show with a narrative ad could work, if done creatively.

The first series of content wraps CW devised was in conjunction with American Eagle Outfitter's line of teen/young adult intimate clothing (bras, tanks, pajamas), labeled "Aerie." The content wraps aired in the fall of 2006 on Tuesday evenings, with *Gilmore Girls* and *Veronica Mars*, two of the most popular and critically acclaimed shows on the network. In the wraps, a group of teen girls (dubbed the "Aerie girls") gossip about the plots of the shows as they are unfolding. While these spots are light-hearted, there is no sense of irony or play present – the girls offer straightforward evaluation of the stories, characters, and actors. This tone, along with the ways in which the girls speak and what they speak about, met with widespread disapproval from viewers, as evidenced in 15 pages of response to a post asking viewers about the ads at The CW Source, a Tribune Company website officially affiliated with CW. Two primary lines of criticism emerged. First is that the Aerie Girls are, in fact, girls – and unrepresentative ones at that. Viewers felt this was missing the fact that many college-aged and adult women watched these programs, and that the teens who were watching had adult sensibilities:

> These girls are beyond annoying. I'm 21, about the same age as Rory [on *Gilmore Girls*], and am well past the age group that the Aerie girls represent, as is my mom, roommate, cousin, and everyone else I know that watches … The more I hear the annoying girls in the commercial, the less I want to find out about their product … (Carrie)

> So sorry to break it to the CW and to American Eagle … I watch them and they are my age and to be quite honest, I feel a tad embarrassed. I don't think that teen girls are that brainless and whiny. Let's get back to corporate ads where ppl [people] try to get us to buy things we shouldn't. (Annie)

> What the CW should do is pull people off the street (girls Lorelai, Rory, and Veronica's ages of course) and ask them what they think about the show, different people every week. (A Person Who Dislikes the Aerie Girls A Lot)

I'm 15, the age this is supposed to be appealing to, but it just makes me mad. I don't want to hear about their own relationships and I definitely don't care about their opinions on the show. I'm perfectly capable of coming up with my own all by myself, thanks. (Stryker)

A second main area in which the CW wraps missed the mark is that they did not thematically fit the programs in question. Many of those complaining emphasized that both *Gilmore Girls* and *Veronica Mars* were famous for their female characters' witty way with words (reminiscent of dialogue written for 1940s romantic comedies) – and the straightforward, somewhat simplistic conversation of the Aerie girls suffered in comparison. In addition, some episodes (especially in *Veronica Mars*) offer intense dramatic moments, and as Teresa put it: "There's nothing as trivial as a story about a girl's rape intermixed with [the Aerie] girls asking how much the lead male works out." This area of critique refers to a point made early on in this chapter: in the end, it is the program itself that must appeal to viewers. Without attending to *why* viewers want to extend their TV experiences in the first place (the show itself), everything else is just "bells and whistles."

As I noted earlier, a key element in successful network branding of Millennials (and their older sisters and their moms!) is demonstrating that the network "gets it" – that the network knows the components of the community in question, from language to attitude. This is something The N has managed more successfully, shifting from their IM interstitials to more self-reflexive, tongue-in-cheek promos resonant of *The O.C.*'s internal textual strategies. The most recent N promos bring together characters from a variety of the network's shows in "therapy sessions," such as "Catfighters Anonymous," "Help for Love Triangles," and "Help for Love Hexagons." As The N's audience has aged with the series, so have the branding efforts. In addition, as Stryker in the above Aerie girls discussion implies, a point of pleasure for viewers is working through the perspectives these texts offer; having a "representative" opinion thrust upon them may rob viewers of this pleasure to a degree. While Millennials are open to the social networking that exposes them to new ideas and opinions, it must be a choice they feel empowered to make themselves.

Conclusion

Who could ignore *the thousands upon thousands of* OC *viewers online? (Ashley, my emphasis)*

The majority of the time I post on the Internet chat boards while a show is airing *so that I can voice my opinions with others (PixieQueen, my emphasis)*

As Anna Everett (2002) emphasizes in her description of a digitextual cultural environment, the literal digital structure of the Internet is built on connections that occur simultaneously: links are always already active and people online are aware of the fact that a seemingly infinite range of possibilities exists when surfing – or, radically oscillating (8). Such an environment is conducive to what we more commonly think of as multi-tasking, a concept that has already undergone cultural refiguring: at one point multi-tasking referred to an ability to move back and forth between different tasks, and now this concept encompasses the notion of actually simultaneously engaging in more than one task. In addition, whereas multi-tasking was once the cultural domain of the "Type A" personality (typically in a business setting), today it is the cultural domain of teens or young adults (typically in a media setting) such as PixieQueen, quoted above.

Of course, within a media setting such as those discussed in this chapter, I would venture to say that younger viewers engaging in multi-tasking do not see what they do as "tasks." As Tarleton Gillespie (2002) suggests, when scholars explore the rise of new technology in a society, it is useful to consider technological tools as artifacts – things that people put to use, with the uses that emerge becoming the key elements to consider. How is the Internet put to use by teens and young adults in relation to television? What assumptions are embedded in these viewers' understanding of the Internet-and-Television and what impact might this have on youth culture and society? How do these same tools operate within the culture of the media industries?

As is evident in this chapter, a dominant use for the Internet and other new technologies in youth culture is communication and sharing, increasingly in the domain of formalized social networking. John Tulloch (1990) argues that television texts have always addressed this human desire for connection with others by emphasizing elements of intimacy in a mode of "interpersonal gossip" that allows for a sense of having "insider status" (206), but I would argue that some forms of television emphasize this more than others and that some social audiences seek this more than others. With programming aimed at Millennials, I would say that a "perfect storm" arises. Individual programs and entire networks have been working diligently to manage the resulting aesthetics of multiplicity that emerges from this perfect storm, primarily through methods of organic invitation that naturalize and tacitly approve younger viewers' expectations of an expansive storytelling experience that gives them a voice.

Series aimed at this market increasingly rely on seriality and large ensemble casts as strategies to offer multiple narrative perspectives, and have matched this with a Millennial understanding of television as part-and-parcel of a larger multimedia landscape that includes the Internet:

> *Lindman (The N):* On a meta-level, when we talk to our viewers about what they like, they say we present teen relationships well [on our shows]. TheN.com allows them to not only deepen their relationship with the brand, but also with each other. We're giving them tools to enhance their experience with our media and with each other –
> *Miller (The N):* I have a word for that! I call that "media badging." It is part of a continuum that has a long history: putting posters up on your wall, playing your music loud out of your stereo, getting a ring-tone, a button on your backpack. MySpace – if you look at the content that's on half of these MySpace pages, it's "I love this! I love that!" Media badging is this great collage trend that has roots back in punk and Warhol. You know – representation and duplication and repetition.

"Collage" was a visual theme that emerged repeatedly in my interviews and research on teens and their Internet-with-TV relationships. Stephanie Savage talked about teen fans of *The O.C.* who "create beautiful collages," and Danah Boyd's (forthcoming) work on teen MySpace users discusses the efforts to which they will go to personalize their pages aesthetically: "teens change their backgrounds, add video and images, change the color of their text, and otherwise turn their profiles into an explosion of animated chaos that resembles a stereotypical teenagers' bedroom" (6). Perhaps teens are always already inclined toward an aesthetics of multiplicity, making these new technologies "useful" to them in terms of expressing their identity (or in expressing an identity they think they should have).

Perhaps this tendency also explains why teen networks and programs have more quickly and thoroughly embraced this Millennial mentality with effective strategies – it is, in fact, a mentality with roots that precede it by several decades. As I have discussed, successful strategies to invite the teen viewer in serve the industry as well as the audience, particularly in a media environment that is moving increasingly towards niche marketing and media conglomeration. If a network can successfully brand itself as a source of authentic, representative storytelling for teens and young adults – and all the attendant expectations for storytelling that teens and young adults have today – that network can often count on long-term loyalty from that social audience.

Of course, any storm, no matter how perfect, raises a host of questions as to what lies in its wake. It is possible that an aesthetics of multiplicity can give rise to learning opportunities for younger viewers, exposing viewers still in the process of "figuring things out" to competing points of view on issues relevant to their lives. While the TV text in and of itself can do this, and while teen and young adult viewers seem to have always found ways to discuss the narratives they pursue, the Internet certainly provides additional opportunities. In the Executive Summary of "Confronting the Challenges of Participatory Culture: Media Education for the 21st Century," Henry Jenkins et al. note that today's new media environment can offer benefits, "including opportunities for peer-to-peer learning ... the diversification of cultural expression, the development of skills valued in the modern workplace, and a more empowered conception of citizenship" (2006: 3). It would indeed be something if websites affiliated with TV shows and networks could help develop such learning.

Clearly, issues of access to the Internet remain important. And, as Jenkins et al. emphasize, a participatory culture immersed in new media *is* becoming dominant among Millennials (and those coming after them); thus, concerns about access need to be accompanied by concerns about helping younger media users develop skills that will allow them to reap the most benefits from this new environment. For example, educators need to find ways to integrate full media literacy into classrooms, and researchers need to explore the full cultural and social ramifications of a dominant youth paradigm that situates intimacy and emotional connection increasingly as requiring technology and a relationship with one or more corporate entities.

The media industries are certainly already researching. Sara Lindman of The N described one study in which that network engaged:

> We actually did a wireless deprivation study, where teenagers could not have cell phones, Internet, anything for two weeks, and they had to keep journals about it. One girl said, "it was like having my arm chopped off."

Seriously! These were the kinds of quotes we were getting. Also, how
lonely they felt. You have to understand, this is a generation that's always
been able to talk on the cell phone or to IM … There's constant, immediate interaction with their peers, all the time. And when they're taken out
of that loop, they feel very, very lonely … This generation and generations
coming up will only be more so this way – the Internet for them has been
a part of their lives for as long as they can remember, and their entire social
interaction is constant, via the Internet and other technologies.

If youth culture involves creating connections through technology to
such a degree, we must consider the socio-psychological ramifications
for teens without access to that technology and the implications for
those who do. In addition, as with anything mediated, ethical issues
abound. One highly publicized "research experiment" raised such
issues in September 2006. Actress Jessica Rose, producers Miles Beckett
and Mesh Flinders, and the wife of the team's lawyer, combined forces
to create a YouTube page for fictional character Bree (dubbed
"LonelyGirl15"). LonelyGirl15 was presented to people as a real
person, a young girl trapped in a strict religious family, venting her
frustrations in a video diary. Some viewers eventually unraveled the
narrative as, in fact, a constructed one aimed at gaining exposure for
the creative artists involved and potentially launching a "web series."
Such a scenario raises compelling concerns. What are the ethics of misleading those with whom you are trying to communicate? What are
the dangers? How can we teach media users in this new terrain to consider such possibilities as they extend their experiences to the Internet –
and how might a constant sense that a story or perspective might be
inauthentic change the way people relate to storytelling?

While this chapter focused on narratives and interpellative strategies
aimed primarily at teens and young adults, I imagine that others outside
the Millennial age range may have recognized some of the viewing experiences related here. At any rate, this demographic will be "all grown up"
soon, and is likely to carry with them into their adult viewing expectations
some of what they have learned TV to "be." In addition, it is evident that
older viewers do watch teen TV, and do in some circumstances form social
networks around such series (as well as others more adult in address). In
the following chapter I will examine programming aimed at adults that has
adopted and "matured" some of the strategies evident in this chapter,
considering how the Internet is impacting the television industry in terms
of genre and in terms of overall network growth and success.

Notes

1 See Brown (1998); Carlip (1995); Pipher (2002).
2 See Hills (2002); Jenkins (1992); Sandvoss (2005).
3 While on the one hand such a claim might be taken to imply that adults invested in such genres are in a regressive psychological state, on the other hand this claim can also be seen as an indication that adult viewers are drawn to such narrative thematics out of a post-liminal awareness that there is always a valid competing point of view – food for thought in an increasingly globalized society of competing cultures. In the concluding chapter I will examine further this notion of the adult fan of any form of media as "retarded" in their psychological growth.
4 An excellent examination of the influence of new media worries on parents' self-reporting of the role of media in their families' lives can be found in Hoover et al. (2004).
5 After an initial wildly successful first season and a solidly successful second, the show's ratings began to decline through this writing (in its fourth season). Many critics attributed this to a third-season abandonment of the show's sense of humor and the addition of melodramatic problems plotted for the central family unit of Ryan, Seth, and parents Sandy and Kirsten.
6 While only airing as of this writing for four years in the US, the series has reached its sixth season, having begun sooner in Canada and also due to the varying release of seasons in the United States.
7 A third incarnation included *Degrassi High*, 1989–91.
8 One might suppose that Ashley (the 16-year-old fan who discussed the existence of fans such as herself who did not fit the image of *The OC* teen) would find her primary point of identification with this character.
9 Ironically, both pointed out, a common pattern on boards was that the first six episodes were the best – all episodes that were written before fan boards began to be examined. In the conclusion I will examine more closely the creative problems that writers, producers, critics, and many fans feel can arise when online commentary is accorded too much weight.
10 Mark Polger created the most visited "unofficial" website for *Degrassi* (Degrassi Online); Pat Mastroiani played teen Joey Jeremiah on *Degrassi Junior High* and currently plays the same character, all grown up, on *Degrassi: The Next Generation*.
11 For example, Clairol Herbal Essences shampoo has been worked into scripts as corporate sponsors of talent shows at the school, rather than as a product to be bought and used by a lead character. In an interview

with writers James Hurst and Brendon Yorke on set on November 10, 2005, they stressed the importance to them and the producers of minimizing more apparent endorsement of products.

12 I explore this storyline largely because the shooting episodes ("Time Stands Still, Parts I and II") aired in the US just as the series was beginning to garner press attention here. Other issues have received comparable extended treatment, from date rape to cutting to gay bashing to abortion – the latter of which led to a wrench in the overall narrative arc of the series in the US, as the actual abortion episodes were not aired here on The N until almost three years later (when later episodes alluding to the decision and its impact on the major characters involved, DVD releases of the directors' cuts, and the availability of the episodes on the Internet made it somewhat ridiculous to hold back). In an interesting parallel, the character who had the abortion, 14-year-old Manny, debated with her best friend Emma about getting an abortion. In the history of the collective *Degrassi* series, Emma was the result of her mother deciding not to have an abortion when she was 14 on *Degrassi Junior High*. In *Degrassi High*, another character, Erica, does have an abortion – an episode that also was not shown in some of the other countries where the show aired.

13 The series also received some funding via their educational emphasis; in 2005, the show was awarded the first annual Shaw Rocket Fund prize for excellence in children's TV, selected by a group of Canadian teens who had been taking classes in media literacy, part of an educational program called "Learning Through the Arts" created by Canada's Royal Conservatory of Music. After the initial wrap of *Degrassi High*, the federal government's Health and Welfare Department helped fund a tour of actors from the Junior High and High School series traveling across the country and speaking to teens about the issues the series had raised. The result was a talk magazine, *Degrassi Talks*, which aired on the CBC in 1991.

14 In 2008, the popularity of The N garnered the programming its own channel, separate from Noggin, on digital cable and satellite.

15 This assumption is supported by research, especially surrounding teen girls' use of IM. See Lynn Schofield Clark (2005).

References

Baym, N. (2000) *Tune In, Log On: Soaps, Fandom, and Online Community*. Sage, Thousand Oaks, CA.

Benjamin, W. (1968) *Illuminations*. Ed. H. Arendt, trans. H. Zohn. Schocken Books, New York (orig. pub. 1955).

Boyd, D. (forthcoming) Why Youth (Heart) Social Network Sites: The Role of Networked Publics in Teenage Social Life. In Buckingham, D. (ed.) *MacArthur Foundation Series on Digital Learning, Identity Volume.* MIT Press, Boston. www.danah.org/papers/. Accessed July 8, 2007.

Brown, L. (1998) *Raising Their Voices: The Politics of Girls' Anger.* Harvard University Press, Cambridge, MA.

Bury, R. (2005) *Cyberspaces of Their Own: Female Fandom Online.* Peter Lang, New York.

Carlip, H. (1995) *Girl Power.* Warner Books, New York.

Chandross, N. (2005) "Degrassi" Becomes A Cult Hit Depicting Violence and Heartaches. ABCnews.com (October 18). www.abcnews.go.com/Entertainment/story?id=1199990&page=1. Accessed October 9, 2006.

Clark, L. S. (2005) The Constant Contact Generation: Exploring Teen Friendship Networks Online. In Mazzarella, S. (ed.) *Girl Wide Web: Girls, the Internet, and the Negotiation of Identity.* Peter Lang, New York, pp. 203–21.

Code, L. (1995) *Rhetorical Spaces: Essays on Gendered Locations.* Routledge, New York.

Elber, L. (2006) New Marketing Model for New CW Network. Washingtonpost.com (September 18). www.washingtonpost.com/wp-dyn/content/article/2006/09/18. Accessed September 19, 2006.

Everett, A. (2002) Digitextuality and Click Theory: Theses on Convergence Media in the Digital Age. In Harries, D. (ed.) *The New Media Book.* BFI, London, pp. 3–28.

Gillespie, T. (2002) The Stories Digital Tools Tell. In Harries, D. (ed.) *The New Media Book.* BFI, London, pp. 107–23.

Gilligan, C. (1982) *In A Different Voice: Psychological Theory and Women's Development.* Harvard University Press, Cambridge, MA.

Goldfarb, J. (2006) MTV Bringing Social Networking to TV Channel (July 24). www.news.yahoo.com/s/nm/20060724/tv_nm/media_mtv_flux.

Hayward, J. (1997) *Consuming Pleasures: Active Audiences and Serial Fictions from Dickens to Soap Opera.* University Press of Kentucky, Lexington.

Hibberd, J. (2006) CW's Ratings Keep Affiliates Happy. *Television Week* 25, no. 44 (November 27), p. 45.

Hills, M. (2002) *Fan Cultures.* Routledge, New York.

Hoover, S. et al. (2004) *Media, Home, and Family.* Routledge, New York.

Jayson, S. (2006) Totally Wireless on Campus. *USA Today* (October 2). www.usatoday.com. Accessed October 9, 2006.

Jenkins, H. (1992) *Textual Poachers: Television Fans and Participatory Cultures.* Routledge, New York.

Jenkins, H. et al. (2006) Executive Summary of "Confronting the Challenges of Participatory Culture: Media Education for the 21st Century." MacArthur Foundation, Chicago, pp. 1–4.

Kronke, D. (2005) Evergreen "Degrassi" (June 29). www.news.degrassi.ca/article.php?a_id=1139. Accessed October 9, 2006.

Mazzarella, S. (2005) Introduction: It's a Girl Wide Web. In Mazzarella, S. (ed.) *Girl Wide Web: Girls, the Internet, and the Negotiation of Identity.* Peter Lang, New York, pp. 1–12.

Mittell, J. (2004) *Genre and Television: From Cop Shows to Cartoons in American Culture.* Routledge, New York.

Morley, D. (2004) *At Home With Television. Television After TV: Essays on a Media in Transition.* Duke University Press, Durham, NC, pp. 303–23.

Morse, M. (1998) *Virtualities: Television, Media Art, and Cyberculture.* Indiana University Press, Indianapolis.

Nicks, J. (2004) Degrassi. In Newcomb, H. (ed.) *Encyclopedia of Television.* 2nd edn., vol. 2. Fitzroy Dearborn, New York, pp. 675–9.

Pipher, M. (2002) *Reviving Ophelia: Saving the Selves of Adolescent Girls.* Ballantine Books, New York.

PricewaterhouseCoopers (2006) The Rise of Lifestyle Media: Achieving Success in the Digital Convergence Era.

Riddell, R. (2006) MTV2 Cues Up Kudocast with Aud Involvement (June 20). www.clickz.com/news.

Ross, S. (2005) Teen Choice Awards: Better Than the Emmys? *FLOW: A Critical Forum on Television and Media* 3 (issue 1). www.jot.communication.utexas.edu/flow/?jot=view&id=932.

Ross, S. and Stein, L. (eds.) (forthcoming) *Teen Television: Essays on Programming and Fandom.* McFarland, Jefferson, NC.

Sandvoss, C. (2005) *Fans: The Mirror of Consumption.* Polity Press, Cambridge.

The O.C. Insider (2006a) Spring 2006 Issue (issue no. 2).

The O.C. Insider (2006b) Summer 2006 Music Issue (issue no. 5).

Tulloch, J. (1990) *Television Drama: Agency, Audience and Myth.* Routledge, New York.

Turner, V. (1982) *From Ritual to Theatre: The Human Seriousness of Play.* Performing Arts Journal Publications, New York.

Turner, V. (1969) *The Ritual Process: Structure and Anti-Structure.* Aldine Publishing, Chicago.

Turner, V. (1967) *The Forest of Symbols: Aspects of Ndembu Ritual.* Cornell University Press, Ithaca, NY.

4

No Network Is An Island: *Lost*'s Tele-Participation and ABC's Return to Industry Legitimacy

The idea that these people – way before they got on this airplane – have interacted with each other either directly or through third parties is one of the cool pieces of tapestry of [Lost]. *(Damon Lindelof, quoted in Snierson (2004: 36))*

As Damon Lindelof, co-executive producer of the hit ABC series *Lost* (2004–), suggests in the above quote, one of the structural dynamics of this show is a sort of "unintentional" and symbolic social networking: characters are somehow connected intimately to each other; they simply haven't found the right forum for figuring out yet that they are meant to be "together." They are in need of a social networking force – and in the case of *Lost*, this force is an airplane crash that strands specific survivors together on an unusual island. Thus, this series operates much like its fans, who network with each other in attempts to unravel the narrative "messiness" of *Lost*. In this chapter, I explore "messy," or complicated, texts such as *Lost*, examining how they rely on obscured invitations to move viewers to the Internet (and elsewhere) in pursuit of narrative enhancements.

A number of shows – both concurrent with this one and preceding it – have drawn on this dynamic of people thrown together through circumstance, with the narrative driven by characters determining how their stories fit together. But *Lost* and other series I explore in this chapter serve as unique examples of successful obscured invitation on two fronts: the timing of their appearance in an era when online social networking had become part of the American cultural landscape, and their role (in conjunction with this timing) in establishing important shifts in the television industry.

As demonstrated in the previous chapter, social networking through new media technology is fast becoming an established element in how teens and young adults relate to shows the industry aims at them specifically; many experts are arguing that this phenomenon is spreading to adults, as well – especially when the center of gravity is a television show. Yet, the series I discuss in this chapter rely less on organic invitation – there is less of an assumption at work that core viewers will "naturally" extend their experience of the text to the Internet or the iPod, etc. Indeed, it may be that, at least at this moment in time, efforts at organic invitation may be too closely associated with teens; to rely on similar strategies would effectively alienate viewers who would be loathe to associate themselves with that demographic.

The programs I explore here also have to escape the stigma of other forms of TV and their demographics, such as soap opera and the fantastic (under which science-fiction and fantasy often fall) and their fans. I use the term "fantastic" in the spirit of Tzvetan Todorov's (1975) understanding of this form of storytelling, from literature – adopting it, however, as a domain or mode rather than a genre. Todorov describes the fantastic as "that hesitation experienced by a person [the reader or character] who knows only the laws of nature, confronting an apparently supernatural event [in the narrative]" (25). Thus, in the fantastic text, a considerable degree of ambiguity exists concerning what is real, what is normal, etc., with explanations wavering between acceptance of the fantastic or a rational explanation for it.[1] I have argued elsewhere that texts which offer competing points of view, conflicting character perspectives, and muddled notions of space and time are well suited to the fantastic, as well as likely to provoke conversation among viewers (Ross 2002). Perhaps more to the point here, this domain of texts has traditionally been denigrated culturally when it comes to television (science-fiction, fantasy, ghost stories, horror, gothic romance). However, it may be the very expansiveness of this domain (i.e., its encompassing of multiple genres) that permits it to exist in the 2000s in programs that can maintain a distance from those traditionally denigrated genres.

It is also important to realize that the "uphill battles" the programs I examine have faced en route to success (critical and/or popular) has had as much to do with their timing in relation to the TV industry's emerging relationship with new media as they have with the cultural status of genres. Thus, it is important to keep in mind that the observations offered in this chapter may indicate less of a permanent trend in terms of traditionally denigrated styles of programming rising to dominance, and more about how the television industry is navigating the opportunities and demands of new media. Still, I do argue that elements commonly found in modern fantastic texts and/ or soap opera "fit" better with the new media imperative of multi-platforming. Thus, this chapter will offer insights into how more mainstream shows can be extended past the TV set, and also into how risky genres (that lend themselves more to such extensions) can become mainstreamed through a convergence of specific industry conditions.

One interesting example of the mainstreaming ("adultifying?") of TV fandom and social networking can be found in the emergence of websites and cable channels or programs devoted to television proper. The E! Entertainment Network launched in 1990 under that name, and today airs on cable featuring *E! News* TV segments hosted by Kristin Veitch; but in terms of television its real strength lies online, where Kristin has a column ("Watch With Kristin") and video segments about TV through a "channel" called The Vine. Watch With Kristin also offers live chat sessions when users can send in questions about their favorite TV series, and wait for the answers if their questions are chosen. Not to be outdone, The TVGuide Channel launched in 1999 and shifted quickly from offering a rolling scroll of what is airing on one's television set to including short programs focused on the TV industry and TV fandom. Their online presence is also, like E!s, even stronger: "Ask Matt" (critic Matt Roush) and "Ask Ausiello" (columnist Michael Ausiello) offer podcasts, blogs, and live chat sessions; writers and stars from TV shows also regularly have blogs posted to the site.

The online tagline for Watch With Kristin is "It's more fun than doing it alone," while TVGuide.com offers a video feature titled "TV WaterCooler" – both emphasizing the pull of social networking. In an interview (July 14, 2006), Ryan O'Hara (President, TVGuide Channel) explained that the website and the channel's shows are focused on guiding TV viewers through the increasing number of viewing choices available to them (providing content about content), and providing viewers with a community where they can chat with other TV fans (from viewers to columnists – and at times, producers, writers, and stars). O'Hara suggested that Internet forums prove especially appealing as they offer unfiltered content (through live chats) and peer opinions on television. This, combined with a sense of community around television, is becoming a more common expectation among adult viewers.

While my own research reveals that 45 percent of those I surveyed report visiting one or both of these general entertainment sites, I am less interested in how common such practices actually are and more in the industry perception that there is a mainstream market for such forums. Online fan communities are no longer necessarily the domain of individuals who self-organize; increasingly, programs and networks are building their own playgrounds for viewers, creating a fundamentally different viewing experience than in the past. As Stacey Koerner, head of "The Consumer Experience Practice" at Global Research Integration, puts it, some corporate entities are seeing the basic paradox of the increased choices that technology has brought viewers: with more and more people watching shows "for them" and with new technologies often creating a sense of disconnect (each person in front of their computer screen), media companies need to provide opportunities for interpersonal connection among their viewers (interview, August 15, 2006):

> The fact that we're reporting on which movies were attended most and which TV shows are being watched most … is really a way for people to understand, "What is everybody else doing? Because I need to be connected, because this technology is *disconnecting* me from people."

How could something I term "obscured" invitation manage to offer viewers anything cohesive or meaningful in terms of connection? With programs utilizing obscured invitation, narrative messiness encourages viewers to seek out the Internet as a domain that can help them unravel the text; online, they can engage in pleasures of prediction and speculation, puzzle-solving, and being part of an "insider" group or community. Jason Mittell (2006b) argues that from the 1990s on, US television has become more narratively complex. He describes such shows as "foreground[ing] ongoing stories across a range of dramas" (32) and that "invite temporary disorientation and confusion, allowing viewers to build up their comprehension skills through long-term viewing and active engagement" (37). While I disagree as to the details of the narratively complex text that Mittell outlines, as well as the "active engagement" that results (and will discuss this further on), his description resonates with my observations of messiness within the text that in turn obscures invitations to engage further with the story beyond the boundaries of the original story.

Thus, the invitation to explore extensions of the text occurs within the originating text itself – it is subtle and non-intrusive to the point of appearing careless, and to "outsiders" it seems as if those engaging in tele-participation are sometimes engaging in wishful thinking (i.e., Is everything really a clue? Do the producers really mean for you to read things in specific ways?). One main point is that, yes, producers and network executives *do* hope you will follow the messiness of the narrative elsewhere, and that your voice will become a part of the narrative mix. However, the strategies of invitation that encourage this must be somewhat obscured, primarily so as not to alienate those viewers who have no interest in following the paths laid out for them. The enhancements offered must not make the experience of the original narrative incomprehensible or frustrating.

Lost is my primary example of a show that has done this successfully. In the fall of 2004, this series became part of two stories: the Internet becoming a part of a Top Ten TV program's narrative experience, and the rebirth of the ABC television network. In the following pages I will unravel how these two stories are connected with each other, and what this might tell us about the TV industry, specific genres, and viewers' understandings of watching TV in this historical moment. ABC's history before the arrival of *Lost* on its schedule was a grim one; for over two decades, the network languished in ratings and respectability as other networks carved out profitable identities. *Lost* and its successful interpellative strategies cannot be examined separately from this context; nor can it be examined without the contextualization of the other hits that arose simultaneously with it (in particular *Desperate Housewives*) and without the contextualization of what was occurring with fantastic shows more generally. And, of course, we cannot examine *Lost* without considering the ways in which the development of multimedia platforms was changing the face of the industry.

Sharing a Messy and Complicated Environment

Transmedia promotion presumes a more active spectator who can and will follow … media flows. (Jenkins 2002: 165)

Not every show is going to work [online]. (Ross Levinsohn, President, FOX Interactive Media, NATPE, January 2006[2])

As I have discussed in previous chapters, by the 2006 television season (*Lost*'s second season), the potential effects of new media technology on television were the talk of the industry. Were some TV viewers being lost to the Internet? And if only some, were these viewers important to the networks? What would TV have to do to avoid suffering some of the problems new media had been posing for the music and film industries? As indicated by the quotes above, one solution that began to emerge was television "getting in on the game," aligning itself with the new developments occurring rapidly around its viewers and assuming that those viewers "can and will follow … media flows." On the other hand, as Ross Levinsohn acknowledges, some shows will be able do this more easily than others, making for a tumultuous environment within the TV industry as professionals attempt to navigate these variations.

This shifting technological, cultural, and industrial environment was very much a part of *Lost*'s trajectory, as this was one of the shows that seemed to be "working" in terms of meshing with the technological times. One possibility for this success is that in a world of DVDs, on-demand viewing, web video streaming, and iPods/iTunes, a serial program has a better chance of surviving. As Mark Pedowitz, the current president of Touchstone Television – which produces *Lost* and *Desperate Housewives* – puts it, these technologies mean the industry no longer has to worry about the "I missed an episode phenomenon" that had previously kept many viewers from following through on an initial commitment to a show (NATPE, January 2006). Further, it is possible that money to be made through offering serials and their extensions via these new technologies could help to offset the loss that typically occurs when attempting to sell serials into syndication.

The television industry had begun experimenting with Apple's iTunes early, with some networks and production companies that were making cult series seeking to stem loss of money through piracy. For example, in 2005 one of the most often pirated series was the new *Battlestar*

Galactica. The process of such downloading was costly and cumbersome compared to iTunes, where one could purchase an episode of *Battlestar* for $1.99 and download it quickly, relatively speaking, to a video iPod. Jeff Gaspin (President, NBC Universal Cable Entertainment, Digital Content and Cross-Network Strategy) noted that the show's availability on iTunes did not hurt its ratings, and in fact may have added "buzz" to the show that was also helped along later by a Peabody Award (NATPE, Faculty Fellows presentation, January 2006).

Other shows needing ratings help began to follow suit across the 2005/2006 television season; one of the top iTunes downloads was the NBC sitcom *The Office*, giving NBC the confidence to renew it and provide it with a better timeslot on the TV schedule. And of course, ABC offered its sophomore hits *Lost* and *Desperate Housewives* early on as well; by the end of this season, ABC also became the first network to offer their hit shows online from their home website – for free, with commercials. *Lost* and ABC's success developed in the midst of this movement, which included a growth of network-created Internet sites offering much more than "merely" the ability to watch an episode. Now there was a mixing online of what Henry Jenkins (2002) describes as the knowledge culture of fandom with the commodity culture of the TV industry, creating an often complicated environment as competing sets of expectations were brought to bear upon the website and upon the show itself.

Still, as Levinsohn notes, not every show is an Internet phenomenon, and some barely make a ripple online. What types of programs can achieve success within this domain? How much of being extendable online comes down to the text itself, how much to the industry, and how much to timing? In previous chapters I have argued that many shows need overt invitation to succeed in this arena (*American Idol*), and that many others rely on organic invitation – which is to say they need an audience already prone to be online (*Degrassi: The Next Generation*). How do shows that wish to avoid obvious appeals or associations with Millennials find ways to enhance their narratives online? What do they "need" to encourage their audiences to seek enhancements?

The rising value of interactivity

"Cult" shows *like* Buffy the Vampire Slayer, The X-Files *and* Lost *are most likely to* have a large fan base and therefore more Internet sites *created about them. They're also* shows you want to know more about … *Shows like* The *O.C. are also the kind of shows that inspire a lot of websites, though they typically consist of pictures and episode summaries, unlike websites for shows like* Lost*, which have more in-depth information about the different elements of the show.* (Genevieve, my emphasis)

I think the show has to have elements that make people want to discuss it, *like a relationship between two characters, or controversial topics, or completely leaving the viewer in the dark, which spawns massive speculation* (Lost). *(Taja, my emphasis)*

Any show with a plot that invites speculation and captures viewers' hearts and/or minds will have an online presence. These days it's not enough to watch an hour of television and then wait a week for the next hour. A large part of the fun is sharing reactions and ideas *about the show with friends, family and co-workers. It's a way to connect with others* … (Oceanblue, my emphasis)

People responding to my survey about the Internet and TV, as seen above, varied in their explanations as to what kinds of shows would do well online, some offering very vague reasons and others a range of specific elements. Overall, though, a common thematic vision emerged: while the specific ingredients might vary, and while disagreements as to genre might exist, "something" about the text or the social audience has to trigger *interactivity*. One might say, as Rick Mandler (Vice President and General Manager of ABC's Enhanced TV) did, that "anytime anyone's talking to their TV" a website is in the making (interview, June 22, 2006). This then raises the question of what, exactly, *is* interactivity when it comes to TV? While I will address this more precisely further on, it is worth noting that genre seems to play a role, with fantastic programs and soap operas carrying an association of *immersion* with any discussion of interactivity. A common industry view is that a viewer cannot interact literally when immersed (or "lost") in the unwinding narratives of the fantastic and soap operas. Any interactivity has to occur after the fact. (Whereas a sporting event or reality series seems to offer more opportunities within the narrative proper when viewers can "leave" the narrative and interact with others and then return to the text.)

Still, regardless of *when* it happens, interactivity appears to be the magic factor in a television series being extendable to the Internet.

And, as evidenced in the last chapter, Millennials have no problem chatting with friends while they are in the middle of watching a show. So what prompts interactivity, then – especially with programs that are not relying on overt or organic invitation? Unsurprisingly, those viewers who self-identified as science-fiction/fantasy fans felt that there was something specific to that genre that prompted viewers to create and/ or seek out websites related to such programs:

> It's hard to put into words. Some shows, usually in the sci-fi genre, have that special energy that just cries out for it [Internet activity], whereas I would find it difficult to get comparable responses for *CSI*. (Jeff)

> It always seems like the fantasy or sci-fi type shows have such a large fan base and the Internet is a way for them to keep the fantasy going. (Angie)

> The sci-fi/fantasy genre is the easy answer since they are the fans most likely to embrace this technology. They tend to be the most passionate about their shows. I seriously doubt that cop or cowboy shows engender the same level of commitment from its fans ... The sci-fi/fantasy genre makes the audience work hard to overcome the suspension of disbelief, which means those people are fully engaged in the story and are more willing to take the extra steps of seeking out those who share their passion. (FarscaperMuse)

As seen here, there is a sense that there is "something special" about this genre and its social audience. Several viewers argued, as respondent Hollyebn succinctly put it, that "sci-fi fans and computers just go together," which raises interesting future research questions in an era where computer use is becoming more and more widespread. More common, however, was a perception among my sci-fi/fantasy fan respondents that the relationship between this genre and its success on the Internet involved a complicated narrative requiring attentive viewing, *and* a continued stigmatization of the genre that breeds fierce loyalty and a need to find fellow "geeks and outcasts" (as many of my respondents described themselves). This explanation resonates with my earlier discussion of cult television; not only does cult fandom operate as an exclusive club of sorts, it tends to involve a small social audience of viewers who are increasingly aware of the history of cult shows and fandom:

> Science fiction has always had a tight-knit community, ever since the early days of *Star Trek*. In our everyday world, science-fiction fans are

generally considered the geeky outcasts, but the Internet is one manner in which we are able to bridge the geographical barriers that leave us scattered throughout the world and instead unite us to share our common love for imaginative entertainment that goes beyond what we are now and instead envisions what we could one day be. (Jessica)

However, one need only look back at Genevieve's quote in the opening of this section to see how current fantastic texts' connection to understandings of cult becomes complicated: "'Cult' shows like *Buffy the Vampire Slayer*, *The X-Files* and *Lost* are most likely to *have a large fan base and therefore more internet sites* created about them." These three programs chronologically have had increasingly large fan bases, beginning with the small numbers of *Buffy* and progressing to the Top Ten numbers of *Lost*. In addition, fans of *Buffy* reported the sense of stigma noted by current science-fiction/fantasy/fantastic fans – but *Lost* fandom is comparatively stigma-free. Something seems to have shifted – in terms of "cult," in terms of the fantastic, and in terms of fandom.

I will leave a discussion of what may have shifted for later. One area to explore here, however, involves the increasing serialization of television. Many of the cult shows that have captured media and scholarly attention across the years have relied on heavily serialized plots, connecting them to the soap opera genre and also to the world of comic books. Regardless of genre, many survey respondents offered the explanation that shows which could capture viewer loyalty and then which could thrive online "had to" have elements (common in serial narratives) that would prompt viewers to approach the program like a puzzle or game:

> Some shows have a certain kind of continuing mystery that is completely taken apart by fans, trying to understand it or find something out – what better to do that with than the world wide web? (Ruben)

> I know that I've heard for *Lost* … that people online are like detectives trying to piece together what exactly happened and making up their own theories. (Sedi)

> Ongoing, intelligent storylines tend to attract people who like to discuss and or/share insights. The easiest way to connect with like-minded people for shows that fulfill the above criteria is through the Internet. (Nicola)

Jason Mittell (2006b) notes the important contextual element of the influence of video games in the rise of narratively complex television shows that operate like games and puzzles, and argues that this gaming environment encourages "a new mode of viewer engagement" whereby viewers focus on plots and events over and above characters and relationships and philosophy (38). In other words, viewers become invested in the show's "operational aesthetics," or how things are put together, more than they are invested in why things happen, what will happen next, or the impact of events on characters and their interactions (35). However, in the responses seen above, viewers' involvement with any mystery or puzzle operates hand-in-hand with a desire to explain and understand things on a more speculative and predictive level that is closely connected to soap operas as much as to video games. In Nancy Baym's (2000) examination of online daytime soap fandom, similar themes of engagement emerge among the group of viewers she studied. Baym argues that soap fandom thrives online because this genre makes interpretive discussions easy; the text appears to be un-authored (and therefore open to interpretation), and the large ensemble cast allows for the presentation of multiple perspectives on issues relevant to viewers.

These traits, of course, are not specific to daytime soap opera. The primary focuses of online discussion that Baym describes can be seen clearly in responses offered throughout this chapter (and elsewhere in this book): personal connections to the themes of the plot; character motivations; and predictions (including creatively expressed wishes). Thus, soap operas, as much if not more than fantastic shows, certainly have a long history of encouraging involved discussion among their fan bases. Kevin Murphy, head writer and co-executive producer for *Desperate Housewives*, notes that the long-term success of soap operas has rested on their promotion of inclusivity and interaction:

> I think soap operas, when they're done well, are very inclusive by nature. You become very, very invested in the show – you feel ownership of these characters. Watching soap opera – it's very interactive. The way people watch our show, they're shouting back at the screen. (Interview, July 13, 2006)

Murphy also noted that any number of shows can work to promote a sense of inclusion, especially with online forums that allow fans to voice their pleasures and their dissatisfactions. Drawing a comparison to comic book fandom, Murphy explained:

> Part of being a fan of something is that it gives you the inalienable right to kick it around. I'm a comic book guy, and that's so much a part of the regular experience of being a comic book reader. Absolutely there's a similarity between comics and soaps – they're serialized. The canvas upon which you tell a story for *Desperate Housewives* is very broad and very long … and as a result, people become regular viewers. And I think that the Internet – the fact that it's now so easy for fans to find other fans – really turns this into a community experience. Plus viewers can fit more in their heads now – they can appreciate, even demand, more involving and complex storylines.

Thus, to a certain degree, the soap opera and comic book text belong to the readers, and a key point of pleasure is sharing opinions with other readers. In the years surrounding the development and success of the "non" soap opera *Lost*, the connection between comic books and programs featuring obscured invitation has become quite pronounced as well. Across the turn of the millennium, it was not uncommon to attend a major comic book convention such as Comic-Con or Wizard-Con and find a show-runner (the executive producer in charge of making a show run smoothly) in attendance for a cult or small hit series. A few years later, it was also not uncommon to find show-runners and cast members of major hits present, as well as of shows about to premiere who were hoping to see their new shows develop *into* major hits.

Several television writers with whom I spoke offered theories as to why this was beginning to occur. Kevin Murphy suggested that introducing a show into a fan environment could help to mark the show as "fan worthy." This is worthwhile in today's cross-marketing and multimedia environment; fans have long been associated with high text loyalty that incorporates purchasing products associated with their text. In addition, if a new program can generate buzz among such viewers, this is evidence that broader financial success might follow across multiple media. As David Eick, the executive producer of *Battlestar Galactica*, explained:

> I think, generally driven, television has become more concept-driven, become more high concept … Ten years ago you wouldn't have been

out pitching something like *24* or *Kidnapped* or *Prison Break* ... [These shows] speak to a more marketing-driven medium ... Nowadays it's all about casting and marketing and high concept, and I think that probably does lead into the genre arena. And the fact that more efforts are being put forth into high-concept and franchisable concepts for television shows leads you into comic books and established characters – and Comic-Con. At Comic-Con, you will find the nucleus of your fan base. (Interview, August 22, 2006)

The high-concept shows that David Eick mentioned as examples all fit the description of obscured invitation in terms of how they operate for viewers; *24*, *Veronica Mars*, *Lost*, and *Battlestar Galactica* all feature complex narratives and large ensemble casts that prompt the kinds of online fan activities I describe in this chapter. Eick hypothesizes that more high-concept shows are being developed for TV because of the industry's need to recuperate profit across multiple venues. Bringing high-concept shows into the domain of the comic book convention "fits," considering many comic books' own high-concept organization. (And certainly some TV shows appear in comic book form, thus making the comic book convention a natural point of marketing.)

But the most advantageous aspect of this form of promotion involves the complicated, serial narratives of the TV shows. High-concept shows have always been a risk, trending towards seriality, and – DVDs and iPods notwithstanding – networks still need a large enough audience watching episodes *as* they air, particularly given the high cost of these series. Rob Thomas, the creator and executive producer of the cult hit *Veronica Mars*, emphasized this when he explained to me why the CW asked him to change the structure of the show for its third season:

I think one of the elements of *Veronica Mars* that's a turn-off for people – they feel like the ship has sailed, if they've missed five episodes, they can't climb aboard ... So I wanted to give more in-points for viewers. In this [new] structure they should never feel *too* far behind. And it also means we'll have bigger clues and fewer suspects – it'll be *easier* for new viewers. It may bum out some of our hardcore fans who watch every week and enjoy the sort of labyrinthian way we plot it. You can love that all you want, but if we're off the air it's a moot point. (Interview, July 18, 2006)

Television marketers are thus turning to comic book conventions, where seriality reigns, and because those attending these conventions will "tell ten friends" (in the words of Eick) – who will each tell ten more friends, etc.:

> We went to conventions and we met them [*Farscape* fans]. They're doctors, physicists, lawyers – we had a really intelligent group of people. They were really smart, but they would get obsessed. We used to do chats, very early, on SciFi.com ... In the beginning I was resistant to the pull, in that these are a vocal minority. But Rock [*Farscape* creator Rockne O'Bannon] and I were talking, and he says: "You know, these people are very influential." (David Kemper, executive producer, *Farscape*; interview, July 15, 2006)

Stacey Koerner ("The Consumer Experience Practice" at Global Research Integration) and Alex Chisholm (MIT) explain that in 2006, mainstream broadcast networks were just beginning to pay attention to online buzz that often emerged from comic book conventions. Network marketers were discovering that people who would talk online about a preview they had seen should be heeded as a marketing force:

> *Chisholm:* The thing is, there are communities out there that exist online. They're the catalyst, they're the carriers ... They start putting it all over the place. So these people are critical, because they're your evangelists. They start spreading the word and creating a buzz, so the interns and producers over at *Access Hollywood* and *Entertainment Tonight*, and the writers at *Variety* ... they're all now feeding into this.
> *Koerner:* This past year [2006] was a complete turn-around. Everyone had "the message," they drank the Kool Aid somewhere around iTunes and *Lost* ... I think that, from an industry perspective, they get it – they know they need to listen – but I don't think they quite understand what they're looking for, or how to operationalize. They look at it mostly as a way of generating buzz or infiltrating "influencers." (Interview, August 15, 2006)

These viewers, labeled "early evangelists" or "carriers" or "influencers," can be counted on to drum up interest in high-risk shows and to potentially affect change in networks' assessments of programs. For example, in the summer of 2006, Koerner and Chisholm hypothesized that the online buzz surrounding the Americanized telenovela *Ugly Betty* convinced ABC to place it in a slot that would guarantee more viewers (Thursdays with the hit *Grey's Anatomy*, as opposed to an original Friday night placement).

An additional "assist" with *Ugly Betty* (and other shows debuting in the same season) occurred within the world of online professional TV critics. I spoke with several television critics working for mainstream newspapers, who explained that the Internet was increasingly becoming a part of their job – especially via blogs and their ability to disseminate buzz about shows before a season even starts. Maureen Ryan of the *Chicago Tribune* feels that a genuine shift is occurring within the TV industry:

> I think, the thing that I see now is the networks trying to harness buzz. They're sending me clips now, trying to do these viral things … They've done outreach to some bloggers. At TCA [Television Critics' Association tour] there were online people there, so, I think that the networks are still trying to feel their way about what all this means, but they certainly see it as a way to increase interest. I mean, look at *Ugly Betty*. This is a show that really was water-cooler chatter … and that pre-season chatter got that show transferred from the death slot on Friday to Thursday, which is the complete apex of television … There's certainly an element of hype for something that was just inside stuff before. You start to get pilots in the mail in June and July – they want you to start talking about it on your blog … I sometimes wonder if that's a good thing – it's so brutal now. You can't put out a bad pilot now – you'll get killed. A lot of the things that used to happen behind the scenes, behind the curtain, are out there in the open now. (Interview, September 13, 2006)

Ryan explains that networks take this risk because today, when a show explodes online as a topic of conversation, this is seen as proof that the program has the legs it needs to survive in the long run. Thus, Ryan argues, networks are cultivating relationships with professional critics who have blogs or online columns, because these online venues are part of key viewers' "expectations of an immersive [television] experience." However, the risk is that, if a pilot is rushed out before it is ready to catch the buzz, there is no going back to tweak or fine-tune the series.

Melanie McFarland of the *Seattle Post-Intelligencer* agrees that the role of the TV critic has become more pronounced via the Internet in recent years (interview, September 20, 2006). "Scripts [for TV shows] have to be 'bloggable'," she explained. There has to be something unique that critics can write about that will capture the attention of viewers who are seeking to enhance their TV experience through reading critics' blogs. McFarland thinks that this can be both a blessing and a curse. TV programs receiving online attention generate buzz (and thus possibly more eyeballs), but they also become subject to intense scrutiny – from critics, and from the viewers who interact with the critics. As Ryan explains, online critic blogs and columns are a new breed of writing: "It's a conversation, not ... preaching from on high." Viewers visit critics' sites, respond to the critic's "take" on an episode or show, and invite other viewers with whom they are socially networked through the Internet to contribute also. It does not take long for a negative evaluation of anything – from an error in costuming continuity to a plot device or character decision – to spread across the Internet.

McFarland feels that this intense scrutiny makes a difference at the network level; certain kinds of shows hold up to scrutiny better than others. In short, the more complicated the narrative, the better a series will fare in the headlights. If a program offers visual and narrative complexity along with iconic characters of some depth, critics (professional and amateur) will devote attention and energy to unraveling these complexities – and less attention and energy to minor flaws in logic or minor idiosyncratic elements of discontent. McFarland argues, in fact, that the Internet's ability to allow viewers to revisit narrative moments repeatedly (be it through reading about those moments or through literally re-watching those moments) has been the most significant development in TV industrially and aesthetically in the 2000s:

> It's almost like, in lieu of video commentary on DVD, you have TelevisionWithoutPity ... There are certain people who watch the show and then they read the entire run-down, because they want to experience it again, and that's been the most interesting thing to me. You know, I used to make fun of my brothers for recording football games that they had watched. That's exactly what some of these sites are for people: you watch it, and ... you have these communities now where you never meet these people online, and you're sitting there discussing a show, and you're going back and forth and pulling out different bits, even repeating something. And that, I think, is one of the biggest changes in television – it changes the way that people experience it in a very fundamental way. I think it's kind of good for producers – I think

it puts the onus on producers to make television better. It's an element in buzz; if your scripts aren't good enough to get people talking online, forget it.

One of the most widely known sites centered on revisiting TV texts, as referenced by McFarland above, is TelevisionWithoutPity.com (TWOP), created by Sarah Bunting and Tara Ariano. What began first as a site devoted exclusively to mockingly criticizing the teen soap *Dawson's Creek* in the late 1990s developed into a site criticizing a broader range of shows (MightyBigTV), and then became a powerful force in TV fan culture as TWOP. As the title of the site suggests, staff reviewers offer commentary on shows in an unflinching manner, engaging in a process that site users have labeled "snarking." (The motto is "Spare the snark, spoil the network.") In other words, reviewers do more than review – they are storytellers who imbue their reviews with sarcastic comments when they feel they are due, and constructive praise when they feel that is due. I spoke with Sarah Bunting about this practice, and she said that what makes such reviews entertaining is that the people they have writing for the site *do* love TV; thus, their criticisms are grounded in a respect for the medium that some "legitimate" critics do not share (interview, August 9, 2006).

However, site visitors do not merely come and read the staff reviews; Bunting emphasized that they come for the sense of community:

> That's the great thing about TV: you have these water-cooler moments ... I remember the *M*A*S*H* finale. I happened to be sleeping over at a friend's house, and it was like: "Silence in the house!" We couldn't go near Mrs. H. for an hour after ... There is an instinct among people, there is a need for this phenomenon – this desire to have someone validate what you've just seen by discussing it in the company of other people.

Bunting believes that this conversational environment allows friendships to form, and even micro-communities with their own distinct cultural characteristics to develop around a specific show. Ben (B-Side) and Joe (J-Unit), who created and manage the website TVGasm.com, feel their site offers similar appeals: they describe TVGasm.com as a forum that mimics the pleasures of watching TV with your friends (interview, July 14, 2006). They found themselves always talking and joking about what they were watching together and thought, "Why not do this on a website, so all of our friends can join in?" As Joe explained, "People want to talk about TV … [It's] the whole water-cooler effect … and certain kinds of shows have more water-cooler moments."

What caught on the most was this site's "snarking" mindset as well. One of their friends posted a particularly sarcastic commentary on the Tony Awards in 2004 that caught on through viral emailing, and quickly TVGasm had multiple loyal communities developing around reality series, melodramas, and fantastic shows in particular. While 37 percent of those responding to my survey indicated that they regularly visit TWOP, several specifically singled this site out as one they had visited once and chosen to ignore because of the snarking mindset, which they found exclusionary in its emphasis on making fun of writers and actors. Indeed, Bunting stressed that the site ultimately is about "wanting to have fun *making* fun of something," and that this approach would not appeal to everyone. One of my survey respondents (PanPan) tried to explain the appeal in this way: "People will come together to make fun of just about anything. Think of it this way – the New York Yankees have a rabid following of fans. But they also have a rabid following of 'anti-fans'."

This approach to discussing TV is remarkably similar to what the "anti" *American Idol* website VoterfortheWorst.com offers – with an actual exchange among viewers built in. As Jonathan Gray (2005) argues about TWOP users specifically, antifandom can provide its own pleasures, ranging from the approval of other antifans (and thus the pleasures of community) to the pleasure of demonstrating what is felt to be a superior intellect and/or level of taste. Thus, snarking may allow actual fans to distance themselves from potentially "low cultural capital" texts and/or to distance themselves from the "low cultural capital" accorded to fandom itself (see Bury 2005). As some of my respondents who did not like such sites pointed out, it is possible that those "ripping a show apart" are actually huge fans who do not want anyone to *think* they are fans – and thus use their activity on a site like TWOP to "prove" (to themselves or others) that they are not intimately connected to the show in question, in a sort of classic process of Freudian disavowal.

Bunting stresses that the monitors of TWOP work to make sure that the boards offer a process of exchange, as opposed to individuals simply getting to "hear" themselves talk:

Sometimes users will go to extreme positions so they can feel like they're being heard. And my only issue with somebody famous showing up is that there is *immediately* a polarization of positions ... The real challenge is to remind people that these boards are supposed to function like a cocktail party conversation, where you want to be listening also and not just wanting to talk.

Some industry professionals indeed feel that the site is more about the most obnoxious person in the room gaining a platform, and then maintaining that platform by criticizing through an entirely negative framework that often discounts the ways in which TV operates:

I don't think they should let people post really horrible things about writers – and I'm not talking about myself ... Like somebody writing something like, they went to college with somebody and they wrote an essay on such-and-such and they're a bad writer. Why is that allowed to be in a public forum? How is that commenting on the show? That's not creating any exciting, vibrant community. (AB showrunner, interview)[3]

They think they know much more than they do. They try to break down the business of the show, how much that writer sucks. They have no idea what that writer contributed, or should be blamed for or credited for. There's a level of presumptuousness and righteousness ... It seems like there's a higher degree of scrutiny and conversation on an episode-by-episode basis ... You know, when I was a kid, I didn't watch TV and then at the end of the year say, "Wow! That was such a great season!" or "Wow! That season really sucked!" It was just on and that was it. There was no TIVO or DVDs of shows. You had to wait four to seven years for syndication before you could watch an episode again. So they're applying this level of criticism that the production process doesn't allow – that isn't fair to how a show gets made. (CD showrunner, interview)

We experienced a bit of a backlash on TelevisionWithoutPity. The joke was that in year one, going to TelevisionWithoutPity was like a tidal wave of love with a million paper cuts. And then it evolved into year two and we decided, "no, it's more like being in a room with a thousand ex-girlfriends." They still recognize that there's something about you that *was* appealing, but now they're gonna tell you what's wrong with you. (EF showrunner, interview)

However, some in the industry have also "felt the love" of the site, developing a symbiotic relationship. Writer-producer Ryan Murphy (*Popular, Nip/Tuck*) was the site's first friendly celebrity visitor in 2000, and his regular posts brought a lot of public attention to the site.

In 2005, writer-producer Rob Thomas (ironically a former staff writer for *Dawson's Creek*) famously announced the renewal of his cult hit teen series *Veronica Mars* to the show's TWOP moderator (John Ramos) even before telling the mainstream press. He knew that word would spread quickly, that this move would show his appreciation for the attention the site had brought to the series, and that such a move would capture the *attention* of the mainstream press (thus bringing mutual good publicity to both the series and the site).

When showrunner EF above describes his/her experiences with the website, (s)he speaks in terms that do indeed conjure up images of a cocktail party – one that might be fun or might be an ordeal: "[It's like] being in a room with a thousand ex-girlfriends." Indeed, even though Bunting sees the cocktail party metaphor as one appropriate to people listening, at the cocktail parties I have been to, people are equally prone to a desire to hear themselves speak as they are to making sure they listen to someone. Thus, *all* of these descriptions seem apt – a sort of love/hate relationship seems to be operating that, while different from the fan speech and tone on other boards, nevertheless suggests a connection with the show in question. These descriptions resonate also with Nancy Baym's (2000) descriptions of soap opera fans playfully engaging in criticisms while still maintaining loyalty to their show.

Unsurprisingly, *Lost* is at the center of one of both TWOP.com's and one of TVGasm.com's more successful "soirees." It is, somewhat paradoxically, the *hit* status of *Lost* that raises so many interesting questions about its successful extensions online. As I have discussed in this and earlier chapters, while my survey respondents and many scholars argue that fantastic series such as *Lost* lend themselves to more intense fan activity than other kinds of programs, it has historically more often been the case that such shows have been niche-market hits, and that corresponding fandom has centered on these texts as "cult hits." What would compel a mainstream broadcast network to green-light a show about a group of people who survive a plane crash only to find themselves on a tropical island populated with inexplicable creatures? What would compel a mainstream network to gamble on a show that seemed destined, at the best, to achieve cult status? And what did this network, in conjunction with writers and producers, do that moved this show past its seemingly inevitable cult destiny?

"Something different" for ABC – and for Viewers

Prior to the success of Lost, *fans of sci-fi were not regarded with much respect. We were those weird "Trekkies ... " The word "fanatic" comes to mind. I guess when other folks consider you a "fanatic" or "obsessed," you get mocked for your passion. (Loretta)*

Lost *definitely stands out from any other show in recent memory ... It has numerous characters that we try to get to know from present time and then through learning their back history, and not all at once – in bits and pieces ... [There is] a big mystery that doesn't reveal everything right away ... The TV market is so over-saturated with reality TV or cookie cutter situation comedy that TV gets stale after a while. That's why* Lost *is such a breath of fresh air. [It] gives us* something different – *something to talk about and be a part of. (John, my emphasis)*

The combination of quotes above from *Lost* fans demonstrates both the opportunities that emerged with this 2004 ABC series, and also the risks. *Lost* carried with it the onus of a potential "Trekkie" or "geeky" core set of viewers, with its fantastic premise and its complex narrative environment of seriality and mystery. But the pilot carried this "burden" at a time when the Internet was burgeoning in relation to television – and thus at a time when the same elements that might attract "Trekkies and geeks" might also attract more mainstream viewers (especially younger ones) through online enhancements.

Just as (if not more) significantly, the show was emerging at a time when there were no mainstream sci-fi/fantasy/fantastic series on broadcast television, allowing it to tap into a lineage of networks turning to this arena as a way to distinguish their program offerings from current television trends – as a way to offer "something different." The 2003/2004 season had been dominated by reality television and by procedurals that offered primarily self-contained episodes rather than continuing storylines (e.g., *CSI*, *Law and Order*), so the fantastic offered a distinctly different generic approach to prime-time broadcast storytelling for viewers. *Lost* offered viewers an escape from the procedurals, promising an entirely serialized storytelling structure that would move back and forth through time with extensive use of flashbacks to develop characters (and indeed slow down plot time to a pace akin to that found in daytime soap operas: the first *season* took place over 44 *days*).

As Catherine Johnson discusses in her book *Telefantasy* (2005), an industrial-historical examination of some of the more successful high-risk sci-fi/fantasy/fantastic shows of TV's past reveals that their success had much to do with strong network support. In other words, the popular conception among cult fans that their shows thrived solely via the perseverance of artistic (often auteurist) integrity in the face of network interference is often a myth – a myth necessary to a definition of cult that relies on the notion of auteurist-based originality of vision. *Star Trek*, for example, fulfilled an NBC need in 1966 for a highly unique show that would appeal to the developing "socially relevant" audience – particularly the females of this audience. NBC actively promoted the show as offering quality via its use and development of continuing characters, which included attractive male stars assumed to be appealing to female viewers. The network also kept creator Gene Roddenberry's emphasis on social issues front-and-center. While the series failed to attract this audience, this appears to have less to do with NBC's support than with competition the show faced from well-established hit sitcoms (*Bewitched*, *Gomer Pyle*).

While the series' ultimate financial success had as little to do with NBC as its initial failure did, it is worth noting that NBC's three-and-a-half season order of *Star Trek* was not a fluke. The network made a deliberate and strategic decision to air a science-fiction series, expecting it to become a solid hit during its original run – something NBC needed, with CBS the dominant network at the time. In the United States, the history of television programming is largely one of periodic risk-taking, with struggling networks taking the risks. Almost thirty years later, FOX's status as the new network on the block would allow for the appearance of *The X-Files*, a science-fiction series that ultimately did much better for FOX than *Star Trek* did for NBC. The show ran for nine seasons, ranking in the top 25 by its fourth and continuing to do well through its sixth. Johnson points out that creator Chris Carter was the darling of FOX; his series had captured for them exactly the audience they were aiming for – viewers of cult cable hits, and "quality broadcast viewers" appreciative of television series with high production values.

While this combined set of viewers did not inherently require a science-fiction series, *The X-Files* would help FOX stand out from their competitors at a time when the networks were dominated by sitcoms (*Seinfeld*, *Friends*) and critically acclaimed dramas offering some seriality (*ER*, *NYPD Blue*, *Homicide*). A series with humor, an intensely serialized conspiracy storyline, polished cinematography, and supernatural and other-worldly dynamics would clearly stand out for viewers continuing to leave broadcast TV for cable. The show also may have attracted cult fans of the short-lived ABC series *Twin Peaks*, created by experimental filmmaker David Lynch for ABC's 1990/1991 season. This series is perhaps known best for its spectacular drop-off among an initially intensely devoted fan base that was purchasing books and holding viewing parties through the first season. About a supernatural spirit able to enter people's bodies and commit murder, *Twin Peaks* was decidedly different and able initially to pull in a healthy number of viewers via its generic hybridity (incorporating elements of soap opera, teen melodrama, science-fiction/fantasy/fantastic, noir, and comedy). Lynch's notoriety as a provocative auteurist filmmaker also allowed ABC to promote the series as "art" (see Thompson 2003).

However, the series unraveled both narratively and in terms of ratings very quickly, and ABC cancelled it early during its second season. Revolving around a central mystery (Who killed Laura Palmer?), co-producers Lynch and Mark Frost disagreed about the structure of this storyline; Lynch wanted to keep the mystery at work, whereas Frost wanted to solve the mystery and develop another (Thompson 2003). The second season result was a compromise that confused and frustrated even the most loyal fans, making both *Twin Peaks* and ABC famous for its failed experiment. In fact, this series would go on to become a benchmark of sorts for every "experiment" that TV – especially ABC TV – would take in following years, in conjunction with the final seasons of *The X-Files*, which critics and fans had come to agree lasted several seasons longer than it should have in terms of wrapping up *its* central mystery. Neither networks nor viewers wanted "another *Twin Peaks*" (unsolvable mysteries) or another "post-Mulder *X-Files*" (prolonging the story unnecessarily).[4]

A notable follow-up example was the even shorter-lived ABC series *Push, Nevada*, one of the first attempts on broadcast TV to integrate the Internet with narrative television during the 2002/2003 season.[5] ABC heavily promoted this series from film writer/producer/actor

Ben Affleck and writer/producer Sean Bailey, which revolved around a murder mystery set in a Nevada town populated by *Twin Peaks*-like characters and rife with *X-Files*-worthy conspiracies. Viewers could attempt to solve the mystery themselves, with assistance from online sites; the first to do so would win one million dollars. The series was unable to gain ratings; it was up against CBS's stalwart procedural *CSI* and NBC's hit sitcom *Will & Grace*. In addition, over the past decade ABC had been losing viewers rapidly, as well as losing more deeply rooted "loyalty viewers" via high-profile cancellations of cult melodrama favorites such as *My So-Called Life* (1994–5) and *Once and Again* (1999–2002). The season before *Push* premiered, ABC had only three programs in the top thirty of the year – and one of those was *Monday Night Football* (Brooks and Marsh 2003: 1472). "Something different" would only take the network so far. ABC needed the right *combination* of "different," at the right time, and in the right places on the network schedule. The network would also have to convince viewers that anything risky they were developing would not be dropped from the schedule too quickly.

During the 2003/2004 season, everything began to come together with these factors for ABC. Some of CBS's and NBC's biggest hits were growing long in the tooth. At the start of the 2004/2005 season, CBS's *Everybody Loves Raymond* was entering its ninth and final season and *CSI* and *Survivor* their fifth; NBC's *Law and Order* was entering its fifteenth, *ER* its eleventh, and *Will & Grace* its seventh. In addition, NBC's strongest performer, *Friends*, had ended its run after ten seasons. These long-term programs were no longer "something different," especially for viewers in the key 18–49 year old demographic – viewers who had become enamored with FOX's *American Idol*, which would begin its fourth season in the winter of 2005, thus not airing against any new fall 2004 series.

It was a good season to be bold, and ABC was ready with two shows that would instantly become associated with *Twin Peaks* – *Lost* and *Desperate Housewives*. *Desperate Housewives* looked to be the safer bet ultimately. The show had been developed over several years by creator Marc Cherry, and daytime and prime-time soap veteran Charles Pratt had assisted in highlighting the soap opera elements in the pilot script, which revolved around the mystery of a suburban housewife shooting herself, and leaving a cryptic note behind for her friends (Carter 2006). Still, the series was darkly comic and dramatic at the same time, posing difficulties as Cherry worked to sell it; network developers were also nervous about the serial mystery. ABC, however, was in no position to be choosy and the script generated excitement with Susan Lyne (President, ABC Entertainment), who had been looking for a show that could capture the adult female viewers of *Sex and the City*, which had just ended its run on HBO (Carter 2006).

Thus, support for the high-risk show came from close to the top, as did support for the riskier project of *Lost*. Lloyd Braun, then Chairman of ABC Entertainment, is responsible for the original concept of plane crash survivors on a tropical island, imagining that a dramatic fictional narrative could be derived from CBS's hit reality show *Survivor*. Bill Carter (2006) describes the rocky route to success for this series, and one wonders how different the subsequent landscape of TV might have been had corporate luck or Braun's tenacity run out. Carter reports that both Braun and Lyne felt micro-managed by their parent company of Disney; people above them with less knowledge of the TV business had final say on which pilots would be developed each season and neither *Lost* nor *Desperate Housewives* was garnering their attention. As luck would have it, in-fighting at Disney during the development season left Braun and Lyne able to make their own choices, clearing the path for Touchstone Pictures to produce both pilots for ABC. The pilot for *Lost* was ultimately sold on an outline developed by J. J. Abrams and Damon Lindelof after an initial script by another writer left Braun unsatisfied. (Abrams had already created *Felicity*, a young adult melodrama, for WB, and also *Alias*, a spy series with supernatural leanings, for ABC.)

The Disney in-fighting trickled down to ABC Television and Touchstone Pictures; Braun removed Stephen McPherson, head of Touchstone, from shepherding the pilot personally after it became apparent that McPherson found the project too risky. Indeed, *Lost* became one of the most expensive TV pilots ever made (over ten million dollars), requiring housing in Hawaii for staff and crew and the transportation of a jet plane's hull to Hawaii where it could be ripped apart for the crash. And Abrams' and Lindelof's high-concept premise immediately made any network executive think of *Twin Peaks*: the survivors were "somehow" connected with each other and there was some metaphysical reason why they had all ended up on an island with mysterious, otherworldly creatures – a reason that would unravel with each season's plot time occurring over less than two months.

But Braun apparently knew a hit when he saw one; unfortunately, by the time *Lost* and *Desperate Housewives* made it to the air, both he and Lyne would be working elsewhere. Disney fired Braun several weeks before up-fronts, when networks unveil shows to advertisers and critics – and Lyne was fired shortly thereafter. McPherson would take over development at ABC, and he would be the one to introduce the world to both of these programs.[6]

McPherson must have been nervous; while *Desperate Housewives* raised interest at the up-fronts, Stacey Koerner reported that *Lost* did not fare as well, befuddling critics and advertisers with its generic blend of horror, action, and the supernatural – as well as its largely no-name cast:

> They show us *Lost*, and it's this thrill-ride, where people are standing on a beach, and someone's getting sucked into an engine, and it's exploding, and there's this mystery element – or is it sci-fi, or is it adventure? Maybe this is *Alias*, but in a weird, sci-fi way? And then they say, "Okay – this is going to be Wednesday at 8 o'clock … And everyone just looked at *Lost* and said, "Never gonna happen. Definitely not at ABC. *Maybe* on FOX." (Interview, August 15, 2006)

However, Koerner's team at Global Research Initiative had recently developed a software program called PropheSEE that measured online buzz building around new series, and the results in the summer before both *Lost* and *Desperate Housewives* premiered predicted both to be hits:

> Essentially, [we] used this technology to monitor online dialogue, whether that be in blogs or discussion forums or news items, to see when specific products [shows] were mentioned, and in what way were they mentioned. We had two metrics: a volume of conversation – how many times there was a conversation about a particular show; and then we had a sentiment score – very basic – positive, negative, neutral. In measuring that over time, together, … we could see which of these scores was contributing to ratings or popularity. But what we found out early on was that we could fairly accurately get a sense of what programs people were interested in, going into a *new* season. So our PropheSEE scores come in [in summer 2004], and Lost is at #2, and I'm thinking, "Oh, shit – this thing doesn't work!" … [But] that's the whole reason we're doing this, to see if there is something that's counter-intuitive to what we already know. (Interview, July 11, 2007)

Thus, people were talking about *Lost* and *Desperate Housewives* via the Internet even before clips of the series began circulating. Fans of

J. J. Abrams were especially excited about his show, and as ABC's promotional campaign kicked in the buzz continued to grow. McPherson worked with Mike Benson (head of marketing at ABC) to create a savvy and intriguing promotional narrative: *Lost* would be marketed with *Desperate Housewives* as one unit, in that ABC was emphasizing their shared sense of mystery and their shared status as "something different" – not just for the network, but for all of television (Carter 2006). In addition, by pairing the generically messy *Lost* with the clearer generic hybrid of *Desperate Housewives*, it is possible that ABC was seeking to distance *Lost* from any association with science-fiction/fantasy.

The marketing itself created buzz. Bottles with notes from stranded islanders began washing up on beaches; flyers with "Have you seen this person?" appeared in malls, featuring pictures of *Lost* cast members in character; and people in laundromats in key markets stumbled across laundry bags with cryptic taglines from *Desperate Housewives* on them saying "Everyone has a little dirty laundry." By creating mystery *about* the mysteries, ABC built up a set of expectations among increasingly interested viewers, enough of who were chatting about all of this online that critics and local affiliates were taking note. In fall 2004, *Lost* debuted with the highest numbers for a new series that ABC had seen since 1995 – and the highest numbers that *any* network had seen in four years – only to be beaten by *Desperate Housewives*' debut one week later (Carter 2006: 305).

While both of these programs changed the status of ABC (and Touchstone) in the eyes of the industry and viewers, and while *Desperate Housewives* has been the higher-rated program, I focus in the remainder of this chapter on *Lost*. It is this program that more closely fits definitions of cult TV – including a more persistent association with *Twin Peaks* and *The X-Files* in the press.[7] *Lost* has also developed and maintained a more intricate and ever-changing multimedia presence, especially via the Internet. While *Desperate Housewives* has numerous fan sites and even a computer game that allows users to become a part of the neighborhood of Wisteria Lane, *Lost* has offered "something different" in this arena as well. As Maria Elena Fernandez (2006a) puts it, "*Lost* has become the test case for the marriage between new technology and creative content," relying on a complicated series of connections between television and other forms of media to enhance the narrative it offers to viewers.

Enhancing the narrative

I think that the Internet has definitely enhanced and maintained Lost's *vieswership. There is so much discussion and theorizing ...* The whole is far greater than the sum of its parts. It just all falls into place. *(Melissa, my emphasis)*

This [Lost] *is the type of show where* you and other people need to come online (together) and talk *about how and what* [sic] *is going on in each episode (or for that matter what's going on entirely) ...* [Lost *is*] *giving the fans of the show something to talk about and also something to think (theorize) about, and the Internet is the easiest and best way for many Lostees to get together and share their love for the show. (John, my emphasis)*

The primary dynamic through which *Lost* enhances its narrative beyond the TV story proper comes back to obscured invitation. If one starts with the enhancements available outside of the actual series (with "outside" a distinction that is becoming harder and harder to make), each can be traced back to the originating text and its "messiness." Verizon, for example, offers two-minute diaries from characters we have not yet seen on the show. The novel *Bad Twin* is "authored" by Gary Troup – a character who did not survive the plane crash, but who had emailed his manuscript to his publisher before he got on the ill-fated flight. Importantly, these "extras" stand alone, in that one technically does not have to be entirely on top of the show to read these other narratives – and more importantly in that one does not need these "extras" to follow the series. This choice maintains a clarity needed given the original text, but as Lorne Manly points out, these enhancements nevertheless "[blur] the line between fiction and reality," mirroring and complementing *Lost*'s complicated and chaotic narrative (*New York Times* 2006).

ABC's own online attempt to formalize tele-participation with this show emerged via ABC's Enhanced TV, run by Rick Mandler. As he explains it, there are differing levels of interacting with TV that appeal to different viewers; ABC designs their interactive sites with this in mind:

We borrowed a design convention from Walt Disney Imagineering, and they design everything with – well, somebody went to summer camp somewhere over there. They design everything with floaters, swimmers, and divers. And so the idea is that the Floaters, they're not looking for all that much. They just want to watch a TV show and maybe get a little extra information, when the thought occurs to them ... The Swimmers – they probably will click through a lot of that information and maybe vote in a poll occasionally, too. And the Divers will drill in. They want more interactivity. They want gaming; they're interested in polls and comments ... It's really hard to tease out who's what and why. It depends on the day and the show. (Interview, June 22, 2006)

ABC's Enhanced TV therefore splits its screen into two, with one side offering a live interactive experience for swimmers and divers. For example, trivia challenges and discussion of predictions can occur on one side of the screen while viewers are watching the show (something swimmers might enjoy). Divers can jump into "Character Challenge" on the other side of the screen, in which they pick teams of characters and then receive points as their team members appear, are featured in a flashback scene, encounter the Dharma Initiative, etc. (and correspondingly lose points as bad things happen onscreen to their characters).[8]

Such designs operate on the assumption that some viewers are approaching the show like a game. One of the most complicated enhancements relating the show to game-playing began in the final weeks of the series' second season, when multiple corporate entities and creative personnel came together to create "The *Lost* Experience," an alternate reality game (ARG) meant to keep viewers invested in the narrative of the show during the summer months when the show was off-air. It is still not entirely clear if this enhancement was a success in terms of satisfying its users, largely because it was never clear if the ARG was being marketed to "regular" viewers or to people who were ARG-savvy. As Jason Mittell (2006a) explains in his examination of the game, ARG players have specific expectations about how these games are supposed to operate, whereas non-ARG viewers interested in pursuing this enhancement as a way to maintain a connection with the show would have a very different set of expectations.

As Mittell describes it, ARG players expect to collaborate with each other, navigating between the fictional world and the real world. However, ARGs traditionally stand alone in the sense that they are not tied to a preexisting narrative; rather, someone creates a narrative for the game that is so intricately embedded in the real world that pleasure emerges for players in attempting to "mine" the real world for what belongs to the game and what belongs to, well, the real world. For those not familiar with ARGs, a fictional example might suffice. An ARG creator might design a narrative about a hidden treasure. Players would hear about this treasure through an online ARG forum; they would then pursue the treasure by following a complex web of clues that would take them through "real yet fictional" websites, magazine advertisements, online articles, etc. (i.e., these items exist – but were created for the game), and also *real* websites, magazine advertisements, online articles, etc. (i.e., preexisting texts that the creator decided to integrate into the game, often deciding as the game progresses). With "The *Lost* Experience," the ARG could not truly stand alone as part of its real world was the fictional world of the show; Mittell argues that because of this, TV fans came to the game with expectations that they would receive insights into the show, whereas ARG fans expected a traditional ARG experience. The result was little of either, suggesting that the game was created first and foremost for the viewers rather than for the ARG community – perhaps in part to distance it from the ARG community.

Producers could not make the game for traditional ARG players without alienating mainstream viewers; and producers could not make the game *necessary* to watching the show – they could only use it as a way to *enhance* enjoyment of the show. Most industry people I spoke with emphasized that, as of 2006/2007 at least, it was not a good idea to make any extension of a television show inextricable from the show – while more and more people are utilizing and taking pleasure in such extensions, most will not take to being *forced* to engage with extensions in order to follow the story. As Alex Chisholm (MIT) explained:

> Each thing has to stand by itself. Whether it's the web experience or the television experience. It has to be able, by its own merits and its own medium, to be sustainable. And what happens with these extensions or touchpoints is that they add *layers* of meaning – it doesn't require the viewer to be in all these different places ... That's what separates the mass experience from the subcultural. (Interview, August 15, 2006)

Mittell does not explain *why* ARG players would expect a traditional game from "The *Lost* Experience"; nor does he offer direct evidence that *Lost* TV fans playing the game were in fact dissatisfied. However, given that the game seemed to exist somewhere in between being an

ARG/subcultural and a "mere" extension/mass experience, would lead me to agree with Mittell. More concretely, Stacey Koerner reported that initial research at her company found that dissatisfaction emerged concerning the intrusiveness of corporate sponsorship into the game – akin to complaints that might emerge if unsophisticated product placement were to appear in the series proper, and suggesting a misunderstanding of the show's fan bases:

> *Koerner:* It's a symptom of everybody throwing stuff at the wall, knowing they need to be in that space, but knowing enough about how to do it and why to do it.
> *Chisholm:* The bottom line is, you gotta understand what's happening with the community and the content before you start.
> *Koerner:* They're [networks and marketers] still looking at it with an eye of "we have to give our fans access any way we can." Their way of looking at it is, "How do we derive more distribution options and capitalize on it?" – as opposed to creating experiences that enable further engagement, deeper engagement. I think they're getting to it, but they don't see it 100 percent yet.

Mittell also suggests that *Lost*'s other enhancements did not effectively blur the line between fact and fiction, thus making any ARG incompatible with the series at an aesthetically functional level. He offers as an example the appearance of *Lost* actors "being themselves" on the late-night ABC talk show *Jimmy Kimmel Live* at the same time that actors "being their characters" appeared. This was a ploy on the part of producers to encourage people to play the new game. On *Lost*, the characters had discovered that a group called the Hanso Foundation appeared to be behind the activities on the island; on *Jimmy Kimmel*, while the stars chatted with the host, a "representative" of Hanso accused the producers of *Lost* of maligning what was in fact a "real" company. Mittell argues that this event (along with others such as "author" Gary Troup having a pre-plane crash Amazon.com interview about "his" book *Bad Twin*) is not complex in the way that traditional ARGs are complex.

I think, however, that this misses an important way in which many viewers approach the show; my own research reveals that viewers see any attempts to play with fact and fiction, both within and outside of the original narrative, as its *own* game (ARG or not). They find events such as the release of *Bad Twin* or the *Jimmy Kimmel* appearances to be an *enhancement* of their viewing experience. They do not "need" these events to be as complicated as the originating text; while they appreciate the ways in which such enhancements mirror the narrative's own messiness, in the end it is the story of the series that propels and supports everything:

> I like the way ... *Lost* reveals some parts of a story but not others, making each episode a link in a chain. That keeps me coming back week after week to see how the story unfolds ... I appreciate the chance to really delve into the story and what's happening to the characters. *The scavenger-hunt for clues* about the island, the characters' pasts, and what will happen next is tremendous fun. (Oceanblue, my emphasis)

Thus, one does not *have* to go online, or buy a novel, or attend Comic-Con to experience the pleasures of puzzling through the show's narrative – but for many watching, doing so is the best way to enhance their viewing experience:

> With *Lost* ... people [go] online to find answers to the many questions this show poses every week. I think it's kind of like a game and it's just fun to learn things you might have missed and hear what other people's ideas are regarding the show because no one really knows what's going on. (Angie)

> I don't usually rush to my computer after watching [TV] ... to discuss it, though there are exceptions: I often get on my computer right after watching *Lost*, because *there is always so much happening in one episode, things are easily missed* and going to forums to talk about the episode helps me catch on with the things I might not have noticed. (Genevieve, my emphasis)

There is a complexity to the text of *Lost* that draws viewers in; people "miss things" because of the scope of the narrative and the manner in which writers make sure that "no one really knows what's going on." For those unfamiliar with the series beyond its basic premise, the narrative and the viewer activities surrounding it can best be described as what Elsa Barkley Brown (1992) (referencing the work of Luisah Teish, 1985) refers to as "gumbo ya ya." As Brown succinctly puts it, gumbo ya ya means "everybody talks at once," allowing different narrative threads to connect (297). Brown finds this concept of communication useful for rethinking women's history because it encourages us to consider that what may sound and look like chaos might hold stories important to a fuller, more nuanced history: "Learning to think non-linearly, asymmetrically, is, I believe essential to our intellectual and political developments. A linear history will lead us to a linear politics and neither will serve us in an asymmetrical world" (307).

While forging a connection between such a weighty claim as this and the way that fans of *Lost* and the narrative of the series interact is a bit of a stretch, I find the connection intriguing. The narrative proper of *Lost* is decidedly "gumbo ya ya" in both structure and content. Episodes focus heavily on flashbacks to characters' pasts, warping the time frame of the show in that, while one season may have shown us 44 days, the flashbacks have contributed years and at times decades. The characters' pasts overlap with their presents, and one character's past might also overlap with another's – even if they themselves do not realize this. Multiple stories intersect as well at the level of intertextuality and allusion, with characters reading books that seem to suggest other ways of reading the series' narratives (e.g., *Watership Down*, the comic book *The Green Lantern*) and with characters' names alluding to philosophers and cultural icons such as John Locke, Jean-Jacques Rousseau, Daniel Boone, and Tom Sawyer.

These overlapping and intersecting narratives have become the center of much online discussion, with viewers attempting to ferret out the references and then explore them. (Who was John Locke? What did he mean when he talked about humans being born with a blank slate?) Another popular topic online is how the characters' past lives figure in their current situation and how different characters' pasts connect. Ultimately, both on TV and then again through Internet sites, in *Lost* there is an approximation of what Teish explains as the goal of "gumbo ya ya": people (characters and viewers) are pondering the importance of the past and its relationship to the present and the future – and that past includes multiple narratives and experiences. For Teish, this is the point of people literally talking at once (not all the time, mind you): fragments of meaning emerge – ideas and moments from the narrative that in and of themselves may seem disconnected, but that upon further consideration may reveal something of value. The messiness requires, after the gumbo ya ya has ended, considerable work on the part of those involved to seek connections where none appear to be present – they use what they "hear" or experience to reevaluate what has come before.

Henry Jenkins (2007) describes something similar in his discussion of transmedia storytelling as being built on "additive comprehension" – each layering on of the story across a different medium both adds to and alters the whole, forcing the participant to reassess the story. As the seasons of *Lost* have passed, the narratives have multiplied – as have the mysteries; mirroring this, websites for the series have proliferated, and within the websites, theories about how things might connect have proliferated. Someone unfamiliar with the show cannot just "jump into" the gumbo ya ya of the show without considering the past of the series – and someone new to one of the many websites available cannot just jump into *that* gumbo ya ya without considering the past of *those* narrative threads. In turn, once one has "jumped in," this changes the complexion of the first round of gumbo ya ya (and so on and so on …).

Of course, *Lost* is not the only show that operates in this manner – but it is the first *hit* TV show since *The X-Files* to offer such narrative complications. And I would argue that *Lost* has surpassed *The X-Files* in this respect, much more deliberately structuring messiness into the text. While *The X-Files* had a central mystery at work, they also had stand-alone episodes that did not necessarily contribute to this narrative. In addition, there ultimately was less ambiguity and contradiction to the text – less gumbo ya ya, that is, and more of a sense that there was a single answer to the questions posed about aliens and the US government.

Lost, on the other hand, emphasizes *constantly* the possibility that there might be multiple explanations for what is occurring to its characters, largely through the competing and intersecting back-stories of its sprawling ensemble cast. These multiplying possibilities lead many viewers online; as Henry Jenkins (2007) argues, stories of such expansive range trigger an "encyclopedic impulse" among readers, prompting them to find ways to organize and comprehend the gumbo ya ya, so to speak.[9] While in the past with cult shows, individual fans might band together to create multiple spaces across which they could share and work on their "encyclopedic impulses," *Lost* was one of the first television programs for which a preexisting structure was used: the wiki. A wiki is an editable online resource that therefore consists of collective contributions overseen by an administrator or team. (The classic example is Wikipedia.) Fans still drive the content, but they do not have to create the website or other infrastructural elements. The result is a more "official" site that focuses on gathering information, while still maintaining a space for community, as evidenced by the call on the *Lost* wiki:

> Anyone can edit Lostpedia. Sign up for an account in minutes to begin editing.
> Not ready to start editing? Help us by discussing, renaming, merging or even deleting articles.
> Add your theories to Lostpedia. Check out all the Theory Pages we have or create your own for existing articles. Be sure to read the theory policy first though.
> Got an idea for something on the wiki? Not sure who to ask or how to go about implementing it? Check out Lostpedia: Ideas and post your ideas there.
> Have fun, there's always articles to edit on the wiki. (www.lostpedia.com/wiki/Main_Page)

Viewers of *Lost* also seem especially eager to work together online at high-profile sites given the additional possibility that the producers of the show might be online, offering a map or guide to viewers:

> The *Lost* creators themselves pay attention to the Internet and the fans who post there ... At last the creators of TV shows – at least a few of them – are beginning to realize that the interaction between fans and their show is essential to the show's continued existence. (Loretta)

> With all the mysteries and literary references and allegories, there is SOOOO much to talk about with *Lost*! Not to mention a large, diverse cast. Also, the creators of the show are somewhat interactive with fans, which strongly encourages fans to get online and talk about stuff. (Melissa)

Given the messiness at work, and the obscurity of clues in the narrative of a show such as *Lost*, the figure of the *listening* producing team is important to the sustained popularity of the show. Both *Twin Peaks* and *The X-Files* suffered when fans began to think that the producers had "lost their way" with their own narratives (pun intended). What to outsiders appears random and careless (constant deferral of answers, constant expansion of questions) can at times begin to appear random and careless to fans as well – a situation that can threaten viewer loyalty, as this online exchange in-between Seasons 1 and 2 demonstrates:

> A: The show could become a victim of itself. It caused such a buzz that it launched many Internet sites where some very devoted fans speculate far and wide what is going on. All of the different theories and ruminations cannot be true ... The saving grace for the writers in that regard is the fact that we here talking about all this via message boards on the Internet, only make up a small percentage of their total number of viewers. The worst prospect would be if they pulled a *Joan of Arcadia* on us, and it could happen. ABC wouldn't really care about finishing it up as planned if the ratings dropped to the point of costing them money. My biggest fear would be that it turned into *The X-Files*.[10]
>
> B: Ahh, please don't even think that! ☺ Seriously, I fear this as well. Hopefully TPTB (The Powers That Be) are smarter than that ... Granted, those of us on the boards talking and speculating about *Lost* make up a small portion of the viewing audience. However, in the back of my mind I'd at least like to *think* that TPTB have some poor intern slaving away reading the boards ... We are the most visible and vocal, for those who are listening. If *Lost* goes the way of *The X-Files*, or heaven forbid, *Farscape*, I'm *done* with network TV other than the NFL, NCAA football, and NASCAR. At least they can't screw that up too bad.[11]
>
> C: It is very easy for network shows to lose their way because of all the pressures from the men in suits who care about nothing but saving money. The networks are underestimating the value of a core group of loyal fans ... [But] it seems to me that the writers are afraid to answer the questions for fear that we won't like the answers they originally wanted to give and are scrambling to come up with some answers they had not originally planned on ... TPTB must give us some answers, however ... We are watching this show for many reasons and "who is getting killed off next for no reason or explanation except to show that the island is really dangerous" is a show killer. DO YOU HEAR THAT WRITERS?

Both Teish and Brown note that if one participant dominates the process of gumbo ya ya, the gumbo ya ya falls apart into meaninglessness for those on the inside as well. This is something that fans express awareness of when they worry about "the men in suits" who can influence the trajectory of a show. But there is a paradox in this: on the one hand, viewers who follow the messiness savor the actual experience of becoming involved in the game of the narrative; on the other hand, their invited involvement gives them a sense of shared ownership – a sense that their investment must somehow in the end be worthwhile. There is still a story at work, after all, and a story for most viewers includes a sense of structure that includes – at some point – a meaningful conclusion. In other words, at some point the "messiness" must evolve into clarity:

> We try to promise the audience – we make this pact with them. Unlike shows like *Twin Peaks* or *X-Files*, that really sort of launched these big mysteries and they didn't really have the answers at the end of the day – we are sort of making the pact that we are really going some place. It will be solvable, we're going to lay in the clues, and you can figure it out at home if you're paying very close attention. So I think that makes it fun for the audience to go online together and share their theories and impressions of what the characters are up to. (Rob Thomas, creator and executive producer of *Veronica Mars*, interview, July 18, 2006)

What groups of fans appear to be asking for is what Stephen Mamber (2003) refers to as implied narrative mapping, "a sense that underlying ... [its] creation was a mapping that's been hidden from us, so we can be representing, in a sense, what's already there but hidden [when we offer our own maps]" (147). With messiness comes the need for some underlying structure – but that structure must, ironically, allow for more complexities to evolve, including the complexities of gumbo ya ya that incorporates the audience's perspectives. As Mamber argues: "A well-designed narrative map cries out to be an *interactive* mechanism *leading one back to the source*" (148, my emphasis). Again, this is not an easy game for anyone to play, because of the number of voices that can become involved in the storytelling process. As Walter Benjamin (1968) argues, "something useful" must develop from storytelling, but trying to find a common thread of "something useful" among producers, network executives, and viewers in a rapidly shifting multimedia environment is easier said than done.

Conclusion

"It's amazing," Abrams says. "The Internet has really changed the way we watch TV. Instantaneously, thousands of people are

interacting and reaching a consensus on what they like and don't like. The scrutiny is mind-blowing, and you'd be moronic not to listen to the fans." (Quoted in Veitch 2005)

As J. J. Abrams notes here, *Lost* has been a part of a larger discussion developing in the industry about how new expectations are emerging among viewers for what television viewing can offer to them. But as I have stressed throughout this chapter, much of *Lost*'s success in terms of its enhancements can be traced to a unique moment in television history that provided room for serial fantastic texts – for high-risk shows – especially at ABC. In addition, it has remained important to rely on obscured invitation in regards to enhancements so as not to alienate those viewers who do not wish to extend their viewing experience past watching episodes on their TV sets – as well as to not alienate viewers who may wish to remain distanced from stigmatized genres and the stigmatization of fandom in general that persists to some degree in mainstream culture. As Mark Pedowitz of Touchstone emphasizes, it is still, ultimately, about creating a network hit that a mass audience will watch; any emphasis on multimedia extensions is secondary to that concern (NATPE, January 2006).

Nevertheless, *Lost* has been a tremendous hit for ABC and Touchstone, in large part due to its enhancements – and where hits go, network strategies tend to follow. Maria Elena Fernandez (2006b) argues that this series provides a new model of the viewing audience for the industry: loyal weekly viewers, and fans who will avidly pursue every avenue of tele-participation offered. To some degree, such a "split" in the viewing audience has always existed for hit shows, growing as the ability for enhancements has. That is, with hit series there have always been what many think of as "regular viewers" and "fans" – or as Rick Mandler of ABC's Enhanced TV might put it, between "floaters," "swimmers," and "divers." What has changed with *Lost* is that networks are now more aggressively courting the smaller audience of fans/divers with online enhancements – and hoping that regular viewers/ floaters might become "fans enough"/swimmers to pursue some of these extensions as well.

In the 2006/2007 season, NBC – after its precipitous drop in ratings at the hands of ABC – demonstrated that it, too, was ready to pursue social audiences of fans. The network had, the season before, experimented with this a bit with their sitcom *The Office*, aggressively pushing the small ratings show on iTunes and then developing online character blogs, actor blogs, and in the summer of 2006 webisodes featuring minor characters. Then, after a serial sci-fi/fantasy show called *Heroes* became a surprise hit for the network in the fall of 2006 (although it was not a surprise to Stacey Koerner's PropheSEE), NBC worked quickly to integrate this series into its new marketing philosophy of "NBC 360" – a vision of the network (and all its sister networks, such as Sci-Fi and USA) as offering viewers a complete media experience across multiple platforms.

Much like *Lost*, *Heroes* lends itself to such an immersive environment: the plot revolves around a large ensemble cast of humans who suddenly find themselves with baffling supernatural powers, drawn together from across the globe to stop a nuclear explosion in New York City. There is also a mysterious organization tracking the heroes down – and it uses the corporate cover of a paper company called PrimaTech Plus. After the show took off in its first season, NBC offered "Heroes 360": viewers can read an interactive graphic novel corresponding to the show (the series features a graphic artist character who paints the future and turns some of his visions into a comic book called *9th Wonders*); they can contribute to a wiki; chat in forums (where of course the most popular topics involve explanatory theories); watch episodes (both with and without commentary); engage in interactive online play while episodes are airing; and apply for a job at PrimaTech Plus via their online application process (which involves calling the toll-free number for the company first, in order to get a code to access the application).

Not to be outdone, CBS has developed a slightly less intense but nevertheless similar experience for viewers of the smaller hit series *Jericho*, about a group of people in a small town who survive a nuclear blast in the United States. Again, the more visited forums revolve around explanatory theories concerning the nuclear blast and the survivors. The enhancements offered for viewers of *Jericho* and *Heroes* resonate not only with what *Lost* has created, but also with Nancy Baym's work on online soap fans that I discussed earlier. As Baym (2000) describes it, "if one understands soap viewing as a game of making meanings from clues, then the collaborative provision of multiple readings and multiple clues has obvious benefit. No longer limited by one's own time constraints and limited knowledge, the game becomes bigger and more fun to play. The more players the better" (93).

This conceptualization of online soap fandom as collaborative play encompasses the different activities that Baym describes as central to the group she studied; it also encompasses nearly all of the activities I have been discussing about a wider variety of programs, demonstrating that what we are seeing today is not so very removed from the genre of soap opera as many might like to think. It also suggests that "things soap operatic" may be at work with the fandom surrounding what Jason Mittell (2006b) describes as narratively complex texts. I would argue that, if fans of narratively complex texts who enjoy considering the mechanisms at work in a show do not have an *equally* strong investment in characters and relationships, at some point the operational aesthetics of that show will become all "bells and whistles" – that is, all style with no substance – and will inevitably lead to viewer *disengagement*.

As Rhiannon Bury's (2005) work on female online fans of *The X-Files* shows, as well as my own research (Ross 2002) on fans of *Buffy the Vampire Slayer* – both series Mittell sees as narratively complex – the relationships between lead characters was a key focus of discussion. Henry Jenkins (2006) also suggests that shows such as *Lost* and *Heroes* demonstrate how "female fan tastes [rooted in characters and relationships and their histories] are reshaping popular television." While I agree with Mittell that the operational aesthetics of narrative complexity encourages online engagement and may distance the narratively complex text from soap opera and melodrama, I believe this distancing is conceptual rather than actual in nature. In other words, viewers are still strongly invested in "things melodramatic" – but the operational aesthetics may provide a rationalization for that enjoyment, much like TWOP's snarking may rationalize investment in a show and in its fan activities.

Of course, ultimately, marketers and network executives are less concerned with issues such as these and more concerned with the monetizing capabilities at work within the growing relationship between and among television, the Internet, and viewers:

> There are a lot of reasons why we're in this business [of Enhanced TV]. Ultimately, I think on the sort of offensive side of the equation, we see this as a chance to bring a really powerful new tool to television marketing ... Layer in interactive television and a digital infrastructure, and suddenly you take the power of television and deliver a brand message and add into it some of the tools of direct marketing being

perfected on the Internet, and you really have the Holy Grail. (Rick Mandler, ABC's Enhanced TV, interview, June 22, 2006)

Marketers are more and more interested in being there at the beginning when something takes off. Websites help them figure that out. Financially, if they get in on the ground floor it's better for them with the fans later. They like the buzz ... It's lightning in a bottle. (Stacey Koerner, "The Consumer Experience Practice" at Global Research Integration, interview, August 15, 2006)

These large complex narratives that these kids consumed in science-fiction space, they're writers bringing that to bear on this next generation. Next, you've got this really interesting push of marketers who are trying to make their message relevant ... So you've got [writers and marketers] almost conspiring now to move this [context of multiple touchpoints] into a business reality. (Alex Chisholm, MIT, interview, August 15, 2006)

While the Internet may not be necessary to such activities, it certainly makes them easier; and it may, through this ease, be making such activities a more naturalized part of the story experience. In short, obscured invitation may segue soon to some blend of overt and organic invitations. Thus it is particularly notable that both CBS and NBC are more obviously encouraging viewers to go online. Extremely telling is CBS's proclamation to critics at the 2007 winter meeting of the Television Critics' Association that they were developing "buzz shows" for the fall 2007 season; in spite of the fact that CBS in 2006 dominated in overall ratings nationwide, they felt they must create shows that people will be talking about online (Bauder 2007). In fact, after canceling *Jericho* after its first season, angry fans used the Internet to mount a campaign that involved sending peanuts to CBS, and CBS granted a renewal to the show approximately two months after its death.

As Stacey Koerner and Alex Chisholm argue, *Lost* is a new brand of program, created by Internet-savvy producers able to build multimedia-platforming into the series in an increasingly organic way – paving the way for later shows attempting to bridge the domains of TV and the Internet:

Chisholm: What's happening is ... at the Comic-Con preview, what they were talking about was how folks like J. J. Abrams, and Sam

Raimi, and Bryan Singer, these guys that are – they're the ones who grew up as fan boys, and they're students of Comic-Con and fan conventions. They've now infiltrated the studio system, and they're bringing what they experienced as kids in terms of moving across all these spaces – they're bringing all that to their own creative development ... So you've got these guys who are really savvy as to how the eco-system works.

While there is not a lot of money at this point to be found in online-based tele-participation in comparison to revenue found via broadcast advertising, being able to set the standards in this arena holds great power – and this is why CBS and NBC were right on the tails of ABC as of 2007. What these three networks are busy developing are strategies for capturing the ways in which cult fans "act" (i.e., buy) without alienating "regular viewers." The results have yielded "mainstream cult" programs (*Lost*, *Heroes*, potentially *Jericho*). These shows' premises run the risk of attracting *only* a traditional cult audience – intensely loyal, highly interactive, but small – but that, in an increasingly Internet-savvy culture, have the advantage of lending themselves easily to enhancements that "regular viewers" will seek out.

As Catherine Johnson (2005) argues, cult TV shows "can only finally be defined through their mode of reception"; it is the *manner* in which viewers *interact with and relate to* a show that lends it its cult status (3). This may complicate academic understandings of cult, but it can help explain why so many of my survey respondents struggled with this concept – many of them describing shows with strong ratings (including *Lost*) as cult shows. While it is not the aim of this book to redefine cult, these industry trends suggest a need for *historicized* understandings of "cult," "cult fandom," and "fandom." If the primary consistent factor across varying understandings of "cult" is tele-participation in the service of exploring all aspects of a show's fictional world, then it becomes important to examine how networks are building environments to support this – but aiming for a larger audience than most cult shows garner. How are such strategies spreading throughout the industry, both in terms of online efforts and in terms of program development? What are the effects of such a shift on understandings of storytelling among creative professionals, critics, and viewers? In what ways might such strategies engender and endanger fans' sense of being part of a specifically bound social audience for a show? In the final chapter I will consider these questions in relation to what appears to be on the horizon for the industry and for viewers in terms of redefining television.

Notes

1 See Christine Brooke-Rose (1983) for further elaboration of this point.
2 Ross Levinsohn has since left this position.
3 To avoid any ramifications, I have marked entirely negative comments about TWOP anonymously.
4 This label refers to the departure of lead actor David Duchovny from the series, a full season after the central conspiracy theory was explained and a full two seasons before the series ended.
5 The true first attempt was from *Homicide* on NBC in the late 1990s, with staff writers working online to offer the first true webisodes. ("Second Shift" detailed the stories of Homicide detectives working different hours than the ones featured on the series proper.) The show also offered a special episode about the Internet that moved the narrative back and forth between the series and the website. However, *Push* was different in that viewers were encouraged from its first episode to integrate their viewing with the Internet.
6 Bill Carter (2006) states that rumor has it that the only reason McPherson did not pull *Lost* from the up-fronts was that Braun called in a personal favor with him—not to mention the ten million dollars the network would have been throwing out the window.
7 Ironically, it was *Desperate Housewives* that in its second season attracted numerous comparisons to *Twin Peaks* due to its critical loss of esteem (though its ratings did not suffer). Critics complained that the show's second-season mystery was not thoroughly thought out and that it detracted from the development of characters and the relationships between them – similar to the complaints leveled against *Twin Peaks*. In fact, Kevin Murphy emphasized when I met with him between Seasons 2 and 3 that the upcoming goal for Season 3 was to maintain an emphasis on characters over and above mystery, avoiding the problem of "stringing the story along artificially ... cheating the audience, sort of like [*Twin Peaks*]" (interview, July 14, 2006). Amusingly, one of the more popular new characters at the center of the new mystery for Season 3 was Orson, played by Kyle MacLachlan – the star of *Twin Peaks*.
8 Amusingly, this game operates much like an online drinking game that began circulating online for *Lost* in its first season (another character appears in someone else's flashback – do a shot; Kate flirts with Jack – do a shot; etc.).

9   For a discussion of how spoilers online factor into the dynamics of information sharing for *Lost*, see Gray and Mittell (2007).
10 *Joan of Arcadia* was a CBS show with a cult following about a teen girl who had conversations with God; the show was cancelled at the end of the second season, leaving viewers stranded without any answers as to why God was speaking to Joan.
11 *Farscape* was a Sci-Fi Network series with an immense cult following that was abruptly cancelled at the end of its fourth season, with no warning to the producers. In the next chapter, I will discuss the efforts of fans online to obtain an ending to the show.

References

Bauder, D. (2007) CBS Execs Looking to Hike Buzz Factor. *Los Angeles Times* (January 18). www.calanderlive.com/tv/sns-ap-tv-cbs-blues.

Baym, N. (2000) *Tune In, Log On: Soaps, Fandom, and Online Community*. Sage, Thousand Oaks, CA.

Benjamin, W. (1968) *Illuminations*. Ed. H. Arendt, Trans. H. Zohn. New York: Schocken Books, New York (orig. pub. 1955).

Brooke-Rose, C. (1983) *A Rhetoric of the Unreal: Studies in Narrative and Structure, Especially of the Fantastic*. Cambridge University Press, Cambridge.

Brooks, T. and Marsh, E. (2003) *The Complete Directory to Prime Time Network and Cable TV Shows*. Ballantine Books, New York.

Brown, E. B. (1992) "What Has Happened Here?" The Politics of Difference in Women's History and Feminist Politics. *Feminist Studies* 18 (no. 2, summer), 295–312.

Bury, R. (2005) *Cyberspaces of Their Own: Female Fandom Online*. Peter Lang, New York.

Carter, B. (2006) *Desperate Networks*. Doubleday, New York.

Fernandez, M. E. (2006b) Island Life. *Honolulu Advertiser* (March 29). www.thehonoluluadvertiser.com/article/2006/Mar/29/il/FP603290312.html. Accessed October 3, 2006.

Fernandez, M. E. (2006a) Television *Chicago Tribune* (January 5).

Gray, J. (2005) Antifandom and the Moral Text: Television Without Pity and Textual Dislike. *American Behavioral Science vol.* 48 (issue 7, March 1), 840.

Gray, J. and Mittell, J. (2007) Speculation on Spoilers: *Lost* Fandom, Narrative Consumption and Rethinking Textuality. *Participations* vol. 4 (issue 1, May). www.participations.org/. Accessed July 1, 2007.

Jenkins, H. (2007) Transmedia Storytelling 101 (March 22). www.cms.mit.edu/mt/mt-tb.cgi/1103. Accessed July 1, 2007.

Jenkins, H. (2006) The Magic of Back-Story: Further Reflections on the Mainstreaming of Fan Culture (December 5). www.cms.mit.edu/mt/mt-tb.cgi/808. Accessed July 1, 2007.

Jenkins, H. (2002) Interactive Audience? In Harries, D. (ed.) *The New Media Book*. BFI, London, pp. 157–70.

Johnson, C. (2005) *Telefantasy*. BFI, London.

Mamber, S. (2003) Narrative Mapping. In Everett, A. and Caldwell, J. (eds.) *New Media: Theories and Practices of Digitextuality*. Routledge, New York, pp. 145–58.

Mittell, J. (2006a) Lost in an Alternate Reality. *FLOW: A Critical Forum on Television and Media* 4 (issue 7). www.jot.communication.utexas.edu/flow/?jot=view&id=1927.

Mittell, J. (2006b) Narrative Complexity in Contemporary American Television. *The Velvet Light Trap* (no. 58, fall), 29–40.

New York Times (2006) Running the Really Big Show: Lost Inc. (October 1). NYTimes.com. Accessed October 3, 2006.

Ross, S. (2002) Super (Natural) Women: Female Heroes, Their Friends, and Their Fans. Dissertation, University of Texas at Austin.

Snierson, D. (2004) Almost Paradise … *Lost*. *Entertainment Weekly*, 795 (December 3), pp. 30–6.

Teish, L. (1985) *Jambalaya: The Natural Woman's Book of pPersonal Charms and Practical Rituals*. Harper and Row, San Francisco.

Thompson, K. (2003) *Storytelling in Film and Television*. Harvard University Press, Cambridge, MA.

Todorov, T. (1975) *The Fantastic: A Structural Approach to a Literary Genre*. Trans. R. Howard. Cornell University Press, Ithaca, NY (orig. pub. 1973).

Veitch, K. (2005) *Lost* in the Moment. *USA Weekend* (May 8). www.usaweekend.com/05_issues/050508/050508tv_lost.html. Accessed October 3, 2006.

Conclusion

The Remains of the Day:
The Future of "TV"

Once Upon A Time ...

I am nestled demographically and generationally between Baby Boomers who grew up side by side with television, and Millennials who have never known TV without cable – and many of whom have never known life without a computer. Ostensibly part of Generation X, I have heard "once upon a time" stories from my parents' cohort about television being "better" in the past – "simpler" somehow having a lot to do with that assessment. I myself now have my own "once upon a time" stories that I offer to my students, waxing nostalgic about the excitement of discovering MTV and recalling days when computers could only be found on college campuses in rooms full of whirring servers and noisy paper ream printers. What are the stories that the next generation of TV viewers will pass on? What will they remember fondly, or not so fondly, about their experiences with television?

In this concluding chapter, I offer some speculative visions about the continued impact of the Internet on TV, examining issues the industry and viewers will face as television becomes more intertwined with the Internet. Yet, as I focus on the future, I am mindful of the fact that so much of the "new" that I have discussed throughout this book has been a continuation of the "old." While my central argument is that the rise of the Internet in US culture has played a role in television increasingly incorporating tele-participation into its framework of storytelling, tele-participation in some form has always existed – from neighbors watching TV at the one house on the street offering a set, to my own personal experience of sneaking over to the house of a friend who had cable before my family did. Regardless of the form of tele-participation, a central story emerges throughout the history of television of tele-participation being a part of the viewing experience – a part of the story.

What I have described in these pages, therefore, is a "chapter" in this story of television that examines a shift in how tele-participation has begun to operate in relation to the rise of the Internet. First and foremost, the Internet's ability to extend the TV text beyond the story on the set has made tele-participation "normative," impacting understandings of fandom (particularly cult fandom) in relation to viewing, and also impacting how the industry understands the notion of the "audience" and how to reach them. Even if viewers are not going online, downloading episodes, or uploading their own creations, they are becoming more and more aware that other viewers are engaging in such activities, and this landscape is becoming a part of a generalized idea of what it means to "watch TV." As this cultural environment solidifies, the industry will continue to seek ways to manage viewers' expectations of and about tele-participation – seeking to match viewers' desires with their own.

Industry Expectations

[Imagine] voting for your favorite American Idol *contestant through your TV and having the votes tallied and reported within minutes on the show. (Maxwell 2006: 36)*

One of the primary tools that the television industry is turning to currently are departments of research and development (R&D) within their own ranks, and outside research companies such as Nielsen and Stacey Koerner's Consumer Experience Practice unit at Global Research Initiative.[1] The old adage of knowledge being power has never been truer than in the 2000s, as television has struggled to keep abreast of its own rapidly changing environment. At NATPE in 2006, a constant call for increased funding of R&D was on the table; as David Mumford (Sony TV's Executive Vice President of Planning and Operations) put it, research can provide some semblance of stability – and as the Internet exploded around and through TV, it certainly had a destabilizing effect (NATPE Faculty Fellowship Presentation).

One key area needing further research according to many professionals at NATPE is better measurement. This was also a common call to arms among viewers responding to my survey:

> The Internet could either add to the Nielsen boxes or replace them. I'm sure some genius could figure out a way to make the statistics fair. I would like to have input on the fact that I'm watching this show or that show because I know that what I watch or want to watch is not what the average Nielsen family watches. (Jeff)

Jeff and other respondents emphasized that there was value today in smaller audiences that engage in tele-participation, as they will exhibit a loyalty to the program that can be monetized – revealing both the logic behind "save our show" campaigns that I will look at further on and the increasing industry-savvy of TV viewers. Nielsen has in fact begun to "overhaul" its methods, phasing out diaries – and phasing in boxes in college dorms, iPod panels, cell phone panels, and Internet ratings through a new initiative the company has dubbed "Anytime Anywhere Media Measurement" (A2/M2). Susan Whiting (President, Nielsen Media Research) observes, in line with what younger respondents emphasized to me, that "it's all about following television content as it moves from device to device" (quoted in Higgins 2006).

Such shifts in strategy from a company as solidified as Nielsen indicate the turmoil the Internet and new technology is creating in the sea of television. The industry is finding itself facing a bigger "Big Picture" than they have before, with more modes of distribution at work. The terrain that David Poltrack (Executive Vice President for Research and Planning at CBS) maps is definitely uncertain, though ripe with potential:

> Traditional viewing – linear viewing in the home – has already been shifting. People are watching from other places; people are watching on other machines. With all these new distribution platforms, how do you manage and measure so that networks get paid? And with network content in all these different places – especially video on demand over the Internet – we have to look to brand the network so that people know "that's a CBS show" or "CBS let me watch my show two weeks later." I really think network branding is going to reappear. This means more competition and better TV. (Interview, July 6, 2006)

Likewise, Henry Jenkins (2006) argues that this shift to multiple points of access for viewers demands that the industry develop more accurate ways of thinking about the audience, shifting from an individualized mindset to a more group-oriented conceptualization:

> Industry thinkers still tend to emphasize changes that are occurring within individuals, whereas ... the greatest changes are occurring within consumption *communities*. The biggest change may be the shift from individualized and personalized media consumption toward consumption as a *networked* practice. (244, my emphasis)

Indeed, changes in distribution of TV programs have included a shift in viewers' expectations about how and when they can access stories, with the primary thematic being convenience: viewers want TV on their own terms – when they want it, where they want it. If a network will not provide that for them, viewers will bond together and take matters into their own hands. This was especially evident among my non-US respondents:

> I really got into the show [*Farscape*] by reading about it online first because it was not being shown on TV in Japan when I was there. There is an entire online international community who come together to talk about anything and everything ... (LisaC)

> *Farscape*, particularly, has a multinational audience, and the Internet is the easiest place to congregate and interact with fans worldwide ... Fans are aware that the cast and crew visited *Farscape* sites to get feedback from [*sic*] their show – the show was made in Australia, but didn't air there until a year after first being made ... (Fehrscaper)

> I now have more friends who live in different countries [because of the Internet] ... These people often see shows long before I get a chance and will tell me about them. That way I can watch out for them being aired over here [Britain] – though I have to wait to talk about them. (Seffy)

> The Internet has allowed me to see some shows I would not have otherwise been able to see. That's actually good news for the biz since I am likely to buy a show's DVDs if I like what I see. If I don't have a chance to see it, then how am I going to know whether to buy the DVDs? (Kirbosi)

Ironically, if the networks were to fully follow Jenkins's advice, it is possible that the communities that develop around sharing texts might fall apart. In fact, each of the respondents above expressed a willingness to pay for access to US programming closer to its original airdates – or even at all – and emphasized the important role of the Internet in relation to the increasing globalization of TV productions. While being deprived might help build a social audience online, most of my respondents would rather have access immediately themselves – and perhaps then form a social audience in some other way, or perhaps not, as occurred with most *Family Guy* fans, as I described in chapter two.

The industry needs to know if meeting these desires can be profitable, and/or if ignoring these demands can result in long-term damage to its relationship with social audiences. Which viewers will pay for what services, and how will any changes affect the advertising-driven structure of the industry? As is evident above, one such area the industry is watching closely involves the use of DVRs and On Demand, and Nielsen is beginning to track how these conveniences are working for viewers. For the first time (2006), Nielsen released a Top Ten list of the most time-shifted programs (shows that viewers recorded and chose to watch later), suggesting there is value in determining which shows viewers will "bother" to view live and which they will postpone viewing. Paul Donato (Senior Vice President and Chief Research Officer, Nielsen Media Research) emphasized at NATPE 2006 that the future of measurement lays in such fine-tuned data, with firms needing to track how and when and how often individual programs are viewed – knowing the details and knowing the larger patterns.

What the value of such data might be falls to other media research entities to determine. Various constituents from within the television industry with whom I spoke think that the ultimate value of such data will support a trend among viewers towards increased On Demand viewing (some online, some via the TV set) and that in the industry will spur individualized marketing:

> Your living room is going to be Internet-enabled, and it's going to be all-consuming. It won't be linear broadcasting – I think the world is all moving to On Demand … You won't be *going* online – you will already *be* online. (Mika Salmi, Atom.com, interview, July 20, 2006)

> I keep thinking we're moving towards a world in which everything is On Demand. And there are a lot of things I love about that idea if it could ever happen. I foresee a day where, if you want *Veronica Mars* – and I'm

not talking about iTunes, but from your home set – you can have *Veronica Mars* for two dollars or you can have it for free if you agree to have the commercials left in it. And those commercials, because you've filled out surveys, are designed specifically *for* you – for your age group, for your income. There are items that you might buy – that you can click on and buy ... You're going to see more shows that are more niche audience that can sell specific advertising. (Rob Thomas, creator and executive producer of *Veronica Mars*, interview, July 18, 2006)

The only way to satisfy advertisers eventually will be to create different advertising per viewer household that can be delivered through the cable box and in turn to the DVR. You pull something up On Demand or from your DVR and there are your ads, suited to your demographics. (David Poltrack, Executive Vice President for Research and Planning at CBS)

In a lot of ways, people today are looking at them [television and the Internet] together. I think the advertising world is talking a lot about cross-media and On Demand, and now TV people are realizing how much promotional value all this has. (Richard Reisman, President and Founder, Teleshuttle Corporation, interview, August 10, 2006)

Business issues arising from such possibilities include the impact of "anytime, anywhere" on DVD sales of TV series. Will consumers stop buying DVDs if they can access a show they are interested in elsewhere, easier and sooner? Perhaps more importantly, which viewers will *continue* to buy DVDs *after* they access a show by other means? Pay cable also needs to start considering such trends as producers and studios consider the potential value of offering movies, concerts, and sporting events online rather than on cable networks. This leg of the industry will also have to contend with a growing demand among viewers for *à la carte* programming that allows them to put together their own cable lineups – potentially to the point of choosing specific series to buy from a network (something several of my respondents expressed a wish for, indicating that the rising cost of pay cable was leading them to simply wait for DVD release, regardless of how good a show was).

One of the more intriguing areas of convergence that emerged between my respondents and NATPE attendees in terms of research can also be linked to the importance of understanding what viewers are willing to pay for. At NATPE 2006, Paul Donato (Nielsen), Stacey Koerner (Consumer Experience Practice), and Ken Papagan

(Executive Vice President of Strategic Planning and Business Development for Rentrak Corps.) all emphasized the value of an engaged, tele-participating audience – and the need to find ways to measure this. Several of my respondents discussed wanting at least the *option* of literally interacting with their TV shows *while* watching, and this is a trend noticed increasingly by many of the professionals I spoke with:

> If you can imagine a Ven-diagram. So the first circle, which is everything in the new world order, I call "Advanced TV," and that's kind of everything made possible by the digitalization of the TV industry. And then a subset of Advanced TV is Interactive Television – and not all Advanced TV is interactive. For example, the technology that can provide a different ad to a different set top box based on household demographics. That's advanced technology made possible by a digital infrastructure … A specific kind of Interactive TV – program-synchronous interactive TV – is what Enhanced TV is. So it's Interactive television tied to a particular program that you would interact with while you watch. (Rick Mandler, Vice President and General Manager of ABC's Enhanced TV, interview, June 22, 2006)

> The fans used to watch *Farscape* on their TV and write to each other while the show was on – not watch it on TV and then go into the computer room later. They were watching it simultaneously with talking – and I think we'll be seeing more of that. (Andrew Prowse, series director, interview, July 15, 2006)

The concept of one-screen interactivity in the United States is bubbling around the edges of TV as of this writing (2007), but has been a staple in Britain for several years. Rebecca Segal (Senior Vice President, Sky Networks) explains that interactive enhanced TV has become part of the British mindset, with SKY viewers able to access "extras" – from products for purchase to cast and crew commentaries to voting and guessing – linked to specific programs (NATPE, Faculty Fellows Presentation, January 2006). Segal notes that interactivity works particularly well in Britain with sports, news, and science-fiction. Co-productions between SKY and US shows (e.g., *The 4400*) give British subscribers interactive experiences with a show, and extra money to producers of a show that fetches less in licensing fees. In other words, higher-risk/potential cult shows can get the money they need to maintain production.

In the States, on the other hand, competing technologies have made it difficult to establish one-screen interactivity (referred to in the US as "Smart TV"); instead, interactivity occurs via two-screen connections, the computer and the TV, such as I described in the previous chapter with regards to ABC's Enhanced TV. This, too, is a newer area of development as TV professionals, as well as some viewers, are still uncertain as to how desirable any kind of synchronous interactive experience is:

> When I mentioned to some of my younger friends that I was participating in a survey about the interaction between TV and the Internet, they immediately said *"American Idol."* It does seem as if the idea of the audience being able to call in or email their votes is becoming very popular ... In the future, if shows like this remain popular, cable TV providers like Time Warner, who already offer Internet service to subscribers, will be offering interactive TV where you just press a button on your TV remote to vote for these shows ... I can imagine watching a TV program on my all-purpose TV set, and Internet chatting as I watch, using the same monitor/TV set – maybe with a second window for Internet chat. Personally, I don't know if I would like that kind of interaction or not ... (Loretta)

> People were oriented toward one-screen interactive ... But there's been a sea change since 2002 – now people at the networks are talking about two-screen interactivity ... I think it makes for a much richer and more flexible media experience. The way I see it ... you've got the user, and right now he's typically either looking at a TV with TV stuff and a PC with web stuff. But increasingly on the PC you can get TV stuff, and people keep talking about putting web stuff on the TV ... The user becomes the center of things, technology serves the user ... The user doesn't want to be limited as to what content they can get from what device and often wants both at the same time. (Richard Reisman, President and Founder, Teleshuttle Corporation)

> There's a recognition [among advertisers] that the PC-based products that we use today are interim, and that the real opportunity is with the remote control and the set top box. Now, maybe we're wrong – maybe with media centers in homes, the PC is going to become the dominant appliance by which people consume media in the household. But I don't think so. And so I think on a *conceptual* level, a lot of advertisers get it, but I think in terms of voting with their dollars, they're waiting for more like what's in the UK with SKY TV to become available in the

United States. (Rick Mandler, Vice President and General Manager of ABC's Enhanced TV)

Narrative shows and interactivity are not necessarily the easiest marriage. The audience doesn't really want to pick the ending ... really people want to be told a story. They want to be told stories that are crafted by good writers, and part of what good writers do is they take you on a journey ... So I don't think people really want to be brought into the process of telling stories. A lot of shows like *American Idol*, reality shows, competition shows, *obviously* lend themselves more to the Internet and direct interactivity. I think we try to figure out what *in* our shows is really compelling to our audience, and sort of serve that up to them in interesting and different ways ... rather than try to make the *show* inter-active. They want to comment on the show and share that – *that's* the level of interactivity we're expecting. I think you want to comment on stories, talk about characters, and predict. (Sarah Lindman, head of production and programming, The N, interview, August 14, 2006)

My friend says that interaction destroys narrative – that an interactive *Romeo and Juliet* would be a failure. Because the power of a story is to transport you to an alternate reality. The moment that you're involved in that story, that narrative, you suspend your normal skepticism and you become immersed in that reality. The moment you're asked to interact, you're sort of taken out of that world, and it breaks the narra-tive flow, you become distracted – let real world things intrude, and [it] destroys the emotional impact because you're being asked to make choices instead of letting the world unfold ... *I* say that's bull shit. Yeah, sure, *one* kind of storytelling involves an immersive suspension of disbe-lief, and interactivity intrudes upon that. But there's a whole *other* kind of storytelling, where you feel as if you're as much of an author as the people who produce the story themselves. And that's very powerful ... It's two people singing in harmony. (Rick Mandler, Vice President and General Manager of ABC's Enhanced TV)

I think it's a pretty wide range of shows suitable for direct interaction. It depends on the nature of the program, it depends on the mood you're in, it depends on what's going on in your life. Probably if you're watch-ing a really intense drama, you won't want to do interaction. But most other kinds of programs – news programs, sports, reality ... The idea is that you can really be flexible. (Richard Reisman, President and Founder, Teleshuttle Corporation)

Clearly, there is little certainty in the industry about whether or not viewers desire direct interactivity – though there does appear to be a loose agreement that some shows, more than others, might lend themselves more to such a desire. One can assume, however, that executives and advertisers will be watching experimentation with *any* kind of show closely. As I began this book, in fact, NBC – having watched ABC's experimentations with *Lost* – announced that their new hit *Heroes* would "go interactive," with viewers able to engage in online activities related to an episode while that episode is airing on their TV set. Both of these narratives would appear to be, from the perspective of most in the industry, the kind that viewers would rather be immersed in *narratively*, with tele-participation occurring after the fact. Thus, a key and obvious future issue for the industry will be working on how to determine when to encourage tele-participation that is literally interactive (i.e., synchronous) and when to encourage tele-participation that is more symbolic in its interactivity (i.e., separate from the time frame of viewing the show).

In the midst of all this swirls an increasing expectation on the part of viewers that a more in-depth media experience is what the future will hold for them, be that interactive literally or symbolically:

> What can the Internet offer for me? ... I really enjoy reading blog entries by the cast and crew; it shows that they are interested in the fans, by taking time out of their schedule to write so that the viewers get a better understanding of that week's episode. (Irish77)

> What I'd like the Internet to offer me, as a viewer, is the ability to provide feedback and learn about the behind-the-scenes stuff that goes into the making of a show, and the reasons behind any large decisions that are made, etc. (Fehrscaper)

> I think they could offer a much more personal insight into my shows, whether through blogs written by the actors and crew to scheduled live web-chats with those same people. The days of just watching a show and maybe buying the DVDs are now gone. (Seffy)

Networks are beginning to attend to the desires of viewers such as Irish, Fehrscaper, and Seffy, with NBC and CBS especially making a concerted effort in 2006 and 2007 to attract what CBS's Executive Vice President of Research and Planning calls the "fully connected" viewer (Shields 2007). CBS's research from 2006 reveals that those viewers with broadband Internet and digital television are more engaged television viewers, in turn more likely to visit websites related to their favorite programs. It is as if the availability created via new media technology promotes and supports a mode of viewing that ostensibly blurs the line between "show" and "extras," sustaining a more holistic story experience. Thus, it is small surprise that NBC has developed its "TV 360" strategy, calling upon the concept of an unbroken circle encompassing the TV set and the computer: Viewers can visit NBC.com for blogs, webisodes, episodes they may have missed or would like commentary on; they can see unaired material created explicitly for the web – including "spin-offs" of network programs; they can even (or so NBC is promising) view pilots for in-development programs and provide feedback to the network about their new projects. CBS viewers can visit InnerTube.com for blogs and interviews and behind-the-scenes featurettes; they can also visit TheShowBuzz. com for entertainment news in general (that of course includes news about CBS programs); they can even venture to YouTube's CBS "channel" for recent clips and highlights from favorite CBS series.

Maureen Ryan of the *Chicago Tribune* sees such experimentation as part of a broader trend occurring in the industry of "a never-ending TV season" (interview, September 13, 2006):

> They're [writers and producers] doing all sorts of extra stuff – they're expected to be multimedia producers as well … I think they're being asked to wear lots of hats right now. Because the stakes are so high, because viewers are expecting and demanding such high quality, the season doesn't end. You reply to fans' questions, write a blog, record a podcast, record a DVD commentary, and oh! Come up with a show that can compete in this incredibly difficult environment.

While, as noted earlier, television companies are restructuring themselves to better divide the labor related to the many extensions that new technologies are providing for TV programs, as of this writing much of this work falls in the laps of writers and producers – and sometimes non-guild writers such as production assistants. The issues of compensation and guild contracts that arise because of such activities are mounting quickly, as networks and guilds argue about whether or not such work is promotional or original – classifications that are key to determining if this work is payable or not. The majority of those I spoke with for this book indicated that the extra work writers and producers are engaging in for their shows will likely be a paramount issue as the next contracts are negotiated; even something as "simple" as offering an episode for sale on iTunes or for free on a network website raises issues of compensation, particularly after negotiations concerning DVD sales left writers severely underpaid:

> For some of the shows, the networks are throwing extra money at them to hire staff to take on these new online ventures ... It's definitely another thing that's clamoring for their [producers'] attention. (Rob Owen, columnist, *Pittsburgh Post Gazette*, interview, September 4, 2006)

> Well, writers should certainly be paid fairly for downloads – that seems fairly obvious to me ... Many people in the Writers' Guild feel that the DVD structure, based upon the previously existing home-video structure – the Writers' Guild has lost that fight for years and years and years ... It may become a showdown. (Kevin Murphy, head writer and co-executive producer for *Desperate Housewives*, interview, July 13, 2006)

> The WGA – we're so out of whack with that – because we missed that step with DVD, it's that much harder to get *in* step for online content. So a lot of the stuff that we do, we did stuff for Verizon, we had to use non-WGA writers ... because they won't pay WGA rates for that work. (Stephanie Savage, co-executive producer, *The O.C.*, interview, July 14, 2006)

> Because it's getting harder and harder for the studios to make money, so the way they rationalize it is, "all this extra content that we're asking from you that we're going to pay you a pittance for is how we are compensating ourselves for the breakdown of our economic model. If *The Office* needs to create content for cell phones to expand viewership, or we can put it on iTunes to get more people to watch – we're doing you a favor." (Josh Schwartz, creator and executive producer, *The O.C.*, interview, July 14, 2006)

> The concern is – there's a need for all this extra content, but who's going to provide it? When you're writing 22 episodes of a television show, there's no time. If you have this other staff that's doing this, does that dilute the original vision of the show because they're not on the true writing staff? Is this counted as work? – is it paid and protected? Because I know that before this stuff got up and running, it was sort of "Oh, let's just write a little something for the Internet." (Julie Martin, producer and writer, *Homicide: Life on the Street*, *Bedford Diaries*, and *Law and Order: Criminal Intent*, interview, August 7, 2006)

"Everything is [becoming] about leverage," Rick Feldman (President and CEO, NATPE) observed at NATPE 2006 (Faculty Fellows Presentation, January). Affiliates worry that offering episodes for sale or for free will rob them of syndicated repeat ratings; advertisers worry that the viewers they most want will pay to obtain episodes without commercials; writers and producers worry that networks and/or studios will walk off with profit rooted in the extra work they are creating; music clearance holders worry that online episodes will allow viewers to strip the music from the digital files they are downloading ... These worries came to a head in Fall 2007 when writers in the Writers' Guild of America went on strike; as of this writing, the strike continues.

This expanded TV universe is also creating new responsibilities for TV critics, now facing readers who expect them to be one step ahead of the game and industry professionals who expect them to assist with publicity and buzz. On one level, TV critics now have more to cover – YouTube, MySpace, and network website offerings are now part of the "television beat" that editors expect their columnists to discuss. Melanie McFarland of the *Seattle Post Intelligencer* (interview, September 20, 2006) and Maureen Ryan of the *Chicago Tribune* both noted that part of their daily routines now involves looking at websites. Much as TV writers are expected to expand their job duties, so are TV critics influenced by the larger cultural quest for immersive TV viewing experiences:

> People are asked to do all sorts of multimedia things without getting compensated – such as writing a blog for their newspaper! ... The Internet has completely changed how I approach my job ... My whole motivation is that I have to help the reader through all this clutter that is going on, to figure out what's good, what they should avoid, what's interesting – and it's a conversation. It's not me preaching from the mountain top. I really enjoy interacting with readers – I get ideas from them. I view it as: "Okay, I have to put this out there. Let's have a conversation about it." I'm not asking people to believe what I believe, and they certainly have a right to disagree with me – and they do so, all the time. Fans expect an immersive experience, and really the networks are catering to that and so am I. (Maureen Ryan)

Rob Owen of the *Pittsburgh Post Gazette* thinks that this different critical environment has also encouraged TV writers, producers, and even network executives to stay more "in the loop" with critics who have blogs, realizing that they have an intimate relationship with viewers who may have considerable power in influencing audience opinions:

> Just as TV show creators are interacting more with their fans than they once did, they're also interacting more with critics than they once did. I'd kept in touch with one TV producer regularly since meeting him in 1995, and at that time that was unusual to have that kind of a dialogue ... Now, you have some people writing about television who are dedicated to nothing but getting scoops and little tiny bits of information out of people who are creating TV shows.

As I described in chapter four, writer-producer Rob Thomas (creator of *Veronica Mars*) told me that he specifically sought out Kristin Veitch (E! Entertainment Television's "Watch With Kristin" online) and Michael Ausiello (*TV Guide* and "Ask Ausiello" at TVGuide.com) because he wanted fans to know that he had to change the format of the show because of increased ratings expectations and new budget concerns. Going to critics who had online columns meant that he would reach the right viewers – and the Internet made it easy for him to find such columnists:

> I did *Cupid* seven years ago [1998] and there was none of this. There was this sense of buzz, but you couldn't measure it or find the source ... And now it's become *real*. You can go on Google and find everyone who's talking about you – your show, your storylines, what you did right, what you did wrong – and that evolution, I had no idea that was out there until six or seven episodes into *Veronica Mars* [in 2004].

In some cases, such attempts can backfire. Maureen Ryan told me about her experience with the FX network and writer-producer Peter Tolan of *Rescue Me* during the summer of 2006, when a scene that many viewers interpreted as depicting the lead male character raping his ex-wife led to an online debate (particularly because the ex-wife appeared to be "satisfied" at the end of the scene). When viewers and also Ryan reacted negatively in online forums, Tolan began responding, fueling the debate; FX contacted Ryan when they read her blog discussions of the growing argument, and offered her an interview with Tolan. For Ryan, this move was an indication of the growing awareness networks are developing about the intimate links that exist between TV and the Internet from the perspective of viewers:

> The last thing I had expected after taking one of FX's flagship shows to task was a call saying, "Do you want to talk to one of the executive producers?" I just couldn't believe it. But I think that's how it is – I think networks are realizing that they have to not only stay on top of stuff, but get out in front of it.

Thus, when a community linked to a public forum is able to "reach" a writer or producer with their reaction to some story element, particularly when "aided and abetted" by a critic with a column, this is much more powerful (and potentially problematic from an industry standpoint) than if one spectator at home mutters to him or herself that they did not like something. As Rick Mandler, Vice President and General Manager of ABC's Enhanced TV, suggests, viewers today desire "a chance to create community around television ... [because] television is part of the fabric of social interaction today" – and the Internet provides an easy route to such creations. Online communities centered on television have been proliferating at an ever-increasing rate since the 1990s, creating and sustaining a formidable presence of critical viewers with which the industry has to grapple:

> I think that the Internet was prone to love and attach itself to certain shows. You saw this even before the Internet with *Star Trek*, when there *should* have been an Internet – and those fans may have even just willed the Internet into existence. They had their cons and newsletters in print, and they had that sense of community ... The Internet really allowed these communities to come together and allowed people to feel – I hate the word "empowered," so – "emboldened" to sort of lay claim to their fandom of certain shows. Not so much that they got to dictate what happened on the shows – it was much more about this feeling that you were not alone. (Sarah Bunting, creator, TelevisionWithoutPity.com, interview, August 9, 2006)

> This is a door that has opened that will never be shut. It may ebb and flow a bit, but this is the Pandora's Box that you can't close. As long as the technology exists, people are going to *create* community around TV. I think that's, at the end of the day, what the real appeal of the Internet is for the fans. Beyond even feeling that they can affect the show, it's

feeling that they are part of a group of people who like the same thing. (Rob Thomas, creator and executive producer, *Veronica Mars*)

My survey respondents consistently emphasized the importance of community creation to them in relation to their shows – and the fact that it was one of their primary pleasures from the Internet:

> If not for the Internet, we couldn't have saved *Roswell*. It was all done through the Internet. And because I could post on the *Roswell* message boards, my life has changed for the better. I have found a community of people from all over the world who share my passion … Perhaps it just makes one aware of all the people watching at the same time in a more immediate way than ever before. (Loretta)

> I'm also someone that has many close friends worldwide now, and I consider some of them extremely close friends. I've even traveled abroad to meet some of them (several times) and they to meet me. The Internet is a very powerful tool for bringing fans of a show together. (Fehrscaper)

As I mentioned in earlier chapters, fans especially come together as a community when their show is threatened in some way. Both *Roswell* and *Farscape* faced unexpected cancellations during their runs that propelled viewers to organize via the Internet. Such organization strengthened already existing communities with something concrete to focus on and with an influx of new community members. The use of the Internet to save series can be tied back to the concept of shared ownership which I have argued that tele-participation encourages. In the following section I will examine some of the more famous Internet campaigns that have emerged in the early 2000s, focusing on how such "tele-activism" reveals intensified versions of what are becoming more common desires and pleasures among viewers – particularly surrounding the notion of shared ownership.

Viewers' Expectations

> At Roswellmovie.net they've organized a campaign to get a *Roswell* movie … People are still asking questions, coming to the sites for news on the DVDs or the movie, and trying to find our Roswellian actors and actresses … (Olivia)

I was very much involved in the Save *Farscape* campaign. I was one of the leading "Scapers" in the San Francisco area ... I even rented out a U-Haul and attempted to park it in the parking lot in front of the Golden Gate Bridge in March 2003 and drop a huge banner advertising the last episode of *Farscape* to be broadcast. Unfortunately park police and M-16 toting National Guardsmen shooed me off! (Jeff)

Saving a show is hard work. It requires many hours of sitting at an ergonomically unsound desk in front of a computer. We needed help. We needed an army. We needed three thousand dollars. We needed an endless supply of iced vanilla lattes. (Allyson Beatrice, "Save *FireFly*," 2005)

The summer before the 2006 television season, critics began to note the large number of serial structure programs entering the competition for viewers in US homes. During the Television Critics Association Tour that July, CBS Entertainment President Nina Tassler had to face down critics who asked her about the network's new show *Jericho*: the previous season, ABC and FOX raised ire among viewers with their cancellations of *Invasion* and *Reunion*, respectively, leaving fans empty-handed in terms of answers to each show's serial mysteries (something CBS had done a year back with *Joan of Arcadia*). Critics wanted to know if Tassler could guarantee that any cancellation of *Jericho* would be followed with at least some kind of wrap-up narratively, perhaps online. They were also wondering if viewers might stop giving new serials a chance for fear that they would be cancelled abruptly. Tassler had to backpedal when she confidently said she didn't think viewers considered such network histories when deciding whether or not to watch a new show – a stance that critics scoffed at.

Indeed, as noted above, critics increasingly have access to viewers' opinions about such network decisions via their blog interactions – and many at the TCA tour had followed the demise of *Joan of Arcadia* on CBS and the subsequent fan campaigns to save the show. And as I have mentioned in previous chapters, market research reveals that fans of cancelled serials often "blacklist" the shows that replace them. Significantly, per the quotes opening this section, the Internet has played a crucial role in fans' abilities to organize when a show in which they have invested is threatened with cancellation, and viewers move especially quickly when they feel that a cancellation has been unfair (i.e., that any failure can be laid at the door of the network). In addition, the Internet has increased access to critics, writers/producers, and network executives themselves, sustaining a community mindset of shared ownership that encourages viewers to fight for their shows.

One of the more inventive (and persistent) fan campaigns in recent years involved the WB's and UPN's sci-fi teen serial *Roswell*, a story about several teen aliens raised as humans in Roswell, New Mexico who are discovered by three teens with whom they attend high school. This series started in 1999 on WB and fans, worried about possible cancellation, organized via the Internet. Fans responding to my survey overwhelmingly expressed the essential role of the Internet to the show being renewed, as represented by Olivia's statement: "In the beginning, if *Roswell* fans hadn't organized over the Internet to send in empty Tabasco bottles to convince the execs that the fans loved *Roswell*, it would probably have been cancelled after the first season and definitely after the second season." Collectively, fans worked to send in thousands of Tabasco bottles (the teen aliens had an affinity); WB renewed the show, and the campaign received a considerable amount of attention from the press. The following year, fans repeated their efforts when WB announced they were not renewing for a third season, convincing UPN to pick up the show – where it ran for Seasons 3 and 4 before cancellation.

As I described in the previous chapter, *Roswell* fandom continued to grow even after its run ended; DVD sales and a successful syndicated run on the Sci-Fi Network expanded the global reach of the series, with fans forming meaningful bonds among each other via the Internet. Viewers desire and enjoy a sense of having an impact with their continued group activities; and even if the current goal of a movie does not come to fruition, *Roswell* fans enjoy continuing the relationships they have formed with each other and to some degree with those behind the series:

> Since we are trying to get a *Roswell* movie, we get feedback from the writers and producers all the time. Also if you listen to the commentary on the DVDs, the cast, writers and producers constantly comment on how the fans helped save the show for two extra seasons. Even as the cast moves on from *Roswell*, people still ask them about their fan base. Almost always they mention the fans of *Roswell* as the ones who have helped them the most. (Kim)

A year after *Roswell* left the airwaves, another science-fiction series became the focus of a concerted and much-publicized campaign that led to a "dream" outcome of sorts. *Farscape* (the Sci-Fi Network) focuses on a human astronaut catapulted through a wormhole into the midst of a cultural and political battle between the organized, warmongering PeaceKeepers and a small band of rebel aliens. The series quickly captured a loyal viewership for the Sci-Fi Network; in fact, it was for three seasons the most successful original series for Sci-Fi, and was in addition their most critically acclaimed show. During these three seasons, David Kemper (executive producer) and Andrew Prowse (series director) worked overtime to build a relationship with their fans, and seemed to me to have genuinely enjoyed the exchanges they were able to engage in (interview, July 15, 2006). This relationship-building served them well when, at the end of the third season of *Farscape*, the network first renewed for two full seasons and then unexpectedly relied on a loophole in the contract to cancel at the end of Season 4.

Kemper and Prowse spoke with me about their show's history as a "fan campaign series" after the program was cancelled in 2003, at the end of its fourth season. The writers, cast, and crew of *Farscape* had an intimate relationship with their fans via the Internet, regularly offering live chats after episodes aired; they were, indeed, a part of the community that had developed around the series. Both felt that their fan base could be seen as part of a growing change in activity among sci-fi and fantasy TV viewers – an increased tendency to be chatting online with others while (or immediately after) viewing – that contributed to a "proprietary mindset":

> I'm trying to remember what we were thinking when this Internet thing hit. In the beginning there was this sense of – the fans were just happy to know that "Oh my God! These guys are talking to us online and he's answering my question!" It seemed like everyone was just happy with that ... Then there was a cult following because they all started talking to each other. Then the Internet sort of morphed to – it became a community of people with a shared interest who can communicate with each other in real time ... And then I think the third stage was, they all got together and went, "Hey! Why don't we use our power as a group?" ... The Internet caused the flow to go the other way – *we* started to get stuff from *them*. And then they became a part of our community, and then they became *proprietary*. Because there's familiarity – the Internet breaks down the wall that Hollywood erects. (David Kemper)

Kemper specifically argued, using almost the exact words that Rob Thomas did above, that the Internet's relationship with TV is "a door that has opened that will never be shut," explaining that future generations of viewers will continue to expect the kind of interaction that *Farscape* viewers had with those making the show and that producers and network executives should be working with, rather than against, this trend.

The cancellation caught everyone, including producers, off-guard. Three months before the decision, Sci-Fi had publicly praised the show and emphasized its importance to the network, seemingly reassuring fans (worried after the network changed the series' timeslot to accommodate the faster-growing hit, *Stargate*). In an almost unbelievable because so dramatic move, producers were told of the network's decision via *letter* literally just as they were shooting the final episode of the fourth season – which ended on a momentous cliffhanger that left the fates of two of the show's lead characters hanging in the balance. Indeed, the episode even ended with the classic words "To Be Continued … " emblazoned on the screen. With no time to rewrite an ending that had been mapped out through Season 5 because of the initial two-year renewal, Kemper and Prowse turned to their community of viewers, breaking the news in an online chat and encouraging them to take action:

> *Kemper:* Yet, as we are, at the end of the line, so to speak, being just the people who make the show and not the corporate entities that fund and air it, we are as helpless as anyone. And we are sad. And we are shattered. And we are sorry. And we wanted to come online and talk to YOU, our core fans who have stood beside us for such a long and great journey. Disappointment is better than anger. Remember that furious people are "nuts." Angry, but civil and controlled people are "fans." (www.farscapeweekly.com/cancelled.html.chat)

Actively including the viewers as a part of the larger process of how decisions can be made, Kemper and Prowse guided fans through the niceties of network negotiations, helping them with how to best make their point about a desire for renewal of the series. They even assisted fans with information about financial investment rules when the idea for continuing the story outside the domain of the Sci-Fi Network arose. (Fans were considering if they could collectively fund the show themselves enough to wrap up the story arc). In the end, the combined efforts of fans, producers, writers, cast, and crew led to a four-hour miniseries airing on Sci-Fi (since bought by NBC-Universal) over a year after the show had ended its official run. The *PeaceKeeper Wars* allowed producers to finish their story and gave fans a satisfying conclusion – and on the way, gave Sci-Fi big ratings. Both those behind the scenes and those watching credit the combined community with the successful attempt to continue the story:

> One of the biggest activities that took place online … was the online campaign to bring back *Farscape* after it was cancelled. The fans of *Farscape* all over the world banned [*sic*] together and raised money for advertisements on TV and in newspapers and magazines, to buy *Farscape* box sets for libraries and hospitals and to the navy, etc. They organized rallies in different cities all over the world … to show support. (LisaC)

Fans responding to my survey explained that one of their primary pleasures as viewers extended past the TV set to their relationship with the creative professionals behind the series. There was a constant sense of being heard – of having a voice – that was interestingly tempered for these viewers; each of those responding emphasized to me that their sense of shared ownership did not mean that they felt they had the right to steer the creative course of the show. They saw their role as providing feedback and support – and the creative professionals' roles were to tell them a story worth watching, and respond to viewer feedback with information, explanation, and discussion:

> They [the writers and producers of *Farscape*] listen, but they didn't change their ideas to fit what the fans wanted. And quite rightly so! I think they looked online as the show didn't air in the country it was made [*sic*], so their only real feedback on whether they'd got things "right" was via the Internet. (Fehrscaper)

> I don't think they wrote specifically to what was being said [online], but rather whether the story they were telling was resonating with the fans. Plus they (and the actors) were actively interacting with the fans by coming online to chat with the fans on a periodic basis. (FarscaperMuse)

> The writers of *Farscape* understood that the story is king, and even if the audience does not like events and/or relationships that occur, if those events and/or relationships serve the story then they [producers] will not be deflected from their ultimate goal. (Nicola)

For *Farscape* producers, their attention to the community of fans and their willingness to discuss decisions and context with viewers made it easy for them to call upon this base when the show was threatened; they had actively participated in community building and successfully negotiated shared ownership. Among the *Roswell* fans who responded to my survey, there was less agreement as to whether or not writers and producers fully embraced the online fan community of the show:

> www.Crashdown.com was a place that writers/producers noticed and supported with parties, discussions, pictures, etc. for the fans. They [producers] admitted to reading some of the fan fiction there as well ... *Roswell* finally had DVDs for all three seasons BECAUSE writers/ producers listened to the fans online. (Lori)

> They did [listen] to a point and that is what kept the show alive. However, they listened to the network more and tried to inject too much of a sci-fi element into the show and eventually destroyed it. (Majiklmoon)

> *Roswell's* producers and sometimes writer, namely Jason Katims, never paid any attention to us – in fact I think he said as much in an interview – which (in the opinion of most of us) is why the show ultimately failed. The season one people (who probably did listen to us ...) were let go or fired. That's when the show started to go in the wrong direction. "The powers that be" paid NO attention to what the fans were saying – or wanting. When you don't give the public what they want, they leave you ... *Lost*, on the other hand, publicly stated at last July's Comic-Con in San Diego, that they read their message boards and find out what the fans are thinking to the point of adjusting the script to throw us off. That's another reason it will survive and succeed. They listen to their audience. (Thanette)

The more pronounced negativity appearing among some *Roswell* fans (versus *Farscape* fans) speaks to the value of writers/producers becoming involved with online communities; *Farscape* producers were able to offer explanations about the vagaries of working in the television industry in a manner that offset some fans' tendencies to demand total ownership of the show (versus shared). One can see in some of the responses above that some *Roswell* fans are attributing decisions to producers that they do not always have control over, or that some fans are making assumptions about the motivating factors involved with decisions. In the absence of information, it could be that viewers are likely to lay all responsibility at the feet of writers and producers while simultaneously feeling that those professionals no longer deserve any ownership of the series.

Awareness of how the industry responds to endangered shows of course involves an understanding of advertisements. I asked those responding to my survey outright if they thought that advertisers and show sponsors pay attention to online communities. The majority of respondents answered that they didn't know – with the primary divergence from this point of view emerging from viewers who had been involved with show-saving campaigns:

> The *Farscape* campaign made sure to make themselves known to advertisers, emphasizing that fans included many women in the target demographic. At one point thousands of dollars in receipts were collected and mailed in to KFC [Kentucky Fried Chicken], which ended up being a major sponsor of the *Farscape* miniseries when it aired. Apple also responded to hundreds of emails by hosting the miniseries trailer on their website. (Kaya)

> KFC has been a very good sponsor to *Farscape* and when *The PeaceKeeper Wars* came out they developed a very sophisticated screen saver free for the fans of the show. The screen saver does not advertise KFC at all. It is just for *Farscape*. (Nicola)

> The sponsors for *Farscape: The PeaceKeeper Wars* decided to back the show because the online fan base impressed them and their determination and coordination in getting more fans for *Farscape* and trying to get our show back. The sponsors for the miniseries approached Brian Henson on the fans' behalf and offered to sponsor *Farscape*. (LisaC)

Even among those who felt that advertisers weren't necessarily paying attention, there was a clear sense that advertisers and sponsors played a primary role in shows' successful (or, more often, unsuccessful) trajectories:

> *Roswell* lived for three seasons thanks to the hard work of the fans, as the network could not keep ad support going strong enough to sustain the series with the ratings it achieved. I think it would be beneficial for sponsors to research the fan base of the shows they support. Targeted demographics and ratings can provide valuable information about a show, but an advertiser's ultimate goal is to gain *buying* customers from the ads

they run. If they know how fervent the fans of a given show are, it's worth their investment to stay the course and support that show even if ratings suggest they should change directions. (Oceanblue)

As Oceanblue's comments suggest, viewers who take part in "save our show" campaigns learn quickly the power of reaching out to advertisers – sponsors become part of the terrain of competing voices about the series. A more often loathed competing voice for fans is the actual network canceling the show, with viewers ascribing human characteristics to The Powers That Be when they vent their frustrations:

> If strong feelings towards the FOX network because of their programming choices is what you're looking for, then check out this site: http:// forums.prospero.com/foxarrested/messages. There are tons of people that are joining the forum at the last minute screaming "FOX, how can you do this?!" and "I just started watching this show when I got the DVD, and I watched the entirety of season one straight through, I loved it, how could I not have seen this before." Pages and pages of letters just like that, and people insulting the executives. (Mike, speaking about *Arrested Development*, personal email)

Here FOX becomes more than a corporate entity – it is a character in an unwinding drama to which viewers hope to eventually write the ending. Thus, at the same time that fans are aware of the power of sponsors, the power of Nielsens, and the power of specific executives, many online discussions surrounding threatened shows demonstrate a need to personify networks especially, with some as villains and others as potential heroes. The tone of such exchanges matches the passion of saving strategies, such as Jeff's attempt to unfurl a "Save *Farscape*" banner on the Golden Gate Bridge, a summer 2006 one-day rental of a ferris wheel to call attention to fans upset that CW had not picked up the show *Everwood*, or the mass mailout of peanuts to Nina Tassler at CBS when that network cancelled *Jericho* in 2007.[2]

Personifying the networks allows fans to vent their frustrations – and thus is not necessarily an indication that fans do not understand the full range of factors involved. This "acceptable paradox" was evident in posts to SaveWonderfalls.com when it looked like FOX would be canceling this series after a handful of episodes (aired out of sequence, no less). Here one can see fans venting "irrationally" about FOX, but one can see also a savvy understanding of how the industry operates:

> I can say, however, that FOX (or as it's known to some fans, "Fux") is NOT the network for a show like *Wonderfalls*. If the unthinkable happens, I really think you all should look toward selling the show to a much more forgiving network like the WB which nurtures quality programming despite what ratings say. (Josh)

> *The X-Files*, which put FOX on the map, would not survive today's network. *Wonderfalls* is a gift from the gods to whomever gives it a chance ... To those who gave it a green light many thanks, to the rest go have a drink with the genius who passed on *Star Wars*. (Chris)

What is occurring here is a sort of negative branding as fans come to associate the network itself with poor decision-making about quality TV. Fans also make it clear that they recognize the power of network branding, following the patterns laid out by market researcher Stacey Koerner (2005): when a show is cancelled, fans will blacklist replacement shows; they will follow stars and writers to other networks; and they will offer loyalty to any network that picks up the show (even if just in syndicated repeats):

> I hope to see you [Caroline Dhavernas, star of *Wonderfalls*] and *Wonderfalls* on TV again soon. But if that doesn't happen, I'm reminded of Claire Danes in *My So-Called Life* and Linda Cardellini in *Freaks and Geeks* (both shows cancelled before their time), the lead actresses continued to higher success. But I sure hope to see more *Wonderfalls*. (Micheline)

> I would like to proclaim my absolute disgust that reruns of a reality show centered on giving ugly women plastic surgery and throwing them into a beauty contest will be aired in *Wonderfall*'s stead [*The Swan*]. *I related with the character of Jaye thoroughly and the news of this is almost enough to want me to throw my TV out the window.* (Olivia, my emphasis)

As one can see in most of the comments in this chapter concerning cancelled shows, and as exemplified in my emphasis in Olivia's statement above, emotions play a significant role in fans' experiences with their series. The shows they will go to bat for are programs that have had a personal impact on them – which is why saving campaigns have

been around long before the Internet. Fans I have observed and interacted with are less often angry about losing power to networks, the
Nielsens, or the sponsors; they are instead upset about having lost
"something useful" per Benjamin, and their statements about saving
shows reveal the continuing importance of storytelling in people's
everyday lives:

> I feel as if I've woken up and found part of my family missing. (Okay,
> I have a family, and they're wonderful, but the feeling is still the same.)
> I feel this way after only getting to know this show through 4 episodes.
> 4 episodes! What am I saying? After the pilot episode, I knew without a
> doubt I'd lost my heart to *Wonderfalls*. Not because it distracted me
> from any humdrum life, but because it added dimension to my sense of
> wonder and faith in storytelling and satisfied my desire for characters
> with depth and humor. (Angela)

> It sounds silly to get upset over TV, I know. But it's not, because this is
> part of a bigger violation of our rights as human beings to share the best
> of ourselves with each other, through creativity and love. (Lyric, in
> regards to *Wonderfalls*)

> I started watching *Joan of Arcadia* toward the end of the first season ...
> I loved the show because it was a mixture of humor and drama and it
> really touched me in a way no show had for a very long time. The day
> I found out CBS decided to cancel the show is when I purchased the
> domain for SaveJoanofArcadia.com. It was too good of a show and
> I liked it too much to just let it go. It was one of the few shows I feel was
> worth fighting to keep on the air. (AngelaW, personal email)

> I tuned in the next week, and the next, and I even remembered to watch it
> [*Wonderfalls*] when it got moved to its new timeslot in its fourth week ...
> And then, before the fifth episode could air, *Wonderfalls* got cancelled.
> It hit me really hard, and I can't explain why – I'd never been terribly
> upset when shows I watched got cancelled, and I'd never even partici-
> pated in a fan campaign for a show before – but I decided someone had
> to save this show ... So I got some friends together, enlisted a profes-
> sional site builder (who agreed to work for free), and started
> SaveWonderfalls ... (Cranberry, personal email)

Thus, bottom line, viewers are *moved* to save shows – quite literally.
There is not a cadre of generic TV fans "out there" who live to save
shows, or who exist to band against networks that cancel any program
quickly or unexpectedly. As both Cranberry and AngelaW note above,

the story of their shows resonated with them in deeply personal ways, compelling them to do something they'd never done before and actively work to save their programs. The descriptions offered throughout this book often suggest the importance in culture of what Lorraine Code (1991, 1995) refers to as "affective knowing": the ability to better understand some aspect of self, others, or society through emotional connection.

For the people responding to my surveys, emotional connection was a key component in what drew them to their favorite programs; I would argue that in fact, it is this element that was most necessary to viewers' willingness to label a program as "quality":

> Making something "topical" doesn't necessarily make it better or more important. In my opinion, people haven't changed much over the course of human history. We still understand stories of revenge, love, regret, sorrow, catastrophe, etc. So in the last analysis, it is the level of emotion that a show creates in the audience that is the first indication of whether or not you have "quality." (Loretta)

> Quality TV is something that entertains, makes me think, and has an ongoing storyline from week to week ... I look at the big picture, and whether I'm gripped enough emotionally to want to keep watching despite the flaws is when I label something as "quality." (Fehrscaper)

> Quality show for me. Hmmm ... Good acting. No hype. Visually interesting to look at either through sets, costumes, makeup and so on. Characters I have strong feelings about – either positive or negative but the positive usually has to outweigh the negative ... Thought-provoking and makes me "work" for the payoff without exerting me ... (Kirbosi)

By extrapolation, this sense of emotional connection as crucial to definitions of "quality TV" for viewers is also key to what drives viewers to move online and extend their experience with the text. This suggests that when viewers find a "quality" show they are more likely to engage in tele-participation. As Sarah Bunting of TelevisionWithoutPity.com notes, one can assess the level of emotional connection by examining the extent to which online participation extends; there are those who will "write and read thirty-two pages on a half-hour show and those who just want to eat a muffin and read a bit about *The Apprentice*."

This element of emotional connection was present also among writers I interviewed from shows with strong online presences when I asked them to discuss what makes for a good story or good storytelling – as evidenced best by this anecdote from David Eick (executive producer, *Battlestar Galactica*):

> The very first network series for television that I was involved with was a show called *American Gothic* ... We get this series order, and here they all come out of the woodwork – I'm getting every *X-Files* writer, horror film director, every director who's done a *Tales From the Crypt* episode, because *American Gothic* is dark and creepy and mysterious. And I'm sifting through all this stuff, this is my first series for a broadcast network, and I'm sort of in over my head. And I start presenting to Sam [Raimi, executive producer] these writing samples and directing samples, and he said to me something that really shocked me at the time. He said, "none of these guys are *moving* me – I don't feel emotionally moved by this work." ... And it occurred to me that we were looking in the wrong places. We should be hiring writers and directors for this series ... who do sophisticated, realistic, emotionally based drama ... Because what happens if you're not moved by the characters, or if the story doesn't touch you emotionally? And I think that simple rule has remained and informed everything I've done since then. Okay, it's interesting; it's political; it's intellectually stimulating – but is it *moving*? Are you touched by it or uplifted by it? And if the answer is "no" or "not yet," then I don't think anything else matters ... That's what you need for good storytelling. (Interview, August 22, 2006)

David Kemper and Andrew Prowse of *Farscape* emphasized the power of emotional connection as well. They described the central theme of their show as well-suited to the practice of online community-building that developed around this series:

> We didn't shy away from the normal aspects of life that are dealt with on "real" shows, like, "I want to sleep with you," "I think you're beautiful and I want to spend the rest of my life with you," ... "Your group says we can't be together" – that's what life is about ... Different people come together not by choice, but later they *choose* to stay together – and they help each other deal with the everyday emotions and issues and the ways in which they can become operatic in our lives ... And so we started focusing on that, and then the science-fiction stuff was kind of easy.

It was kind of "Creature of the Week" and that gets resolved, but what didn't get resolved was the dramatic tension of the relationships. Viewers could emotionally connect with that.

Both of these series have been lauded by their fans and by critics as "quality" television shows; because of this, and because classical notions of quality traditionally rest on the notion of pure artistic vision, I was interested to see what writers, fans, and critics thought about the possibility that Internet feedback might disrupt writers' ability to engage in quality storytelling. As I discussed in chapter three, for example, the writers of *The O.C.* felt that FOX's desire to attend to viewers' online demands for changes in the show got in the way of the stories they wanted to tell. If tele-participation supports a sense of shared ownership among viewers, how much right do viewers think they have to actively shape the show? Do they simply want to be heard, or do they also expect writers and producers to consider seriously (and potentially attend to) their ideas?

> I think viewers have always felt that they deserved to be heard. But I think the first people we want to hear us are the TV Executives who try to run their shows by the numbers instead of by the quality. TV Executives (FOX is notorious) cancel shows in a few episodes just because it [*sic*] doesn't have the numbers at the beginning. They do not care about content or quality – unless it sells immediately. The people who should most readily listen to the viewers are the producers and writers of a show. The smart ones (*Lost*, *24*) do listen. And that has only happened thanks to the Internet … In my opinion, most of them don't pay much attention. Producers and writers on *Roswell* boasted how they DID NOT listen to the fans. And this was insulting and distressing. It's no wonder the quality went down since they were not paying attention to what their audience wanted. (Loretta)

> As a viewer I don't think I have a "right" to be heard by TPTB [The Powers That Be]. It's their show, their money, their vision. That would be like saying I have a right to tell a songwriter how to write a song or a painter how to paint a picture. On the other hand, I think TPTB are making a mistake if they don't open up some avenue to listen to what the fans and other viewers have to say. Who knows, it might actually improve the quality of the sludge they throw at us year after year. (Kirbosi)

> A right to be heard – no. The people that make the shows have the right to make it how they wish, and there are examples of times when a show

was ruined because writers tried to please all the fans and ended up pleasing none. However, I do think producers and writers would be foolish not to listen to their viewers … (Fehrscaper)

(Response to Fehrscaper): I agree that the writers trying to please the fans can be detrimental to a show but they should know what their viewers think of a show. If their fan base is gone … no show … If they understand what the viewers see, they can enhance it or come up with new ideas from what their fans discuss. (Irish77)

(Fehrscaper response): I agree that writers should know what their viewers think of their show. I just don't think viewers have a right to be heard. It's a privilege – not a right …

(Irish77 response): Why shouldn't the viewers be heard? If the writers know what the fans think of their show then the fans are being heard, correct? It's a privilege for me to watch their particular show? When I have thousands of other programs to watch on any given night (besides owning about a hundred movies that I could choose to watch also) it is my right (or option) to watch a show instead of changing the channel …

(Fehrscaper response): You're misunderstanding me. I think viewers should be heard. Most definitely. But I don't think we have the right to demand to be heard. Ultimately, it's the people that make the show that have the right to decide whether they care enough to listen to their viewers or not. And if they don't listen, then they deserve to lose their show to poor ratings etc. But is should always be their choice whether to listen or not.

(Irish77 response): Agreed on all points ☺

One can see in this series of opinions patterns that have become dominant throughout this project. Viewers share a sense of ownership with each other and with writers and producers, especially when writers and producers foster this through online interactions. Tellingly, viewers feel that their ownership philosophically trumps that of the network's when the network is not prioritizing quality – suggesting that in today's multimedia environment, networks would be wise to brand themselves as offering forums for viewer feedback and interaction, as MTV, The N, and CW have. But perhaps most telling is the genuine sense of respect most viewers express for the *art* of storytelling in television; viewers may participate – at times even directly (e.g., *American Idol*) – in the development of a story, but they ultimately see any shared ownership as *necessarily* unequal in nature, lest quality suffer.

One might surmise that time spent online exposes viewers to widely varying opinions and suggestions, the range of which makes it clear that if a writer were to respond to them all, chaos would ensue. Thus, it is wiser for writers and producers to use the Internet as a barometer of what is and is not working and why:

> I mean, that's the incredible thing about how we live and work right now, too – the ability to get feedback from our audience for us is constant. We have tons of dialogue with them through the message boards and that lets us know if something is going right or wrong. (Sarah Lindman, head of production and programming, The N)

> I particularly want to know what the criticisms are – I want to know what isn't working, what fell short, what didn't resonate in the way we intended, what's confusing – all those questions I'm very interested in. So I'll check in with the Internet from time to time, particularly if I hear there's an overwhelming response to something, or if I'm particularly curious about whether something we tried worked. I will check because it's the quickest and most effective way to get an opinion. (David Eick, executive producer, *Battlestar Galactica*)

> I think people are trying to keep up with viewers' demands. I know that even the producers of *Criminal Intent*, they do sort of track the Internet, and I know they do that with *Lost* ... I think it's sort of fun to check in and see what the fans are responding to, but I think ultimately, as a writer, it has to be the story that *you* want to tell, that is *your* vision. If you try to write to please everyone, it's a sure-fire way to drive yourself mad. (Julie Martin, producer and writer, *Homicide: Life on the Street*, *Bedford Diaries*, and *Law and Order: Criminal Intent*)

Indeed, this was the stance of virtually every writer and producer I interviewed: the Internet is a useful tool to gauge how viewers are experiencing the story (especially specific elements), and even useful to explain at times what motivates writers' decisions. But ultimately, as David Kemper of *Farscape* put it, "Artists have a responsibility. *We* are the storytellers":

> The fans would be, "Here's what we want," and it would be up on a bulletin board ... And our theory was that they don't actually know what they want. They say, "this is what we want," and we say, "well, we're not going to give it to you, 'cause we're crafting the story, *we* are the storytellers. You're not professional storytellers. You want instant satisfaction ... We created this and you like it. You have to trust us that

we can keep it something that you'll be interested in. And we can't succumb to a small faction that are vocal, 'cause it will ruin the show."

The worst thing you can do is take any one opinion or any small segment of opinions, and use it to drive you. Because I think ultimately that those people who sit at computers and write those messages don't *want* to drive you. Even if they say to you, "you *must* do this, show maker," or, "you must *never* do *that*, show maker," what they really want you to do is what you want to do: they really want you to tell them a story. (David Eick, executive producer, *Battlestar Galactica*)

Now we've entered the age of the Internet, where you can really get in-depth – you know, they take you behind the scenes, meet the creators ... People are aware these shows are written, and they have a more sophisticated relationship with the show ... You also feel a sense of anger when the writers do something that would not have been your choice, or a sense of elation when it's "Oh! I'm so happy the writers finally did that!" And I think that the Internet gives you a way to articulate that ... But there is nothing that we're doing different in our show to accommodate that. I often advise other writers, "don't look at the chatrooms if you can't take it." I don't look at the chatrooms and fan stuff because it would just make my work harder. I would end up adjusting the way I approach my day-to-day work ... I would end up pandering ... You never want your work to become the product of soulless committee thinking, which it would if you became a slave to the Internet. (Kevin Murphy, head writer and co-executive producer, *Desperate Housewives*)

Television critics I spoke with agreed with this approach, emphasizing that writers' and producers' primary responsibility was to tell a good story:

We ask television producers a lot if they go online and read what people say, and the majority of them say they don't ... You have a story arc and pretty much there's no going back. Plus, you have a vision, and people are either on board with that vision or they're not ... I think your obligation to your viewers is to do exactly what you set out to do from the beginning. The fact that with the Internet, everything is instantaneous, really, really decreases the amount of thought, really careful thought, that goes into something before you send it out into the universe. Just ask any TV critic. (Melanie McFarland, *Seattle Post-Intelligencer*)

It's definitely becoming increasingly common [for showrunners and writers to talk with fans online]. Showrunners break down into two camps: the "I want to interact with my audience as much as possible" camp and the "I don't want to hear anything that they're saying" camp … I think maybe it's like audience testing. You could use online commentary to get a sense of whether or not you're headed in the right direction … I'm not sure that they have an obligation to listen to fans; I think their primary obligation should remain to make a good TV show, and to put the bulk of their energy into that. (Rob Owen, *Pittsburgh Post Gazette*)

Writers and producers are expected to be on top of fan reaction. I would say that it's a rare TV show that doesn't have someone on staff who is deputized to patrol message boards to check out fan reactions and things like that. So I think they're expected to at least take account of fans. Some people go so far as to interact with fans … It's a really fine line to walk. I think if you're a really creative person, you really have to follow your vision … You get into the hall of mirrors, where there are so many opinions that you can't focus and concentrate on what it was that *you* wanted to do. So it's a fine line. Certainly fans have more say over things than they ever have and they use that power, more and more. (Maureen Ryan, *Chicago Tribune*)

This general sense of hesitancy is tied, as one can see above, not only to the practice of listening to fans by following what they say online, but also to the practice of listening to fans by directly interacting with them in online chat sessions and indirectly interacting with them in forums. As I discussed in chapter three, Josh Schwartz and Stephanie Savage of *The O.C.* worried about the influence of message boards on the network; they also worried about the dangers of interacting with and responding to fans online:

We talked about the relative value of giving out *our* point of view of what the show's about, what our intentions were, and then the relative value of, does this just create another site or nexus for negative comments, or is it possible to have a real conversation and forum where people feel that you're sharing your thoughts with them? (Stephanie Savage)

As I noted earlier, Peter Tolan's interaction with fans after *Rescue Me*'s contentious "marital rape" episode led him eventually to Maureen Ryan in the hopes that a critic might be able to assist with the damage done by this interaction. When fans online took Tolan and creator and executive producer Dennis Leary to task for the episode, Tolan (to use Rick Mandler's terms for Enhanced TV at ABC) "dove" into an arena of interactivity at TWOP that he could barely doggy paddle in – he was simply unprepared for the critical mindset that he met at this site. Users expected him to account in some way for the episode within the larger context of the show – they wanted to "swim" with him – but Tolan only wanted to offer his point of view (that the scene in question was not a rape) and then leave:

> I was actually reading those TelevisionWithoutPity boards the day that he [Peter Tolan] started posting, and it was just mind-blowing to me. What's funny about that whole experience is that he later said, "Oh, that was the worst decision I ever made – to interact with fans." And that makes me laugh, because the fans, *I* thought, were ridiculously nice to him. I mean, there *were* people who asked pointed questions, but he mainly ignored them. Someone would ask a very cogent question about rape culture, or women on the show … and he would answer like softball, you know? He would just say, "Well, that's just beating a dead horse – let's move on to another topic." (Maureen Ryan, *Chicago Tribune*)

What Ryan notes here is a key element in the dynamics of community that most viewers operating online seem to expect now: intimacy via connectedness. If a writer or producer or star chooses to go online and speak with viewers, those viewers expect to have a real exchange with them. In my earlier research with *Buffy* and *Xena* fans, there was more of an emphasis on the auteur – a less distanced auteur than classical literary and film theory describes, to be sure, but someone nonetheless who might *at most* "drop in" to a fan site, offer information and insight, and then leave rather than stay for anything more intimate and in-depth. With my more recent respondents, however, the expectations for intimacy and connectedness are heightened; and while this dynamic revolves primarily around the community online, it applies to *anyone* entering that space.

This sense of connectedness, in fact, is what propels so many viewers to tele-participate; and this tele-participation can in turn prompt a further sense of connection that does not de facto "turn off" a viewer's ability to "think straight":

> *Farscape* was sensitive to the fans. To their credit, that sensitivity did not mean compliance to their wills, but *Farscape* more than any other show felt connected. The cast and crew seemed to reach out just as much as the fans did, and it remains to this day my most positive fan experience. (JessicaJ)

JessicaJ's description of her experience with *Farscape*, like those of so many viewers discussing their experiences with television in this book, exemplifies what Benjamin says every good story ultimately must do in order to become useful: it must take an experience and make it the experience of those listening.

Of course, not every television series has an online forum with writers, producers, and actors actively engaging with viewers, though I certainly think this is becoming more common than even five years ago. And not every viewer will feel compelled – perhaps not even once in his or her life – to find forums and participate in some way with a show. In fact, for most of my respondents, tele-participation rooted in emotional connection is a mark of fandom that sets them apart from "regular viewers":

> It's really difficult to say what it is that separates us from the regular viewer. Perhaps one becomes a fan when he/she ceases watching the show simply as eye-candy and to actually care for the characters of the show in question. When the person ceases being a couch potato and actually pays attention to the quality of the writing and dialogue of the show. When the person suddenly feels the ability, or need, or both to discuss the show with anyone he/she encounters that [*sic*] may be interested. (Jeff)

> I think of a "true fan" as someone who tries to catch each new episode of a series, knows the names of all the characters and their relationships with one another, has kept track of the storylines, and, most importantly, feels a connection to one or more of the characters ... In short, I guess a fan has some sort of emotional attachment to a show and its characters. I don't think a fan has to engage in any specific activity besides watching the show, but most fans like to discuss the show with other fans in real life ... or online. (Llamacran)

> If anything, being a fan can be an attitude, because your behavior and feelings may unintentionally revolve around a program. You become "one with the network" or "one with the program" to the point that you may grow a sense of upsetness [*sic*] or anger if you miss it. (Animation1)

For most fans, then, fandom is about participating somehow with the story and becoming part of a literally social audience surrounding the show. Yet, the majority of fans I worked with also feel that Internet communities are not only something that separate the fan from the regular viewer, but something that operates to "mainstream" fandom – working to blur the line between fan and regular viewer:

> I think society's attitude towards fandom is changing now, thanks mainly to the Internet. Fandom used to be the realm of the geek … Now, with the Internet offering anonymity, it gives other people the chance to view fandom with a safety cushion … So the role of the geeks and the nerds is diminishing as they're replaced by, pretty much, everyone. (Seffy)

> It seems like almost everyone watches *some* TV, and even people who wouldn't identify themselves as huge fans of a show seem to like going online and discussing their opinions of which *American Idol* contestant deserves to win or whatever. (Llamacran)

> I recently saw a commercial for arthritis pain-killer with Leonard Nimoy and what he needed to do was greet the fans in the audience with the Vulcan hand signal. That assumes everyone knows not only who he is, but also his role on *Star Trek* and what the hand signal is. Also you may have seen the commercials with William Shatner and Leonard Nimoy for that travel service – Priceline? It would not be amusing if no one knew *Star Trek* and about *Trek* fans. (Loretta)

This collective sensibility is in line with Henry Jenkins's argument that "as fandom diversifies, it moves from cult status towards the cultural mainstream, with more Internet users engaged in some form of fan activity" (2002: 161).

In addition, and as Animation1's description above connotes, a level of devotion can emerge with such a sensibility that any network executive and their advertisers would be thrilled to find ("one with the network … one with the program"). I have argued throughout this book that industry professionals in the 2000s have begun to understand the quite literal economic value of such audiences, at times actively courting tele-participation (overt invitations), or tapping into preexisting tendencies of tele-participation (organic invitations), or modeling interactivity and social networking (obscured invitations). Collectively, these strategies promote pleasures of shared ownership that correlate to the pleasures of sharing stories. In my final section, I offer some concluding thoughts about the potential cultural and social benefits of such an experience for viewers, the potential artistic benefits for creative professionals, and of course the economic benefits for the TV industry.

The More Things Change ...

I see a very long and intertwined relationship between the Internet and TV. Both from the perspective of direct interaction between fans and the makers and producers for TV shows which is occurring now, and the budding rise of TV shows being converted to play on people's iPods to be downloaded for a fee. It may not be long before the boundary between the Internet and TV will become so blurred as to be indistinguishable from one another. (Jeff)

The real impact of the Internet is that people can communicate all over the country and all over the world right after (or before) they watch a show. And a million people urging their friends "don't miss it" OR "skip it" can possibly make or break a show's ratings. Word of mouth has been replaced with "word of the Internet." (Loretta)

To entertain should not be taken lightly. One can learn through entertainment. I don't know how many industry and academic people share this view of the value of entertainment. I wish more would. (Aena)

The intricate cross-linkages of cultural forms ... are the industrial response to the heightened value of both interactivity and play for audiences. (Marshall 2002: 69)

The television industry, bottom-line, seeks to please its viewers. What I have discussed in this book is a shift occurring within the industry and within viewers' lives that appears to be influencing what television viewers are coming to expect from the industry in terms of what pleases them. It is my contention that the rise of the Internet (and particularly broadband connections) has stimulated a likely already-present desire among viewers to participate to a larger degree in the experience of storytelling – whether by influencing narrative decisions, or by understanding the process of creation more fully, or by sharing thoughts and feelings with both creative professionals and fellow TV viewers.

A cursory glance at one's daily newspaper, magazine, TV show, or child sitting at the computer reveals that the Internet is involved directly with how an increasing number of us are "playing with" TV – including how those in the industry are playing. Networks are pulling clips from YouTube because of copyright protection issues – and setting up their own sites for viewers to visit for clips and promos and special webisodes. Some networks are even creating their own Web Channels, where original programming can be found; some of these shows are being shifted to TV, while others await the mainstreaming of a device than can beam computer content to the viewer's TV set. Sports fans are watching March Madness games at CBSsportsline.com, "paying" with their demographic information. Advertising companies and networks are working together to set up social networking capabilities for their viewers, beyond the domain of teen audiences. Fans of new shows are setting up websites that will be ready to kick into high gear the moment their show becomes threatened with cancellation. Writers, directors, and producers seeking to break into the industry are bypassing television momentarily, using the Internet to promote their own work – and some of them are landing paid work in the industry. TV-oriented websites are even popping up unexpectedly, as when Conan O'Brien made a joke on his late night comedy show about a fictional website called hornymanatee.com; NBC legal experts advised that the show's producers create the website rather than risk a lawsuit for naming a domain that did not exist (and that a fan might buy and put unsuitable content on).

Growing research on online fandom in the arena of marketing is confirming what fans and some scholars have long known: fans' activities online culminate in making the text their own through shared endeavors of saving, rereading, redistributing, discussing, and recreating (Koerner 2005). The Internet is not a precondition to this arena of activity, with fandom stretching far back into the history of media. So what, really, has changed because of the Internet in terms of tele-participation? What drives people to use the Internet to participate with TV, and what happens when viewers' desires meet up with those of creative professionals and also those of industry professionals?

I believe that what I have described in this book is a fundamental shift in how viewers, industry professionals, and creative professionals are coming to understand TV in the age of the Internet. While this shift is by no means completed, the increasing pervasiveness of the Internet in everyday life, and the opportunities it has created for viewers in particular, indicate that what the reader has seen in these pages is hardly a fluke. Key among these changes is the development of an aesthetics of multiplicity. Shows that have marked tele-participation feature narratives with multiple points of view, typically through the use of ensemble casts, and often, but not always, through complex narrative structures. These programs also often focus on incomplete stories, typically by relying on seriality and interruption.

This internal, narrative aesthetics of multiplicity is certainly nothing new; we have seen such structures at work in cult shows from earlier decades in television, as well as in soap operas – whose roots stretch back even further into comics, among other storytelling forms. It is the combination of such narrative forms with the Internet's capabilities to extend the text, and viewers' experiences with that text, that has effected the most fundamental changes in how TV is being understood. On the one hand, the Internet provides easy opportunities for viewers to find others with whom to talk about shows. On the other hand, the Internet's digital capabilities allow both viewers and industry professionals to expand upon texts in unique ways that permit elaboration and retellings of the original TV text. This environment combined with a growing awareness in the industry that viewers who seek social interaction with other viewers, and who seek elaborations and retellings, are viewers who exhibit great loyalty to those providing them with these opportunities. The industry then cultivated an expansion of an aesthetics of multiplicity, connecting the Internet to television, and bringing together – often unintentionally – the voices of viewers, creators, and industry professionals. As Rick Mandler of ABC's Enhanced TV put it:

> If there's one thing we've learned from the Internet, it's that there's a lot of value for people in community, and that social interaction is really important, and that television is part of the fabric of social interaction ... *American Idol* without voting is a good show; with voting and with talking online, it's a hit.

Thus, by the early 2000s, an ever-growing number of shows were tapping into viewers' desires to socially interact and to continue the story of these shows. In addition, storytelling began to bypass TV in some instances, with entrepreneurs using the Internet to provide space for user-generated content – space that captured consumers who had been drifting away from TV (in particular, young White males). And more and more often recently, UGC has been reconnecting to television as the larger corporate structure of media industries has literally brought these separate domains into the same fold – thus complicating understandings of television and tele-participation.

What brings these different modes of tele-participation together from the perspective of viewers are understandings of storytelling that emphasize shared ownership among *literally social* audiences – social audiences that increasingly include the voices of creative professionals, critics, and industry executives in tandem with the voices of viewers. Of most interest to me, given the pleasures and displeasures and new expectations I came across in my research, is a continued need to examine Walter Benjamin's (1968) notion of storytelling as offering "something useful" to those listening. Among my respondents at least, tele-participation has brought most a range of "things useful" that they directly connect to the concept of storytelling. Benjamin stresses that sharing stories is necessary to the healthy functioning of society as it allows us to come as close as we can to experiencing others' situations. I asked respondents to tell me if they thought that storytelling was dead in the sense that electronic media, as opposed to oral storytelling traditions, curtailed the ability for people to "talk with each other about the story, change the story even, apply stories to our lives":

> I don't think storytelling is dead. Just think how many people watch *Lost* each week. And those same people chat about it online and share thoughts. How is that so different than going to a play and doing the same thing? Or listening to the bards who had to sing their tales and stories since most folks could not read? ... People will always tell stories and create myths. I think this is human nature. (Loretta)

> Storytelling is not dead. Just look at all the fan fiction that's out there! ... In the same way, episodes are discussed, evaluated, examined in minute detail, argued over, and sometimes compared with your own life ... My daughter is a good example of how storytelling is alive and well. She often plays games based on her favorite books, sometimes on what she's seen on TV, and we often discuss TV shows and films we've just watched together. (Fehrscaper)

> I think storytelling is far from dead ... The massive amounts of forums dedicated to all things TV and film related is incredible. It enables people from all over the world to interact and tell their own stories. This in turn can generate new ideas and plotlines, collaborations between people of different cultures and backgrounds, [and interactions] based on the sole fact that without these websites and forums we never would have met. (Irish77)

At the very least, for an increasing number of viewers, tele-participation supports one of Benjamin's criteria for good storytelling: it provides people with the "ability to exchange perspectives" (83). While it is utopic to imagine that this is what all tele-participation results in, it is "useful" I think for all of us – viewers, scholars, writers and producers, critics, and even (perhaps especially) those running networks and websites – to consider the value of such a simple thing as sharing different stories. Writers, especially, are thankful for the opportunities that a focus on tele-participation has afforded them creatively, from being able to create and sustain a cult hit because networks and advertisers see the value of a highly tele-participating audience, to being able to use the Internet (at least for now) and possibly On Demand in the future to escape the confines on creativity that broadcast networks and the FCC support:

> I, as a show creator, might be able to create this product where my tastes and sensibilities aren't limited by the very confining limits of traditional broadcast Standards and Practices. (Rob Thomas, creator and executive producer, *Veronica Mars*)

> There was some concern, right before we were going to air, that the show [*Bedford Diaries*] was in danger of violating some FCC regulations; the Janet Jackson case had just been overruled, and a couple of big shows had just been hit with fines ... Everyone at WB just panicked, and they said, "Well, we can't air this show as it's cut together now" ... I guess as sort of a compromise with him [executive producer Tom Fontana], the network said, "We can't air the show without cutting some scenes – we can't risk the indecency fine. But we will air, since it's not subject to FCC regulation, we will air your original episode over the Internet." (Julie Martin, producer and writer, *Homicide: Life on the Street*, *Bedford Diaries*, and *Law and Order: Criminal Intent*)

> There's a sense among writers and users that there's still a lot more freedom creatively on the Internet, because it's *not* regulated by the FCC. Because of that, you have people – well, you know, there's some people who say, "Yeah, but that just means you have more poop jokes" – and it's true, there are. But it also means that there's more a sense of being unfettered. And if you have something that's a success and even if it's a little less PC than what people would expect to see on TV, the networks are keeping a very close eye on that. For networks, it's becoming a farming ground for new, original talent. (Melanie McFarland, *Seattle Post Intelligencer*)

Thus, the Internet's role in the promotion of tele-participation has opened some doors, providing a forum where the voices of writers and viewers can be offered and heard – where stories that might not be told otherwise can emerge. Simon Assad of Heavy.com feels especially strongly about the Internet's ability to promote the sharing of stories and via that to return people to a tribal form of community, less fettered by institutions:

> The Internet has changed the way we do business, the way that we live our lives, and the way that we communicate and interact with each other. Take the notion of "community." Take a real traditional view of community in the past … Tribes of maybe fifteen or twenty people, sharing stories, passed down through the ages, everybody knowing each other – bonding and looking out for each other … Then cities grow and governments start organizing our communities, and it's harder to bond and share. Online, it's again about actually relating to somebody on a level where you have some things in common, and it's very easy to share and communicate. (Interview, August 11, 2006)

The power of the Internet to promote a sense of community – unfettered community – around media texts is a strong and persistent rhetoric among those whose careers revolve around the same – including academics such as myself. It is a lovely vision, as outlined by Henry Jenkins (2006):

> Fans envision a world where all of us can participate in the creation and circulation of central cultural myths. Here, the right to participate is assumed to be "the freedom we have allowed ourselves," not a privilege granted by a benevolent company, nor something they are prepared to barter away for better sound files or free Web hosting. Fans also reject the studio's assumption that intellectual property is a "limited good," to be tightly controlled lest it dilute it's value. Instead, they embrace an understanding of intellectual property as "shareware," something that accrues value as it moves across different contexts, gets retold in various ways, attracts multiple audiences, and opens itself up to a proliferation of alternative meanings. (256)

I quote from Jenkins at length here because this description touches upon several key tenets of this book. However, while resonating with many of my own descriptions, there are also important differences between what Jenkins sees and what I have observed as I researched

for this book. While certainly viewers are increasingly seeing their TV
texts as stories that they share with writers, producers, and networks,
they are not necessarily prone to reject the advances of a "benevolent
company." Indeed, one of the key truths that should be evident from this
project is that the very definition of "fan" is shifting, with many shades
of gray emerging whereby multiple and sometimes contradictory
understandings of fandom exist. For some, Jenkins's description is the
"correct" one, but for others this is too restrictive. Even Sarah Bunting
of TelevisionWithoutPity.com – a fervent TV fan if ever there was
one – is not opposed to the commercialization of fandom, having co-
written a book based on the website and sold the domain to Bravo, a
cable channel affiliated with NBC-Universal:

> We totally are sell-outs. We've been dying to be sell-outs since we were
> 24 … I was really trying to make a career out of it; some of these guys
> [running fan sites] had a much more abstract, utopian vision for the
> Internet, and were genuinely disgusted when that didn't happen. And
> I can sort of see their point, but I also feel like, "adapt or perish."
> (Interview, August 9, 2006)

Jenkins's somewhat laudatory description of online fan communities
also glosses over the "truth" of any community, as noted by many
researchers in their looks at online TV fans: in order to create a community, a boundary must exist that separates those within from those
(with)out. Among my own respondents, disparaged texts and their
disparaged fan bases remain as prevalent as ever:

> Which TV genres do I watch? Certainly not reality shows. Are they
> REALLY based on reality? Animation? Some, but I'm very particular …
> I find anime from Japan far more enjoyable to watch than the light-
> weight stuff you get from FOX … Soap Operas? Oh please, let me out
> of the room! … Scifi? Did someone say scifi?! Bien sur, mon amie! That's
> what I'm here for. (Jeff)

> Much to my deep regret, soaps and reality TV are production winners
> here [in the UK], so are more culturally acceptable … I very rarely watch
> anything other than science fiction. If there are no sci-fi shows on the
> TV, it generally gets turned off and I'll go on the computer while listen-
> ing to music (my kids have their own TV and cable boxes). I watch TV
> as a release from real life, and there's no finer way to escape reality than
> the escapism of sci-fi … I have often wondered why on earth anyone

would want to watch a soap? I can't understand why anyone would want to watch a programme that reminds them of their problems in an attempt to get away from their problems for an hour or two. It's a huge Bug-bear of mine (I absolutely detest soaps) and has led me into more than a few arguments. (Seffy)

I don't watch much reality TV. I have sporadically watched *American Idol* and that Great Race but not much else. I don't like the idea of being nasty to someone to win a game. I find it distasteful and I find most reality shows contrived and not realistic at all ... I watch the ABC soaps – not every day but whenever I can ... Science Fiction/Fantasy ... This is my favorite genre and I watch and have watched every Sci-Fi or Fantasy show ever on TV. (Loretta)

I do not watch "reality" garbage (and don't apologize for calling it that – you really don't want to send me down that road in public), nor soap operas. I watch some animation, *Simpsons* once in a while, always watched *Futurama*, but have no interest in the rest due to subject matter (*Family Guy*) or style of animation (anime, Disney). (Kirbosi)

Thus, traditional dynamics of taste remain firmly ensconced within fan communities, replicating attitudes long-held by members of the general public, critics, and scholars as well. The power of becoming a "taste-maker" does not translate to a total emancipation of previously untoward pleasures. For example, there is little understanding among non-fans and scholars of the variety of reality shows that exist on television, with all reality shows and all of their fans lumped together as rooted in dynamics of revenge and unhealthy competition that stimulate unrealistic fantasies of fame and attention.[3] The notion that some reality shows might prompt intelligent discussion does not appear often in popular critical, academic, or fan discourses.

Finally, it is important to keep in mind the central focus of this book – the ways in which the television industry is *managing* viewers' desire to tele-participate, and indeed to some degree *creating* a desire to tele-participate. As Alex Chisholm of MIT succinctly put it:

An executive's idea of community is a market. It's not Pierre Levy's collective intelligence community ... It's this whole question of how do you layer and leverage your media investments. (Interview, August 15, 2006)

As Mark Andrejevic (2004) cautions, it is important to consider and study the ways in which the promise of tele-participation is interpreted by *all* of those involved. To a certain and considerable degree, the television industry is using the promise of tele-participation to maintain economic power in the face of the Internet as a threat to television's viability as the primary storyteller in US culture. Given the might of the television industry, it is important that viewers and educators remain literate and informed about tele-participation, something that Jenkins (2006) emphasizes heavily.

This book has dissected primary strategies of invitation that have developed via a conversation of sorts between people working in and around the media industries, and viewers coming to terms with the role of the Internet and other new media in their everyday lives. The "newness" of all this raises important issues that need to be examined in research that I hope this project will spur in some small way. In pursuing this line of research, one key area for future study must be the issue of access: if the "Millennial Way" is becoming the normative way of engaging with stories, we need to examine the impact on those who do not have broadband, or who are not trained to feel "at home" with new technologies of communication – what Jenkins (2006) refers to as a "participation gap" (23). We need to continue exploring the impact of online social networking on our cultures, particularly for younger people. I think special attention should be paid to tracking the development of virtual worlds connected with TV texts: How might understandings of social networking be altered by the ability for a viewer of the teen docu-soap *Laguna Beach* to go on a date with a star of the show at MTV's "Virtual Laguna Beach?"

We should also be exploring the *potential* of TV's relationship with the Internet to provide us with stories that typically go unheard in popular culture, especially given the changing racial demographics of the generation on the heels of Millennials. We should be exploring the ways in which online discussions of television shows may be prompting viewers – and writers and executives – to see the value of offering and attending to competing perspectives on issues ranging from identity and experience, to politics, to authenticity, to power, to how best to develop a character or plot. I believe that there is great cultural and social value in much of what we are seeing with tele-participation, and I believe that the human – dare I say "inherent" – desire to share stories with each other can help to prompt real conversations among those invested in tele-participation.

It was in this spirit of optimism that I designed this project to bring together the voices and perspectives of not only TV viewers, but also of critics, writers, producers, entrepreneurs, network executives, and marketers. And I can certainly attest to the fact that the more economically invested people I spoke with are as passionate about storytelling and sharing stories as they are about maintaining a solid margin of profit. As we continue to explore how TV and its stories will change in conjunction with the Internet (and whatever comes next), it will serve us well to think of storytelling as an essentially social activity, involving many different constituencies, with the power to make us think and feel and sometimes even to act. We may be making TV differently, and watching TV differently, and thinking about TV differently ... But in the end, we seek a story that resonates for us. Whatever lies "beyond the box," our social responsibility to both provide and interrogate what stories come forward – and also *how* and *why* they come forward – is a narrative that must always and forever remain "to be continued ..."

Notes

1　Within a year, this unit was folded into others in a restructuring of the company. Koerner believes this is to the detriment of the company as it does not allow audience research to receive the full, focused attention that it should.

2　Fans originally had wanted to place the Ferris wheel, symbolic of two main characters' relationship, in front of the CW offices. They instead found a school parking lot and donated some proceeds from the rides they gave to a school arts and music program. (The series had featured a teen boy pianist.)

3　For example, in an anthology on reality television, Reiss and Wiltz (2004) argue that "reality TV viewers do not watch the shows so they can talk about them with their friends." They determine instead that fans fantasize about achieving fame themselves, and then seeking revenge on those who have wronged them/underestimated them in life (25).

References

Andrejevic, M. (2004) *Reality TV: The Work of Being Watched*. Rowman and Littlefield, Lanham, MD.

Beatrice, A. (2005) Save FireFly. Online work-in-progress from forthcoming book (2007) *Will the Vampire People Please Leave the Lobby? True*

Adventures in Internet Geekdom. Sourcebooks, Naperville, IL. Available at www.allysonbeatrice.com/firefly.html. Accessed February 23, 2007.

Benjamin, W. (1968) *Illuminations.* Ed. H. Arendt, trans. H. Zohn. Schocken Books, New York (orig. pub. 1955).

Code, L. (1995) *Rhetorical Spaces: Essays on Gendered Locations.* Routledge, New York.

Code, L. (1991) *What Can She Know? Feminist Theory and the Construction of Knowledge.* Cornell University Press, Ithaca, NY.

Higgins, J. (2006) Nielsen – Follow the Video. *Broadcasting and Cable* (June 19). www.broadcastingcable.com.

Hills, M. (2002) *Fan Cultures.* Routledge, New York.

Jenkins, H. (2006) *Convergence Culture: Where Old and New Media Collide.* NYU Press, New York.

Jenkins, H. (2002) Interactive Audience? In Harries, D. (ed.) *The New Media Book.* BFI, London, pp. 157–70.

Koerner, S. (2005) Listening to Fan Voices. Family Friendly Programming Forum, presentation.

Marshall, P. (2002) The New Intertextual Commodity. In Harries, D. (ed.) *The New Media Book.* BFI, London, pp. 69–81.

Maxwell, A. (2006) The New Prime Time. *Home Theater* (June), pp. 36–44.

Reiss, S. and Wiltz, J. (2004) Fascination with Fame Attracts Reality TV Viewers. In Balkin, K. (ed.) *Reality TV.* Greenhaven Press, Farmington Hills, MI, pp. 25–7 (orig. pub. 2001).

Shields, M. (2007) CBS: Serious Web Users Bond With Prime-Time Shows. *MediaWeek.com* (January 4). www.mediaweek.com/mw/news/recent_display.jsp?vnu_content_id=1003528040. Accessed January 5, 2007.

Index